Classic Patisserie:
An A–Z Handbook

Je dédie ce livre
à ma femme, Helene
avec tout mon amour

Classic Patisserie:
An A–Z Handbook

Claude Juillet

OXFORD BOSTON JOHANNESBURG MELBOURNE NEW DELHI SINGAPORE

Butterworth-Heinemann
Linacre House, Jordan Hill, Oxford OX2 8DP
225 Wildwood Avenue, Woburn, MA 01801-2041
A division of Reed Educational and Professional Publishing Ltd

℞ A member of the Reed Elsevier plc group

First published 1998

British Library Cataloguing in Publication Data
Juillet, Claude
  Classic patisserie: An A–Z Handbook
  1. Pastry   2. Cake
  I. Title
  641.8'65

ISBN 0 7506 3815 X

Typeset by Avocet Typeset, Brill, Aylesbury, Bucks
Printed and bound in Great Britain by
Biddles Ltd, Guildford and King's Lynn

PLANT A TREE

British Trust for Conservation Volunteers

FOR EVERY TITLE THAT WE PUBLISH, BUTTERWORTH-HEINEMANN
WILL PAY FOR BTCV TO PLANT AND CARE FOR A TREE.

CONTENTS

FOREWORD

It is with the greatest of pleasure that I have agreed to write the foreword for this book by Claude Juillet. It is a book which will delight and interest anyone who has a love for the art of patisserie.

It was in my position as a member of the Academie Culinaire de France, and also as the Curator of the Bibliothèque Culinaire de France which is one of the most comprehensive collections of books on gastronomy in Europe, that I first met Claude Juillet. The library is housed within Château Grignon near Paris. Professionals from all over the world visit the library, many to carry out research, others just to browse through this unique collection of books.

Claude spent many hours within the library researching his book and we had long discussions about gastronomy. Over the years our friendship has grown, firmly cemented by our mutual love and commitment to gastronomy but, in particular, to patisserie.

To promote the profession of patisserie has been my life's work, and it is through books such as this that this highly specialized craft will be brought to the fore.

This book highlights the fact that patisserie is a truly international craft and has evolved throughout history to the fine art we know today. It is of educational and historical interest and is full of amusing anecdotes, and will assuredly whet the reader's appetite to find out more about this wonderful craft. Any book which achieves this I wholeheartedly welcome to ensure that this old and most beautiful craft will survive and continue into the future.

I wish my good friend Claude and his little 'pièce de résistance' every success.

Monsieur S. G. Sender
Membre de l'Academie Culinaire de France

INTRODUCTION

Les beaux arts sont au nombre de cinq, et le plus grand est la patisserie
– The fine arts are five in number and the greatest is patisserie.

> Marie Antoine Câreme
> 1784–1833

The idea for this book started many years ago when, as a young man, I left my native France to work as a patissier in an hotel situated on the west coast of Scotland. Scotland is a land rich in history and culture, but what was the greatest revelation to me were the similarities that I discovered between the culture of my native homeland and the country which was later to become my adopted homeland through marriage, Scotland.

Scotland and France have been inextricably linked as allies as far back as the twelfth century. However, it was the period affectionately referred to by the Scots as the Auld Alliance which was to have a profound and lasting French influence at every level of Scottish national life. For example, the French influence during that period penetrated into the Scottish legal and ecclesiastical system, an influence which has survived until the present day, but much more interesting to me in my chosen profession, was the degree of French influence in Scottish cuisine and also in the usage of Franco–Scottish domestic terms in the kitchen.

In my work, time and time again I was to come across Scottish recipes which were undoubtedly of French origin, but over the years had been modified and adopted by the Scots as their own. Often the name of the dish was a corruption of the French name or the dish had been given a new English name. I was intrigued, a seed was firmly planted and so the thirst for knowledge began. How had patisserie spread from country to country? Where did it originate? How had it evolved? What was the etymology of the names? So began my quest for the answers to these questions and as I researched the subject over the years, a rich and fascinating tapestry of the history of patisserie unfolded before my eyes.

This book is a direct result of that research, a culmination of informal notes which I have made over the years in my work and in my travels. It is not only a history of the main classic patisserie recipes, but a description of each patisserie and etymology of its name. It became apparent at an early stage of the research that in order to understand the evolution and spread of the craft, it was also essential to understand and have a knowledge of the history of the commodities used. The craft of patisserie evolved gradually as different and exciting commodities were discovered and became available to man. They were used to experiment and create new recipes. Without these raw commodities, patisserie would not have evolved and so the book also includes main commodities used in patisserie.

Patisserie has evolved over thousands and thousands of years and can be traced as far back as neolithic man, but it was the great ancient Egyptian, Greek and Roman civilizations which were mainly responsible for the evolution and spread of the craft, although it must be acknowledged that the ancient Chinese also had a knowledge of patisserie.

However, it was the Roman civilization which perhaps played the most important part in the evolution of the craft and its spread throughout Europe and across the Channel to Britain. The Roman culture and language had a lasting influence in the cuisine and culinary terminology of their conquered peoples. From all corners of their vast empire they brought back an endless variety of raw commodities to be used in their cooking.

As early as 400 BC the Pastillarium corporation was founded in Rome, these ancient craftsmen were the equivalent of the patissiers of today. After the fall of the Roman Empire, the evolution of patisserie as a craft was to become a slow and gradual process.

Historical events such as wars, invasions and marriages between members of the European royal households all played a significant part in the evolution and spread of the craft. Another important contributory factor were the great explorers, merchants, ancient craftsmen, famous gastronomes and cookery writers who either directly or indirectly were an invaluable part of the whole process.

For example, in the eighth century the Moors invaded Spain on the European mainland, they left in their wake an eastern influence on western cuisine and culinary terminology. The eastern invaders also brought with them a wealth of new and exotic commodities which were to transform western cuisine throughout Europe.

Two hundred years later the English culture was also to undergo a dramatic and lasting influence from foreign invaders. The Norman Conquest of 1066 resulted in an influx of French culture which was to permeate the English language, cuisine, culinary terminology, eating habits and customs. This French influence was to continue long after the Norman invasion by their successors over the centuries. This French influence has survived until the present day.

Europe and Britain have had a long history of conflict, neighbouring countries warring against each other in an attempt to extend their borders and so strengthen their position in Europe. Old enmities were not resolved by conflict, but alliances and peace were often achieved by arranged marriages between the members of the different European royal households. These marriages were not only a union of two people, but also a union of two cultures. These self-imposed royal exiles brought with them to their new homelands a retinue of their own chefs, courtiers, recipes, culinary terminology and customs which ultimately enriched the culture of their adopted homelands.

The great explorers and merchants of the fifteenth and sixteenth centuries were responsible for the expansion and growth of Europe during this period. Explorers such as Christopher Columbus and Marco Polo, with their great voyages of discovery, opened up the New World and all its culinary treasures to the Europeans. The great sea-faring nations such as Holland, Spain and Britain had established new trade routes between Europe, the East and the Americas. What ensued was a toing and froing of languages, customs, cuisines and culinary terms from every corner of the world, a huge melting pot of cultures. An abundance of new and exotic commodities were imported to European and British ports, thus enabling chefs in the west to experiment and create a myriad of new recipes, patisseries and baked goods with the endless supply of delicacies hitherto unknown in the west.

Not to be forgotten in the evolution of patisserie are the world renowned gastronomes whose life's work was dedicated to the craft of cookery, such as the great medieval cook Taillevent who transformed and refined the art of cooking which existed in the Middle Ages. His writing and recipes laid down a firm foundation for his successors to work upon.

However, the golden age of patisserie will forever be associated with France in the eighteenth and nineteenth centuries, when two of the world's greatest chefs and gastronomes transformed the craft of patisserie into an art form. Antoine Câreme founded French Haute Cuisine and spent much of his life perfecting the craft of patisserie and creating new recipes. His greatest love was patisserie and his elaborate and monumental display pieces are still regarded by professionals today as masterpieces. He not only promoted patisserie in his practical work, but also in his published writings.

Antoine Câreme's successor was Auguste Escoffier who totally transformed French Haute Cuisine into the much lighter Classical Cuisine. It is to him that we owe a selection of classic French patisseries such as the soufflé and a selection of delectable ice cream coupes. Escoffier was a prolific writer and one of his books, *The Culinary Guide*, which was published in English in 1902, became known as the cookery bible of chefs throughout the world. These two French gastronomes left a wonderful heritage to future generations.

The latter half of the twentieth century has heralded an explosion in global communications, worldwide travel and immigration of peoples throughout the world. Never before in the history of man have we been exposed to such a multitude of different cultures and cuisines and we have embraced them whole-heartedly, resulting in a cultural impact never experienced before. Today, more than in any other period in history, we are more knowledgeable and adventurous about cooking. Through education we have become more aware of the wonderful legacy of gastronomy which has been handed down to us by our ancestors, a legacy which has been highly valued and respected by craftsmen in the twentieth century.

The foundations laid down in gastronomy by chefs such as Antoine Câreme and Auguste Escoffier remain today. However, in the twentieth century highly innovative chefs have contributed to further evolution in gastronomy. For example, in the sixties the French chef Paul Bocuse promoted a new art form in the presentation of food called Nouvelle Cuisine which transformed food on a plate into a painting on a plate. It was to change the traditional presentation of food forever. He was followed by a series of highly creative international young chefs who were to leave their highly individual stamp on twentieth century gastronomy.

Patisserie is also part of that legacy and today the art has been lovingly guarded by dedicated patissiers throughout the world, who in their endeavours individually or collectively have promoted and contributed to its evolution, ensuring that it will survive and be passed on to future generations – patissiers such as Michel Roux, L. J. H. Hanneman and my dear friend S. G. Sender who has kindly written the foreword to this book, whose lives have been dedicated to the art of patisserie and whose passion and love of the art has been such an inspiration to generations of young patissiers.

I hope in some small way through the publication of *Classic Patisserie: An A–Z Handbook*, I too have contributed to the promotion of patisserie, for that has been my main aim in writing this book.

Classic Patisserie: An A–Z Handbook provides the reader with an easy to use reference book which is in the format of a dictionary on this specialized subject which is educational, informative and interesting. The book contains over three hundred entries giving detailed information on the main classic international patisseries; it also includes entries on the main commodities used in their production. Each entry gives a definition, history and wherever possible explains the etymology of the name. Many entries include amusing anecdotes.

It illustrates to the reader how the art of patisserie has evolved throughout the ages up until the present date, highlighting the important contributions made by numerous countries throughout the world to this truly international art.

This book will not only appeal to the professional, craftsman, artist or student, but also to everyone who has an interest in patisserie and its evolution. It is a book for the inquisitive; for those who want to know more about this highly specialized subject.

I truly believe it will be appreciated by readers throughout the world and not only in English speaking countries because patisserie belongs to us all.

As we go forward into the millennium, I am confident that this wonderful legacy, the art of patisserie will continue to evolve throughout the centuries and give joy and pleasure to future generations. I salute the generations of fellow patissiers who have contributed to this legacy.

Claude Juillet

Biographical information

Claude Juillet was born in Saint Germain-en-Laye in Paris in 1945. At the age of 16 he served a three-year apprenticeship at the renowned establishment Aux Vikings, Neuilly sur Seine in Paris. This was followed by further industrial experience in a series of exclusive restaurants in Paris such as the Tour Eiffel, Drouant, Fouquets, and Pre-Catalan.

In 1968 he left France in order to widen his experience in the catering industry. He secured a contract with British Transport Hotels, and worked in the world-renowned Gleneagles Hotel and Turnberry Hotel in Scotland. Whilst working at the Turnberry Hotel in Ayrshire, he met his Scottish wife Helene, who was teaching at a local grammar school, Irvine Royal Academy. They were married in 1970 and five years later opened their own patisserie/restaurant, the Swiss Cottage in Ayrshire, Scotland.

In 1982 he left the catering industry and entered the teaching profession. He was appointed as a lecturer in catering in the Faculty of Humanities, Hospitality and Science at Newcastle College in 1982. He gained his Certificate in Education at New College, Durham in 1986 and also holds the Diploma in Hotel, Catering and Institutional Management. He has a Licentiateship in City and Guilds, holding certificates in Cookery, Patisserie and Bakery. He is also a qualified NVQ assessor.

His present post at Newcastle College involves teaching in a variety of catering courses. However, his specialist subject is patisserie and throughout his career he has won gold and silver medals in sugar work displays at national competition level.

ACKNOWLEDGEMENTS

S. G. Sender, Curator of the Bibliothèque Culinaire de France, Château de Grignon, for providing research facilities at the Bibliothèque.

The Hotel and Catering Institutional Management Association (HCIMA) and the Cookery and Food Association (CFA) for kindly agreeing to endorse the book.

Carole Lancaster for typing the original manuscript.

PLATES

A

∾ AGAR ∾

Is also known as Agar Agar and is extracted from a red-coloured seaweed, especially *Gelidium* and *Gracilaria*. It is a vegetable gelatine substance and is used in the catering industry as a meat stabilizer, for emulsions and in the manufacture of jelly, jam and cream.

History

The seaweed is gathered on the shores of Russia, the United States of America, China, Japan and Malaysia. The word 'agar' is of Eastern origin. The weeds are washed, dried and finally boiled in order to extract the agar. Today, it is marketed in sheets, strips and also in powdered form. Nowadays, a seaweed called *Agae Gelidium* is gathered around the shores of the British Isles and is used like agar.

∾ ALLSPICE ∾

Is the berry from the *Pimenta Dioica*, an evergreen tree which grows to a height of ten metres. The berries are gathered from the tree before they are ripe and are allowed to dry, and can be either powdered or used whole. The spice is usually used in the powdered form to flavour a variety of sweet and savoury dishes.

History

Pimenta Dioica is native to the West Indies. The plant was introduced into Spain in the fifteenth century by the famous Spanish navigator and explorer, Christopher Columbus (1451–1506), on a return journey from the New World.

∾ ALLUMETTES AU FROMAGE – CHEESE STRAWS ∾

Allumettes au Fromage are made from either savoury shortcrust pastry or puff pastry. The pastry is rolled, egg-washed, then dredged with grated Parmesan cheese and Cayenne pepper and cut into strips which are rolled by hand into a corkscrew shape. They are then baked and cut into smaller strips for serving. Allumettes au Fromage are served as an appetizer with an aperitif before a meal.

History

Allumettes au Fromage originated in Brittany, a district in the north-west of France. The French cities of Rennes and Viré are famous for the production of the savoury and produce different varieties which are exported throughout France and abroad. The savoury can also be made with anchovies or spiced almonds.

≈ ALLUMETTES – SACRISTAINS ≈

The recipe is identical to that of Allumettes au Fromage, but egg-washed strips are rolled in castor sugar or icing sugar and are then baked in the oven until they become caramelized. They are then served as an accompaniment to sweet mousses, coupes and iced desserts.

History

They were created by a Swiss patissier called Planta, in the middle of the nineteenth century, in Dinan, a town ten miles from the city of Saint Malo in Brittany, France.

≈ ALMOND – AMANDE ≈

Is the oval, edible, nut-like stone which is obtained from the green fruit of the *Prunus Amygalus*. The tree is native to West Asia. There are two types of almonds, the bitter and the sweet variety. The nut is extremely versatile. Sweet almonds are used in cookery and confectionery. Oil extracted from bitter almonds is used mainly for flavouring purposes. Almond oil is also used in the production of cosmetics.

History

Almonds originated in Mesopotamia, which was the Ancient Greek name for the land to be found between the two great rivers, the Euphrates and the Tigris, which today is now part of Iraq. Here the great civilizations of Samaria and Babylon existed. The Greeks were probably responsible for introducing the nut into Europe. A dozen or so varieties of the nut were known during the time of Pliny the Elder, a Roman historian (AD 23–AD 79). The bitter variety of the nut was served at the beginning of a meal as an appetizer and also to incite people to drink more wine during the course of the meal. Almonds were widely used in the ancient world.

They were introduced by the Crusaders into England after the first Crusade, at the beginning of the eleventh century. The English have always loved the nuts. In the late thirteenth century the English royal household consumed almost fifteen tons of almonds in one year alone! Almonds were extremely versatile and were used in a variety of sweet and savoury dishes in medieval Britain. They were highly valued because they were also extremely rich in protein. The nuts were eaten whole, or blanched and used as a decoration. Ground almonds were used in cookery as a thickener for sauces. England was a highly religious country in the Middle Ages, and religious festivals such as Lent were strictly adhered to by the mass of devoutly religious people. During Lent meat, which is rich in protein, was strictly forbidden in the diet and only protein-rich almonds were used as a meat substitute in a variety of medieval Lenten dishes. The demand for almonds by the English during that period resulted in the nuts being imported from Europe on a massive scale. Almond paste or marzipan was created in Italy in the middle of the fourteenth century and its popularity spread throughout mainland Europe and finally across the Channel to England.

∾ AMANDINE ∾

Is a small flan or tartlet made with sugar paste and filled with a mixture of eggs, sugar, butter and ground almonds. The Amandines are then baked and may be dredged with icing sugar or glazed with boiling apricot jam. The French recipe for Amandines closely resembles the English recipe for Bakewell Tarts.

History

The Amandine was created in 1608 by a French patissier called Raguenau, who lived in Paris, not far from the Bastille. When he had perfected his recipe he opened his own pastry shop, called Mousquetaires du Roy – *Roy* being the old French word for *roi*, which translated into English means king; *mousquetaires* translated into English means musketeers. The success of the new pastry shop was immediate; the small Amandines were sold by the thousand. Raguenau became a wealthy man with the proceeds from his new creation. He started to lose interest in his pastry shop and became involved in the theatre and wrote a series of plays. Alas, the plays were unsuccessful, and, bankrupted, he moved into the country and died penniless. However, his Amandines have remained one of the most popular cakes in France today.

∾ ANANAS CHIBOUST ∾

Ananas Chiboust is also known in France as Vacherin Turk. The gâteau has a Genoese sponge base which is decorated with candied pineapple slices. The surface of the gâteau is piped with Italian meringue. It is then placed under a salamander or in a hot oven to allow the meringue topping to become golden brown in colour.

History

Ananas Chiboust was created in Paris in 1867 in a small patisserie belonging to a Monsieur Le Fèvre. One day he was presented with a basket of fresh pineapples by a close friend. Pineapples were something of a rarity in France and were regarded as a luxury fruit. Monsieur Le Fèvre decided to display the exotic fruit in the window of his patisserie. After a few days the fruit began to deteriorate and could no longer be used as a display. He removed the fruit from the window and asked his patissier, Félix, to create a new recipe using it. Félix was at a loss; he had never seen a pineapple before and certainly had no idea how to prepare and cook the strange fruit! He decided to explain his dilemma to the Tournier, Gaëton Jeannin, who specialized in making the dough and pastry within the establishment. Jeannin was equally puzzled, but thought that the first task in hand was to remove the thick, hard skin. He was delighted and surprised when the succulent yellow flesh of the fruit was revealed. The pineapples, however, were not fresh, so he removed the cores, cut the pineapples into slices and candied the fruit. He decided to use the exotic fruit as a decoration for a gâteau and create a new recipe with it. He decorated the surface of the gâteau with the candied pineapple rings and had the inspiration to pipe the gâteau with Italian meringue and brown the meringue topping in the oven. Italian meringue had been created at the beginning of the nineteenth century and was used in such classic recipes as Omelette Norvégienne. The French adored patisseries and desserts made with meringue, and during this period meringue-based desserts were extremely popular and fashionable.

Monsieur Le Fèvre was so impressed by Jeannin's new creation that he promoted him to Chef Entremetier. In France, a gâteau is referred to as an entremet and an Entremetier is a patissier who specializes in making gâteaux. Jeannin christened the gâteau Ananas Chiboust, as a mark of respect to his friend, the Parisian patissier Chiboust, who created the classic Gâteau Saint-Honoré.

∾ ANGELICA – ANGÉLIQUE ∾

Angelica Archangelica is a perennial herbaceous herb which grows to a maximum of two metres in height. It originated in northern countries such as Iceland and Russia. Today, angelica is grown extensively in France, Italy and in some parts of Britain. The hollow green stems are candied and are used for decoration purposes in the production of baked goods and desserts.

History

Angelica was introduced into Scotland in the middle of the sixteenth century by the French. The plant was thought to have been brought over to Scotland by the young Mary Stuart (1542–1587), who was Queen of Scotland from 1542 to 1567. Mary had spent much of her young life in France and later married the French Dauphin who became Francis II of France. He died tragically shortly after their marriage, leaving Mary a widow. The links between Scotland and France, however, had started long before this period and went as far back as the twelfth century.

It was the period known as the 'Auld Alliance' in the sixteenth century which was to have a dramatic impact on Scottish cookery and culinary habits. The 'Auld Alliance' between Scotland and France was cemented by the marriage of Mary's father, James V (1512–1542), who was King of Scotland from 1513, to his first wife Magdalène, who was French. The union was short-lived; the delicate Magdalène died two months after their marriage. His second wife, Mary of Guise-Lorraine, was also French and was a member of the nobility; they were married in 1538. Mary of Guise bore him a daughter, also called Mary, who was later to become the beloved Mary, Queen of Scots. It was Mary of Guise who was responsible for starting to introduce French recipes and customs to the Scottish court in Edinburgh. The two countries became inextricably linked, and this French influence was to continue after Mary of Guise's death through her daughter Mary, on her return to Scotland in 1561 from France to claim the Scottish crown. The young Mary brought with her from France a retinue of French servants, chefs and courtiers.

The Scottish court in the sixteenth century was based at Edinburgh Castle, and it was in this eastern region of Scotland that the French influence was at its greatest. Scotland had changed during Mary's absence and had become a Protestant country which had embraced the new religion. Mary found the Scottish court oppressive and dull. The new religion was also very restrictive, and Mary's lavish entertaining and strange French customs were frowned upon by many of the Scottish lords. Despite this, it was during this period that the French influence was indelibly stamped on Scottish cookery and eating habits. Many Scottish noble families employed a French chef, as it was thought to be highly fashionable during that time.

A separate small court was established at Craigmillar Castle, which was a few miles away from Edinburgh. It was there that Mary escaped from the oppressive Scottish court to spend time with a small, select group of her trusted attendants and servants, many of whom were French. The castle and the surrounding community was nicknamed 'Little France' by the Scots. It was in the gardens of Little France that for the first time plants such as angelica and sorrel were brought over from France and planted in Scottish soil. The angelica plant is said to flourish still in this small corner of Scotland – a lasting testimony to the old friendship between Scotland and France.

❧ ANISEED – ANIS ❧

Aniseed is the seed of a hardy herb plant, *Pimpinella Anisum*. The plant grows to a height of approximately fifty centimetres. It grows in France, Spain and most European countries and is also cultivated in Greece and Egypt. The seeds are used as a flavouring in bread, pastries and also in the production of alcohols such as Pastis and Ouzo. The wonderful French liqueur Anisette is made with the herb.

History

Aniseed has been used by man to flavour food for thousands of years. The Romans used the flavouring in their cookery; at that time the herb was imported from Croatia. The Greek mathematician Pythagoras (580 BC–500 BC), recommended the herb as a flavouring in cookery, but it was not until the twentieth century that it became widely known to the British public, when it was used as a flavouring for sweets called Aniseed balls. The pungent flavour of these small, brown-coloured balls was instantly recognizable and proved to be a great favourite with children.

∾ APICIUS, MARCUS ∾

He was a renowned Roman gastronome.

History

He was born in 25 BC, during the reign of the Roman Emperor Tiberius (42 BC–AD 37), Emperor from AD 14. Marcus Apicius wrote several cookery books which were published around AD 5. The main source of material for the books was gastronomic cookery. In one book there is a recipe for a cake which is made with honey, milk and eggs, which are then beaten and cooked slowly in an earthenware dish, over a stove. It seems that this was probably the first recipe published for baked egg custard! Marcus Apicius opened the first school of cookery in the world.

∾ APPERT, NICHOLAS ∾

He was a French scientist.

History

He was born in 1749 and invented the method of canning food in 1812. He opened a canning factory and by 1818 was successfully canning meat, vegetables and soup. He published a book about food preservation in 1810. He died in 1841.

∾ APPLE – POMME ∾

Is the edible fruit, *Malus Pumila*, of the apple tree belonging to the family *Rosaceae*. The apple of today is the descendant of the wild crab apple, which was tiny and extremely sour to taste. Through the ages the fruit's colour, size and taste have changed out of all recognition. There are several thousand varieties of cultivated apples throughout the world. The three main groups of apples are eating, cooking and cider apples. Eating apples include

Cox's Orange Pippin, Golden Delicious and Granny Smith's. Perhaps the best known cooking apples are Bramleys. The trees grow best in countries with a cool climate and they require plenty of rain. The main apple-producing countries in the world today are England, France, Ireland, New Zealand, Australia, the United States of America and Canada.

Apples are rich in vitamin C and are a good source of pectin. Their versatility is unsurpassable in cooking and in the production of baked goods and desserts. Apple-based desserts and pastries such as Apple Snow, Apple Charlotte, Apple Strudel, Apple Pie and Apple Turnovers have all become classic recipes and their popularity has remained undiminished over hundreds of years. Because the fruit is rich in pectin, it is ideal for the production of jams and jellies. Eaten fresh, the apple is the most popular fruit on the market today. Baked, poached or stewed, it makes a delicious dessert and is often served with a custard.

Apples are also used in the production of alcohols. England and France both produce great quantities of cider. In the south of England, the highly intoxicating cider known as Scrumpy is produced. Normandy, a region in the north of France, is renowned not only for its wonderful cider, but also for its delicious apple brandy which is called Calvados.

History

The French word for apple is *pomme*, which is a derivative of the Latin word *pomum*, meaning fruit. In Germany the fruit is called *apfel*, in Holland, *appel*, and in Sweden, *apel* – the spelling of the name of the fruit changing as it spread across Europe. Apples have been known to man since the beginning of time and have been referred to as the 'forbidden fruit' since time immemorial. In the book of Genesis, Adam, the first man, who was created by God from dust, was banished with his companion Eve from the Garden of Eden. Adam and Eve had succumbed to temptation by eating the first apple from the Tree of Knowledge of Good and Evil.

Ancient civilizations had knowledge of apples. Greek mythology is full of tales about the fruit. For example, the Apple of Discord and the Apples of Hesperides are mentioned in Greek myths. The Egyptians also appreciated the fruit. During the reign of Rameses III (1198 BC–1167 BC), who was the Pharaoh and ruler of all Egypt, apple trees were cultivated along the banks of the River Nile. Etruscan farmers were later responsible for developing new varieties of apples.

More than a thousand years later, the Romans boasted of more than thirty different varieties of apples. Maltius, a Roman officer and a close friend of Augustus (63 BC–AD 14), Emperor of Rome from 27 BC, was immortalized when a variety of apple was named after him. The Mattianes apple was a popular variety of apple in ancient Rome. Other varieties during that time were the Manlienne, Claudienne and Appiene. Apples were eaten raw by the Romans or sometimes they were boiled in water and wine or baked in the ground beneath ashes. Apple compote was a popular sweet of the

Romans. One of their favourite drinks was a type of alcoholic cider made with apples, similar to our cider of today. The apples at that time were very sour and had to be sweetened with honey, as sugar was not known to the Romans.

The apple tree spread throughout Europe and it was the Romans, during the invasion of Britain, who started the cultivation of apples on the island. By the Middle Ages, apples were widely cultivated in Britain. However, they were usually cooked during this time and were not eaten raw. The fruit was baked in pies or tarts and sweetened with lashings of honey or sugar to make them edible. It was not until a much later date that the sweet, juicy apples we know today were cultivated.

The apple was introduced to the New World by the early European settlers. Because of the long sea voyage across the Atlantic to America, it was impossible to take cuttings of the apple trees as they would have withered and died. The early settlers took the pips of apples to plant in their new homeland.

This ancient fruit is surrounded by myths and legends. Perhaps one of the best loved legends concerning the apple is about the Swiss archer, William Tell, who lived in the fourteenth century. He refused to salute the Hapsburg Badge at Altorf on Lake Lucerne which was a symbol of Austrian authority in Switzerland, and was ordered by the Austrian ruler, Gessler, to place an apple on top of his young son's head. The apple was to be used as a target, in order to test William Tell's competence as an archer. The first arrow shot by William Tell with his crossbow succeeded in hitting the apple and splitting it in half; his son escaped unhurt. He aimed the second arrow at Gessler and the arrow pierced his heart, killing him instantly.

∾ APPLE CONNAUGHT – POMMES CONNAUGHT ∾

Is a sweet which consists of apples and custard. The apples are sliced and then baked in a buttered earthenware dish. The custard is baked separately in another buttered earthenware dish. When both dishes are baked, the cooked apple slices are arranged over the custard. The dish is then glazed with a mixture made of golden syrup and water, which is thickened with arrowroot. The syrup is coloured with red colouring. Apple Connaught is served cold.

History

The sweet was dedicated to General de Gaulle (1890–1970), who was the leader of the French forces during the Second World War (1939–1945). The General fled from France during the German invasion and crossed the Channel to England, in order to organize a free French fighting force in Britain. His headquarters for a period were at the Connaught Hotel, Carlos Place, Mayfair, and Apple Connaught was created while the General was based at the hotel.

∾ APPLE DUMPLING – POMME EN CAGE ∾

The apple is peeled and cored. The centre of the apple is then filled with sugar, sultanas and butter and flavoured with cinnamon or cloves. The apple is then covered with shortcrust pastry or rough puff pastry, brushed with egg-wash and baked in the oven. The Apple Dumpling is usually served with hot custard sauce.

History

This apple dessert originated in the district of Normandy, an area of France which is famous for its apples. In Normandy the dessert is called Bourdelot. The same dessert is made in other regions throughout France and many have their own regional names for the dessert. However, Pomme en Cage, which literally means an apple in a cage, is the name used throughout France. When the dessert is made with pears instead of apples, it then becomes Douillon. The dessert was introduced into Britain by the Norman invaders during the time of William the Conqueror (1027–1087), King of England from 1066.

∾ APPLE PIE ∾

Made with shortcrust pastry, it is usually a double crust pie which consists of a base, apple filling and a pastry top. It is made on an ovenproof or a tinfoil plate. The filling is made with sliced fresh apples which have been partially cooked in water with sugar. Often today, tinned apples are used for the filling. The apple filling can be flavoured with cinnamon. The pie is brushed with egg-wash and then baked in the oven. When cooked, the surface of the pie is liberally dredged with castor sugar. It is cut into wedges and can be served either hot or cold. It is delicious accompanied by custard, fresh cream, or ice cream.

History

Surely Apple Pie must be the king of all pies. This classic English pastry dates back to the sixteenth century. As early as the twelfth century, pies were made in England, but they always had a savoury filling. It was in Elizabethan England that apples began to be used as a sweet filling in pies. During this period in England, fruit was never eaten raw as it was thought to cause infection, and therefore was always thoroughly cooked before being used as a filling for pies, or in the production of fruit fools or mousses. The apples were cooked for a long period of time in wine, which was sweetened with honey, sugar or spices. There were a variety of different pastries made during this period – for example, the Elizabethan chefs made rough puff pastry and rich shortcrust pastry. The fruit pies were elaborately decorated with flowers and leaves. The recipe for Apple Pie first appeared in an English cookery book in 1590.

In France, however, the equivalent of Apple Pie is known as Tarte au Pommes and was made as early as the fourteenth century. The filling for the pie included apples, dried figs, raisins and sweet white wine. The mixture was flavoured with spices such as cinnamon, ginger and anise. The medieval cooks sweetened the apples with dried fruits and wine because sugar was so expensive. The French, therefore, were making sweet fruit pies two hundred years before the English. The pies were free-standing and were made with two rounds of pastry: one round acted as a base on which the filling was placed and the other was used as a covering. The surface of the Apple Pie was gilded with saffron and it was then baked in the oven.

In the eighteenth century the early English immigrants took the recipe to America, where it was to become immensely popular. Today, it is regarded by the Americans and the rest of the world as a typical American dessert and they have adopted it as their own. This is borne out by the expression 'as American as Apple Pie'.

∾ APPLE SNOW ∾

This is a cold sweet which is made with a mixture of cooked apples and meringue. The cooked apples are gently folded into a meringue mixture, then spooned into individual glasses or sundae dishes. The surface of the desserts is decorated with piped whipped cream.

History

This classic English dessert dates back to Elizabethan England, when a variety of desserts with meringue toppings were christened Snowes, because the white meringue resembled snow. It was also during this period that eggs were discovered as a raising agent and began to be widely used in baked goods and in cookery dishes.

∾ APPLE TURNOVER – CHAUSSON AUX POMMES ∾

Apple Turnovers can be made with either shortcrust or rough puff pastry. The pastry is rolled into small circular shapes, one half of the circle is covered with apple purée, the remaining half is pulled over the top of the filling, in order to enclose the apple purée and obtain the familiar half-moon shape of the pastry. The pastry is then egg-washed and baked in the oven.

History

The French name for the pastry, Chausson aux Pommes, translated into English means a slipper filled with apples. The pastry was so called because it resembled the shape of a shoe which was extremely fashionable in France at the time of its creation. The English name, Apple Turnover, of course refers to the fact that the pastry is turned over on top of the apples in order to cover the apple filling. Apple Turnovers were first made in Britain in the fifteenth century and at that time were known as Apple Pasties. The method of cooking the pastry was also different, as they were not baked, but were originally deep fried in oil.

∾ APRICOT – ABRICOT ∾

The apricot is the yellow-fleshed, edible fruit which comes from the tree, *Prunus Armeniaca*. The tree is closely related to the peach, plum and cherry trees. The fruit itself resembles a small peach and is yellow to orange in colour. It is a rich source of vitamin A and minerals, especially when dried, and also contains iron, calcium and potassium. The kernel is used to produce apricot brandy. The apricot is a very versatile fruit. It can be eaten fresh and is used extensively in the making of tarts, pies and confectionery. It can be conserved, especially in the production of jams and jellies, and can also be dried. One of the most popular recipes which includes apricots as its main ingredient is Apricot Condé, which is a rice pudding, decorated with apricot halves which are then glazed with boiling apricot jam.

History

The fruit originated in China. It was then introduced into Armenia and Persia, where the fruit was known as the Sun's Egg. The fruit was sold by the Romans at the price of one dinar for each apricot, thirty years before the birth of the great Roman historian Pliny the Elder (AD 23–AD 79). The Roman legions introduced the fruit into the northern countries of Europe during the Roman invasion. However, it was not introduced into Britain until the mid-sixteenth century. The French writer, Alexandre Dumas (1802–1870), who was also a fine gastronome, discovered and wrote about the healing properties of the fruit. He described how a special tea made with the fruit cured inflammation of the stomach.

∾ ARROWROOT – MARANTE ∾

Arrowroot is a starchy substance obtained from the roots of various plants and tubers. It is used as a thickening agent for puddings and sauces. Unlike sauces thickened by cornflour, which tend to be cloudy, sauces thickened by arrowroot are clear. The starch is easily digested and is often recommended for invalid cookery. Today, arrowroot is mainly produced in the West Indies, on the island of St. Vincent.

History

The plant is a native of tropical America. The word 'arrowroot' is derived from the Indian word *araruta*, meaning root. The Indians of South America used the arrowroot, *Maranta Arundinacea*, not for culinary purposes, but for medicinal purposes. The starchy substance was used as an antidote on wounds caused by poisoned arrows during battles.

Arrowroot was not known in Europe until the nineteenth century. Since then, the thickening agent has been used extensively in the kitchen for puddings and sauces. It has always been recognized for its easy digestibility and healing properties, and subsequently a variety of recipes emerged, specifically for invalids or convalescing soldiers. During the Victorian period in England the use of arrowroot in invalid cookery escalated, and these dishes were recommended in the diet of wounded soldiers convalescing in the aftermath of the Crimean War.

～ ARTOIS, GÂTEAU D' ～

The gâteau is made of puff pastry, which is rolled into two strips. One strip is brushed with apricot jam, over which almond cream is spread. The sides of the pastry strip are egg-washed, then the second strip of pastry, which is slightly larger, is placed on top. A criss-cross pattern design is obtained by using the point of a sharp knife. The gâteau is then egg-washed and baked. When cooked, the gâteau is brushed with hot apricot jam and the sides are decorated with nibbed sugar.

History

The gâteau was created over a hundred years ago in the former region of Artois, in the north of France, hence the name Gâteau d'Artois. Arras was the capital city of the former region.

～ ATHOLE BROSE – HEATHER HONEY ～

Is a type of soft sweet or drink, which consists of oatmeal, heather, whisky and cream or eggs.

History

Athole Brose is a Scottish creation. Scotland is a land full of wonderful myths and legends, and the story of how this recipe was created is no exception. Brose, quite simply, is a term used to describe oatmeal which is added to boiling milk or water and is then seasoned with salt. It is thought to have been introduced into Scotland by the French – the English word 'brose' is a derivative of the old French word *broez*. Brose has long been regarded as a typical Scottish dish, and in Scotland there are a variety of different Brose recipes which vary from region to region. In this particular recipe Athole refers to the Earl of Atholl who, according to the well known Scottish story, created the drink during a Highland Rebellion in 1476. He allegedly devised a plan to capture the rebel leader Ian McDonald, Earl of Ross. The story goes that the Duke knew of a well on the rock face of a local mountain from which the rebel leader drank. He cunningly filled the well with a mixture of whisky, honey and oatmeal. McDonald, typical of a true Scotsman, could not resist the whisky concoction and indulged himself to such an extent that the Duke, who was lying in wait to ambush him, surprised him and captured the intoxicated rebel leader!

James I (1566–1625), who was King of England from 1603 and King of Scotland (James VI) from 1567, was a great lover of the drink. He was reputed to have consumed large quantities of alcohol, and probably Athole Brose was a great favourite of his because of its alcoholic content.

B

∼ BABA AU RHUM – RUM BABA ∼

Is a small bun made from a fermented dough and flavoured with currants which have been flambéed in rum. The buns take their shape from the dariole moulds in which they are baked. When cooked, they are soaked in a hot syrup made with water, sugar and the zest of oranges. The syrup is sometimes flavoured with spices such as cinnamon and cloves. The Babas are then sprinkled with rum and glazed several times with boiling apricot jam. As a final decoration, half a glacé cherry and a piece of angelica are placed on top of the Baba.

History

The Baba as we know it today developed from the Kugelhopf. It was originally created in the early eighteenth century in Poland and was introduced into the French district of Alsace-Lorraine by Stanislas II (1732–1798), who was King of Poland from 1764 to 1795. He was the father-in-law of Louis XV (1710–1774), who was King of France from 1715. The pastry was christened Babka in Polish, which when translated into English means an old, bent woman. It was given that name because it resembled the shape of an old, bent woman. The dough at that time was made with rye flour and, when cooked, it was soaked in Hungarian wine. The Polish King adored the Babka, preferring it to be soaked in a very sweet white wine and flavoured with saffron. Years later, he renamed the pastry Ali-Baba, from the beautiful story *Ali-Baba and his Forty Thieves*, which was written by Edmond Galland. Gradually, over the years, it was shortened to one word only, Baba.

In 1835, a Polish baker called Sthorer brought the recipe for the Baba to Paris. He opened a patisserie in La Rue Montorgeuil which specialized in making Babas, and added Smyrna raisins and currants to the original recipe. When cooked and while still warm, they were sprinkled with rum instead of the traditional white wine, thus becoming Baba au Rhum. Today, Baba au Rhum remains a classic French dessert and is renowned worldwide.

∼ BAKED ALASKA – OMELETTE NORVÉGIENNE ∼

This is an ice cream dessert which is either bombe or oval shaped. The ice cream is sandwiched between layers of sponge which have been soaked in alcohol. The sponge is masked with an Italian meringue and is decorated with piped meringue. It is then put into a hot oven or under a salamander until the meringue is light golden brown in colour. Before it is served, the dessert is sprinkled with alcohol or a liqueur and set alight. The type of alcohol or liqueur used is determined by the flavour of the ice cream – for example, coffee, praline or chocolate ice cream should be flambéed with rum and vanilla ice cream should be flambéed with Kirsch. There are many different types of Baked Alaska, and the name which is given to the dessert is determined by the flavour of the ice cream used.

History

The Chinese created the first type of ice cream thousands of years ago and they were also the first to create a type of hot ice cream dessert which consisted of ice cream enclosed in a layer of pastry and baked. The date of this first hot ice cream dessert is unknown.

It was not until 1860 that a Parisian chef created a hot dessert made with ice cream which was covered in meringue and then baked in the oven. He christened his new creation Omelette Norvégienne, which translated into English means Norwegian Omelette, probably because the meringue resembled snow, and Norway to the French is a land of snow. The Americans renamed the ice dessert Baked Alaska, because the white meringue bombe-shaped dessert resembled the bombe-shaped igloos which are built from blocks of ice and are the traditional homes of the native Eskimos of Alaska, the forty-ninth state of America.

∾ BAKEWELL TART ∾

Is a flan made with puff pastry trimmings which are brushed with jam and filled with a mixture of eggs, sugar and butter. It is then baked in the oven and dredged with icing sugar, or the tart can be coated with water icing or fondant icing.

History

Bakewell Tart was originally known as Bakewell Pudding. The well-known and extremely popular English tart was created by accident by a female cook working in the Rutland Arms Hotel, Bakewell, Derbyshire. The cook was making a flan with left-over pastry trimmings covered with jam. As she had a surplus of eggs, sugar and butter she decided to mix them all together and fill the flan with the mixture. She melted the butter, added the sugar, then the eggs, the mixture was beaten thoroughly, then poured into the flan ring and baked. The Bakewell Tart had arrived!

∾ BAKING POWDER – LEVURE CHIMIQUE ∾

Is a chemical raising agent consisting of cream of tartar and sodium bicarbonate. Cream of tartar is a by-product of wine making.

History

Baking powder was invented by the English chemist, Alfred Bird (1813–1879). His wife was allergic to yeast and he decided to try to create a substitute for yeast. The result was baking powder. In the eighteenth century, bicarbonate of soda or potash were used in conjunction with sour milk as chemical raising agents.

∾ BANANA – BANANE ∾

The banana tree is not a tree as such, but is a fibrous plant. When the plant is a year old the flowering stem emerges. At the end of the stem are sterile male flowers and further up the stem are female flowers which develop into seedless fruit without being fertilized. When growing in the wild, bananas depend upon bats for pollination. All cultivated bananas are hybrid, sterile varieties. The banana plant produces approximately thirty kilograms of fruit, which is around two hundred bananas. The banana *Musaceae* family is native to the island of Sri Lanka.

The banana is used widely by the patissier to flavour cakes, bread and pastries, and many desserts use bananas as the main ingredient, for example, the classic desserts Banana Split and Banana Flambée. It is one of the most popular fruits eaten raw on the market today.

History

Banana plants probably originated in Asia, although the word 'banana' is not of Asian origin. Bananas were cultivated in prehistoric times. As far back as 600 BC, bananas were cultivated in India. The plant was introduced into China from India seven hundred years later. It is recorded that by the year AD 600, the banana plant was cultivated in the Arab States, and eventually it was introduced into Africa.

In the early seventeenth century the fruit was introduced into Europe. Although it had been known to the ancient Romans hundreds of years before this date, they regarded the banana as an exotic fruit which remained a subject of controversy. By the middle of the century the banana had arrived in France; however, it remained a luxury fruit and was not widely available to the French until the nineteenth century. The banana was brought back from Bermuda to Britain in the middle of the seventeenth century. However, it was to remain an extremely rare and expensive fruit for a long period of time, available only to the wealthy. It was the Spanish, during their expeditions to the New World, who introduced the fruit to the Americas.

∾ BANBURY CAKE ∾

Is made with rough puff pastry which is rolled out and cut into round pastry shapes with a pastry cutter. The pastry shape is moistened around the edges with egg-wash or cold water. A filling is made with butter, mixed peel, demerara sugar, currants and mixed spices. A spoonful of the mixture is placed in the centre of each pastry round. The edges of the pastry are drawn together up to the centre and are sealed together by pinching the pastry. The cake is then flattened by hand, turned upside down and rolled lightly with a rolling pin. The surface of the cake is egg-washed, slits are made on the pastry with the point of a sharp knife and the cake is then baked.

History

A type of cake very similar to the English Banbury Cake was brought back to England by the Crusaders in the thirteenth century from the East, and the English adapted the original recipe. The Banbury Cake originated in the town of Banbury in Oxfordshire, where it became a speciality of the region. Elizabeth I (1533–1603), Queen of England from 1558, adored the small cake and it became extremely popular during her reign. The original recipe differs slightly from the recipe of today; the original filling was made with a mixture of butter, mixed peel, demerara sugar, currants, mixed spices, sponge cake crumbs and flour, and the filling was flavoured with rum.

∽ BAP ∽

A bap is a small bread bun. The traditional recipe contains flour, salt, lard, yeast, sugar, milk and water. The ingredients are mixed into a soft dough which is covered and allowed to rise. The dough is then kneaded and divided into small rounds, which are then brushed with milk to glaze, or dusted with flour if floury baps are desired. They are then allowed to prove for fifteen minutes before baking. Baps are served for breakfast.

History

The recipe for the bap was created in Scotland. The meaning of the word 'bap' is unknown, although the word is of Scottish origin. The bap was created hundreds of years ago, probably as far back as the sixteenth century, and was the traditional bread bun served for breakfast in Scotland. By the eighteenth century, breakfast in Scotland was a lavish affair and could not be surpassed anywhere else in the world. The Scottish breakfast had an international reputation and could include cold meats, cheeses, eggs, kippers, bannocks, baps, oatcakes, honey, marmalade, jelly and, of course, a huge bowl of piping hot porridge seasoned with salt. The bap's reputation was further enhanced by being mentioned in the Scottish novel *The Bride of Lammermoor*, written by Sir Walter Scott in the nineteenth century.

∽ BATH BUNS ∽

Are small buns which are made with a yeast dough consisting of baker's flour, yeast, margarine or butter, sugar, salt, milk and eggs. Sultanas and candied peel are added to the dough. The buns are liberally sprinkled on the surface with nibbed sugar and currants before baking. This topping of sugar and currants is what distinguishes Bath Buns from other yeast buns.

History

The buns are named after the city of Bath, where they were first created, probably during the eighteenth century. During this period, Bath was an extremely fashionable and elegant city. The inhabitants of Bath were very sophisticated and cultured, both in fashion and in their eating habits. They were renowned for their appreciation of good food, and it was during this period that such wonderful recipes as Bath Buns and Sally Lunns were created.

∽ BATTENBERG CAKE ∽

Is an oblong-shaped sponge cake which is covered in marzipan. The sponge is made in two different flavoured squares which are divided into four oblong sections. The four oblong sections are sandwiched together with apricot jam. The oblong shape is then brushed with apricot jam and covered with a thin layer of marzipan. The sponge is made in two different flavour combinations of vanilla and chocolate or vanilla and strawberry. These two colour combinations give the cake its distinctive diagonally-shaped sections, which is the main characteristic of the cake and is extremely effective.

History

The cake was created towards the end of the nineteenth century and was probably named after the Prussian noble family of the same name. It was Victorian England, and there were extremely close links between the two countries during this period. Queen Victoria had married Albert, who was the second son of the Duke of Saxe-Coburg-Gotha, in 1840. The link was strengthened further when in 1884 her grand-daughter, Princess Victoria, married Prince Louis of Battenberg. Only one year later, the Queen's youngest daughter Princess Beatrice married Prince Henry of Battenberg.

∽ BATTER – PÂTE A FRIRE ∽

A batter is a mixture of flour, eggs and a liquid, which is usually milk. The main ingredients are put into a bowl and beaten together until a coating consistency is obtained. A batter may be used to coat sweet or savoury foods before cooking. The foods are usually shallow fried or deep fried. If the batter is used to coat savoury foods, it is seasoned with salt and pepper. When the batter is used to coat sweet foods, it is seasoned with sugar and spices. There are several different types of batter, which are listed below:

1 Plain flour, salt, yeast, water or milk.
2 Plain flour, salt, egg, oil and milk.
3 Plain flour, salt, egg, oil, milk and baking powder.
4 Plain flour, salt, egg, oil or melted butter and whisked egg whites.

Batters can also be used to make pancakes, crumpets, waffles, Yorkshire Puddings and Toad-in-the-Hole.

History

The English word 'batter' is a derivative of the French verb *battre*, which translated into English means to beat, describing the method of mixing the ingredients together. The French word for batter is *Pâte à Frire*. *Pâte* translated into English means paste and *frire* comes from the French cookery term *friture*, which in English means frying food in fat. Batters have been made since ancient times. The Romans made waffles with batters which were called *obelios*. The first Crusaders, on their return from the Holy Wars in the Middle East, introduced into Europe a recipe for coating foods with a batter and then frying them in deep, hot fat, commonly known today as fritters. Crêpes, which are also made with a basic batter, date back to early civilizations.

∾ BAVAROIS ∾

Is an egg custard which is made with egg yolks, milk and sugar. Gelatine is then added and finally lightly whipped cream. The whipped cream makes the mixture very rich. Some patissiers add Italian meringue to the mixture to reduce the cost. The Bavarois mixture is usually flavoured with vanilla essence, but other flavourings may be added to the mixture, for example, coffee, chocolate or praline, or often the Bavarois is flavoured with liqueurs. A Fruit Bavarois can also be made, using fruit juice or fruit purée, gelatine, lightly whipped cream and sugar; this type of Bavarois is usually flavoured with liqueurs or alcohol. The dessert is usually decorated with whipped cream, fresh fruits, glazed fruits or chocolate shapes, depending upon the type of Bavarois being made. The Bavarois mixture can also be used as a filling in desserts such as Charlotte Russe, Empress Rice, tortens and gâteaux. If the Bavarois mixture is poured into a dariole mould which is lined with sponge fingers or bread slices, it is then called a Charlotte. Bavarois is therefore an extremely versatile mixture.

History

Originally the Bavarois was not a dessert, but in fact was a drink. It was created in the middle of the eighteenth century in Paris. The story goes that the Princess of Bavaria, who lived in Paris during that period, frequented the famous Parisian café called Chez Protocope. She always ordered a sweet tea, which was made from a syrup flavoured with Maidenferne. The proprietor of the café named the drink Bavaroise in her honour. Eventually, at a later date, milk and cream were added to the drink and whisked together until frothy. Some time later, eggs were added to the drink and a Crème Anglaise was produced. The recipe was changed once again when gelatine and fresh whipped cream were added, and new flavourings such as chocolate, coffee and liqueurs. From a simple flavoured tea, a new dessert had been created.

∾ BÉCHAMEL SAUCE ∾

Is a basic white sauce which is made from a roux of fat and flour, to which boiling milk is added. The milk is flavoured with an onion studded with cloves, giving the white sauce a distinctive flavour. The sauce is then seasoned with salt and pepper, brought to the boil and allowed to cook until it thickens. Béchamel sauce is a basic white sauce to which other flavourings may be added to obtain a variety of sauces. For example, if cheese is added to a Béchamel sauce it becomes Sauce Mornay, if mustard is added, it then becomes a mustard sauce. The sauce is used widely by the Patissier Traiteur in France in the production of a variety of savoury dishes, such as Parmezanes and Croque Monsieur.

History

Béchamel sauce was created in France by the Marquis de Béchamel, who was Head Waiter to Louis XIV (1638–1715), King of France from 1643. The sauce was created to accompany a turbot which had been cooked for a royal banquet. It became extremely popular in Britain in the nineteenth century and was used in a variety of dishes by the Victorians.

∾ BEETON, ISABELLA ∾

Isabella Beeton was a famous English Victorian cookery writer.

History

She was born Isabella Mary Mayson in 1836 in London. She changed her surname to Beeton when she married Samuel Beeton, a young English publisher, in 1856. After her marriage, the young Isabella produced *The Englishwoman's Domestic Magazine*, which contained articles on dressmaking, cookery recipes and women's issues.

However, it was the publication of her first book called *Household Management* in 1860 which earned her the reputation as one of Britain's most knowledgeable cookery writers. The book was an immediate bestseller, and in 1865 the revised edition of *Household Management* was published.

Isabella Beeton died at the age of twenty-nine, only nine years after her marriage. In that short time she had given birth to four children and had also managed to write a book of mammoth proportions. A truly remarkable achievement for one so young.

⮾ BISCUIT ⮾

Today, biscuits are consumed in large quantities – the perfect partner for the British cuppa! They can be either sweet or savoury. Mechanization has meant that the shapes, flavourings and fillings of biscuits are endless. The main ingredients used in the production of biscuits are flour, fat, sugar, eggs, milk or water and flavourings. The biscuit has become an integral part of the British diet.

History

The word 'biscuit' is French and is a derivative of the old French word *biscut*. The English adopted the French spelling of the word in the eighteenth century. A type of biscuit dates back to Roman times, but they did not resemble the biscuits with which we are familiar today. The original biscuits were made with wheat flour and water. They were baked until they were so hard that in order to make them edible they had to be dipped into wine. It was an ideal food for the Roman soldier who was often on the march for long periods of time, as it was the only type of food which could be carried easily, did not need to be cooked and could be kept for months – in fact, perhaps the first convenience food!

As far back as AD 800, the biscuit was an important item in the French diet. The French Emperor Charlemagne provided his soldiers with biscuit rations during campaigns. In the ninth century in France, Charles III (879–929), who was King of France from 893 to 922, saved Paris, which had been besieged by the Vikings, by giving silver and gold to the Vikings, who then allowed the distribution of biscuits to thousands of Parisians who were dying of hunger.

As late as the seventeenth and eighteenth centuries, biscuits remained hard and not very appetizing. Under Louis XIV (1638–1715), who was King of France from 1643, the French peasants nicknamed biscuits the 'stone bread of the Turks'. During this period, biscuits were to remain the ideal convenience food for European soldiers and sailors, primarily because of their long-lasting quality. In 1792 they were distributed to the French army as rations, on the orders of Napoleon Bonaparte. They were to remain the staple diet for soldiers and sailors for many years.

It is interesting to note that even today the habit of dipping or 'dunking' biscuits into tea or coffee in order to soften them still continues, in much the same way as the Roman soldiers dipped their biscuits into a glass of wine to soften them thousands of years ago. Old habits die hard!

∾ Biscuits a la Cuillère – Sponge Finger Biscuits ∾

These biscuits are made with a light sponge mixture consisting of egg yolks, sugar, flour and whisked egg whites. The mixture is put into a piping bag and piped into finger shapes onto a greased baking tray and dredged generously with icing sugar before baking. The biscuits are baked until dry. They are used in the recipe for Charlotte Russe and are also served as an accompaniment to sabayon, ice creams and a variety of mousses. In France, it is the tradition to serve Biscuits à la Cuillère with a glass of champagne.

History

Biscuits à la Cuillère were created in France at the end of the seventeenth century. Charles Maurice de Talleyrand (1754–1838), a French statesman and a fine gastronome, suggested to Antoine Carême, the famous French chef, that the shape of the biscuits should be changed as he was unable to dip the original sponge biscuits into his glass of Madeira wine. Carême was puzzled as to how he could mould the sponge mixture into the correct shape, as this was before the invention of the piping bag. Then he had a flash of inspiration. Using a large funnel he poured the mixture through the funnel allowing it to be pushed through onto a baking sheet, thus obtaining the finger shapes with which we are familiar today. Talleyrand praised the new shaped biscuits which allowed him to dip them into his glass of Madeira wine after a meal. The biscuits were an instant success, and today in France the habit of dipping biscuits into a glass of wine is considered polite. However, today it is usually a glass of champagne.

∾ Biscuit Glacé – Iced Biscuit ∾

This iced dessert does not in fact contain any biscuit mixture. Egg yolks and caster sugar are whisked together over a bain-marie, like a Genoese sponge mixture. Italian meringue is added to the mixture, and finally lightly whipped cream. Today, the meringue mixture is often omitted. The mixture is poured into either a round or rectangle mould and frozen. The dessert is decorated and is usually accompanied by an egg custard. The dessert can be flavoured with alcohol or liqueurs, flavoured essences or chocolate, for example.

History

It was created towards the end of the eighteenth century by Tortini, an Italian who lived in Naples. The dessert is called a biscuit because the method used is similar to the method for making biscuits.

∾ BLACK BUN ∾

Black Bun is also referred to as Scotch Bun. It is a pastry case which has a rich fruit filling and a pastry top. The pastry is used to line a cake tin into which a heavily fruited mixture is placed. The mixture consists of dried fruits, mixed peel, chopped almonds, baking powder, plain flour, soft brown sugar, spices and salt. The ingredients are bound together with an egg and some brandy. A pastry lid is placed on top and the bun is baked in the oven. The bun should be made several weeks before use, as the flavour improves with age. It can be stored for up to six months because of the amount of fruit used in the filling and the alcohol content.

History

The name Black Bun was given to this pastry because of its intense, rich, dark colour caused by the heavily fruited filling, hence the name Black. Bun is an old Scottish word which is a derivative of the French word *bugne*, which translated into English means hump (Ref.: *Le Petit Robert 1*, 1972). Originally it was a twelfth cake, and was traditionally served on the Twelfth Night after Christmas, commonly known throughout the Christian world as the Day of Epiphany. The eating of a festive cake on Twelfth Night was an ancient European custom upheld by Christians in France, Britain, Holland and other European countries up until the eighteenth century. For example, the Galette des Rois was the traditional twelfth cake eaten in France on the Day of Epiphany and was the equivalent of the Scottish Black Bun. The Black Bun was reputed to have been eaten on the Day of Epiphany by Mary Stuart (1542–1587), who was Queen of Scotland from 1542, at her court in Edinburgh Castle in the sixteenth century.

Over the years, the tradition of eating Black Bun on Twelfth Night has died out in Scotland and today the bun has become part of Scotland's Hogmanay celebrations. It has become a tradition in Scotland that anyone who passes across the threshold after twelve o'clock midnight on New Year's Eve will be welcomed with a wee dram of whisky and a generous slice of Black Bun or a piece of shortbread!

It is interesting to note that as late as 1745, in Scotland, a law was passed which prohibited Scottish bakers from producing any rich buns or breads except for occasions such as Christmas, Easter, weddings, christenings and funerals!

∾ BLACKBERRY –
FRAMBOISE SAUVAGE / MÛRE ∾

Is the fruit of the prickly shrub of the bramble, *Rubus Fruticosus*. The blackberry is rich in vitamin C and minerals.

The patissier uses the fruit extensively in the making of flans, tartlets, fruit bavarois, fools, mousses and sorbets. It is an ideal fruit for jam and jelly making as it is extremely rich in pectin. Blackberries have a wonderful flavour when eaten raw and are widely available for purchase. However, blackberry gathering is a popular activity with many British families as the fruit grows wild throughout Britain. In fact, such is the popularity of gathering blackberries that, in the Northeast of England, the third week of October is known as blackberry week. In France, the fruit is used to produce a liqueur called Crème de Mûre.

History

Blackberries have grown in the wild since antiquity. The fruit is known as a blackberry in England, but in Scotland is more commonly known as a bramble. The fruit is native to northern parts of Europe. It also grows extensively in Asia. Today, the blackberry is cultivated extensively in North America.

∼ BLACK FOREST GÂTEAU – GÂTEAU FORÊT NOIRE ∼

Is made with a chocolate Genoese sponge which is cut into three layers with a sharp knife. The sponges are soaked in syrup which has been flavoured with Kirsch. A filling is made which consists of strawberry jam, whipped cream and black stoneless cherries. The sponge layers are then sandwiched together with the filling. The surface and the sides of the gâteau are masked with whipped cream. The sides are then covered with chocolate vermicelli, or grated chocolate, and the surface is decorated with chocolate curls or flaked chocolate and dredged with icing sugar. There are many variations of this recipe.

History

The Black Forest Gâteau originated in Germany, probably in the Black Forest, a mountainous forest region in Baden-Württemberg, West Germany, hence its name. The gâteau became extremely popular in Britain in the middle of the twentieth century, and towards the end of the century remains a favourite dessert of the British.

∼ BLANC-MANGE ∼

Is a pudding which is made with milk or water, ground almonds, caster sugar, egg yolks, gelatine, and sometimes whipped cream is added. The addition of cream makes the pudding richer. Usually the mixture is poured into individual dariole moulds or into a large dariole mould and allowed to set in a refrigerator. The Blanc-mange is then turned out of the mould and decorated with whipped cream and glazed fruits.

History

Blanc-mange is a recipe which dates back to ancient times; a similar recipe was known to the Romans. The pudding was named Blanc-mange because of its perfect white colour. Blanc-mange is a French word. Originally it was spelt Blanc-manger: *blanc* when translated into English means white and *manger* is the French verb which means to eat. Gradually the R ending of the verb was dropped and the pudding became known as Blanc-mange.

At first the pudding was savoury, not sweet. It was introduced into Britain during the time of William the Conqueror (1027–1087), King of England from 1066. The savoury pudding was made with a mixture of diced chicken, almonds, milk and rice; all the ingredients were white in colour. The pudding was to remain a savoury dish for hundreds of years. In the fourteenth century, the famous French chef, Taillevent, stated in one of his cookery books that 'Blanc-mange was beneficial to people who were sick and it aided their recovery'.

The change from a savoury to a sweet dish was a slow process. Chicken was the first ingredient to disappear from the original recipe. At first honey was used as a sweetener and was later replaced by sugar. At a later date, gelatine was added. By the seventeenth and eighteenth centuries, Blanc-mange was a popular sweet pudding in France and Britain, especially with the aristocracy. Françoise d'Aubigné, Marquise de Maintenon (1653–1719), who was the second wife of Louis XIV (1638–1715), King of France from 1643, adored the white, sweet pudding and it was always served at royal banquets during her reign. Another member of the French aristocracy, the Marquis de Cussy (1767–1841), who was made a marquis by Napoleon (1769–1821), declared that 'Blanc-mange is the best pudding of all time'!

Blanc-mange was to remain an extremely popular pudding of the British up until the middle of the twentieth century. However, the recipe has been changed over the years. Arrowroot and then cornflour were introduced into the recipe as a thickening agent. As artificial colourings were introduced, the pudding, which had always been white in colour, was made in a variety of different colours, making a nonsense of the pudding's name. Today, Blanc-mange has disappeared from the British table.

∾ BLIND ∾

To bake blind is a cookery term used to describe the method of baking pastry flans or tartlets. The pastry tins or flan rings are lined with the pastry and are then covered with greaseproof paper. Dried peas or beans are placed in the centre of the greaseproof paper in order to hold it down. A recent invention is the use of aluminium baking beans. The weight of the beans prevents the pastry from rising whilst baking. When the pastry is cooked, the filling is then added.

History

As far back as the thirteenth century, flans and tarts were baked blind. However, the pastry was made to such a stiff consistency that no support moulds such as flan rings were used. The free-standing pastry flans were baked blind in the oven and when cooked, the filling was then added.

∾ BLUEBERRY – MYRTILLE ∾

The wild blueberry is to be found all over the northern hemisphere. It is the fruit of the bushy plant belonging to the genus *Vaccinium Myrtillus*. The fruit grows where the soil is acid and arid. The plant produces masses of white flowers, which are followed by dark-bluish small berries. Today, the plant is widely cultivated and produces much larger berries. The berries are a rich source of vitamins A and B and are especially rich in vitamin C.

The berries are extensively used by the patissier in the production of fruit coulis, ice sorbets, tarts, flans, pies and also in the making of jam and jelly. Because of its wonderful colour and attractive appearance, the fruit is used in the presentation of gâteaux and sweets. Eaten raw, blueberries are excellent and are full of flavour.

History

Blueberries have grown in the wild since prehistoric times and have been a source of food to man since that time. Probably the European wild blueberry originated in Denmark, as *bil* is a derivative of the Danish word *bolle*. In Scotland they are known as whinberries or blaeberries – *blae* is an old Scottish word for blue. In America the blueberry is also known as the huckleberry, a name which was immortalized by the American author Mark Twain, who wrote *Huckleberry Finn*.

For centuries the fruit has been recognized for its medicinal properties. It contains substances which lower the amount of sugar in the blood. It is also reputed to soothe intestinal problems. An interesting fact is that during the Second World War (1939–1945), British night-fighter pilots were given blueberries as part of their diet in order to improve their night vision. It is the skin of the fruit that contains substances which improve night vision.

The patissier uses the fruit in the production of cheesecakes, mousses, fools, crumbles and sorbets. The fruit is also used in the classic American pastry, Blueberry Muffins.

∾ BOMBES GLACÉES – ICE BOMBS ∾

Are ice cream desserts. Bombe refers to the spherical shape of the mould in which the dessert is made. The mould is lined with ice cream and then filled with a bombe mixture. The bombe is turned out of the mould and decorated with whipped cream, glazed fruits and angelica.

A basic bombe mixture consists of egg yolks, whipped cream and syrup. Sometimes an Italian meringue is added to the mixture. It is flavoured with alcohol or a liqueur. There are a variety of different flavours and each flavour has its own name. For example:

Dame Blanche

Consists of a vanilla ice cream filled with a bombe mixture flavoured with almonds.

Bombe Javanaise

Consists of coffee ice cream filled with a bombe mixture flavoured with banana.

Bombe Singapore

Consists of strawberry ice cream filled with a bombe mixture flavoured with pineapple.

History

The Bombe Glacée was created by an Italian called Tortini in Naples in 1798.

∽ BONBONS LIQUEURS ∽

A confectionery made with sugar syrup which is flavoured with alcohol or a liqueur. The flavoured syrup is poured into special trays which are filled with starch. The starch is imprinted with the desired individual bonbon shapes. The flavoured syrup is poured into the shapes and is allowed to stand for several minutes before the surface of the tray is lightly dredged with starch. The tray is then placed in a warm cabinet, at a constant heat of 30 °C to 40 °C, for twenty-four hours until a crystallized shield has formed around the bonbons. The bonbons are then coated with fondant, marzipan or chocolate, or a combination of two of these.

History

In Paris in the nineteenth century, the most fashionable pastry shops in the capital were all situated in the Rue de Lombard. It was in one of these patisseries that Bonbons Liqueurs were first created by a French patissier called Gile. The recipe for the bonbons was created purely by accident. Gile specialized in confectionery, an art which was of Italian origin and had been introduced into France during the time of Catherine de' Medici (1519–1589). Experimenting in his kitchen one day, he filled a tray with icing sugar and made small individual imprints into the icing sugar. He then poured a cooked sugar solution into the small shapes. Gile decided to place the tray in a warm cabinet for several hours, in order to allow the sugar solution to set. However, he forgot about the tray until a few days later. He discovered that a sugar coating had formed on the outside of the bonbons and the inside was of a pouring consistency. Realizing the potential of his discovery, he repeated the process several times in order to achieve perfection. Finally, he cooked the sugar solution to the 'soft ball' stage, which is around 107 °C or 225 °F. This time, he made the small imprints for the bonbons with the keys to the kitchen of the patisserie. This resulted in bonbons which were key-shaped, with perfect soft centres. Gile is quoted as saying 'Here is the key', meaning he had discovered the process to make bonbons with a hard outer shell which contained perfect liquid soft centres. It was at a later date that alcohol and liqueurs were added to the recipe. Today, the syrup or liqueur solution used for the bonbons should have a density of between 30 and 31 °B.

∾ BOUCHÉE A LA REINE ∾

Is a puff pastry case which has a savoury filling. A bouchée is, in fact, a small vol-au-vent. The bouchée is made in two different sizes. The first size can be popped into the mouth and eaten. The second size is for one person only, usually served as a hot entrée at the beginning of a meal and eaten with a knife and fork. The traditional filling for the bouchée is a chicken velouté sauce to which diced cooked chicken, mushrooms and diced cooked sweetbreads are added. A variety of other savoury fillings include seafood, cheese savoury and vegetable savoury.

History

Bouchée is a French word, which translated into English means mouthful. The name refers to the size of the small pastry, which consists literally of one mouthful. *A La Reine*, translated into English, means of the Queen. The small bite-sized bouchée was either created by Queen Marie Thérèse, who was the first wife of Louis XIV(1638–1715), King of France from 1643, or his second wife, who had at one time been his mistress and was called the Marquise de Maintenon. She married the King in 1684.

The larger bouchée was not created until much later, probably during the time of the French chef, Antoine Carême (1784–1833). During this period, the bouchée was also made with a sweet filling of pastry, cream and nuts.

∾ BOULE DE NEIGE – SNOWBALL ∾

Is a petit four which is made with marzipan, chopped glacé cherries and flavoured with Kirsch. The mixture is rolled into tiny marzipan balls by hand, then rolled in icing sugar.

History

This particular petit four got its name because of its resemblance to tiny snowballs. It was created in the twentieth century.

∽ BOURDALOUE TARTE ∽

Is a flan which is made with shortcrust pastry. Pear halves are placed on the bottom of the flan and are covered with frangipane. The Bourdaloue Tarte is baked in an oven and can be served either hot or cold. Before serving, the tarte is dredged with icing sugar.

History

In 1824 a new patisserie opened near the church called Notre-Dame de Lorette, in Paris. It was in this patisserie that the first recipe for a baked dessert made with frangipane was created in 1850. The new dessert was called Entremet Bourdaloue. The frangipane mixture consisted of ground almonds, sugar, eggs and vanilla flavouring. A few years later, poached apricots were added to the recipe. By the twentieth century, the dessert was totally transformed. The original baked dessert was replaced by a shortcrust pastry flan with a filling of pears and frangipane and was christened Poire Bourdaloue, which later became Bourdaloue Tarte.

∽ BRAZIL NUT – NOIX DU BRÉSIL ∽

Brazil nuts are the nuts of the *Bertholletia Excelsa*, which belongs to the family *Lecythidaceae*. The nut is very rich in oil and is extremely nutritious; it contains vitamins B and E, minerals and protein. The tree grows up to thirty-five metres in height and is native to countries in South America, mainly Brazil. It produces a fruit almost the size of a coconut which, when ripe, falls to the ground. On impact the fruit breaks and opens, revealing the seeds or nuts, which are then gathered. The trees grow in the dense jungles of the Amazon basin, and the natives who gather the nuts wear special hats to protect themselves from the falling fruit. The nuts are used widely in the production of chocolates and sweets, and are one of the most popular nuts which are eaten in their natural state.

History

The nut takes its name from the country of its origin, Brazil. Brazil was a Portuguese colony from AD 1500. When Napoleon invaded Portugal in 1807, John VI (1769–1826) had become Regent because his mother was declared insane. John VI decided to flee to Brazil and did not return to Lisbon until 1821. During that period the Portuguese brought back from the New World a variety of foodstuffs unknown to the Europeans. It is highly probable that they introduced the nut into Europe at that time. The name Brazil nut was not known until the nineteenth century.

∾ BREAD AND BUTTER PUDDING ∾

The pudding consists of stale bread slices which have been buttered. The crusts of the bread slices are usually cut off. The buttered slices are placed neatly at the bottom of an ovenproof dish, slightly overlapping, and are sprinkled with raisins or sultanas, or a combination of both. An egg custard which has been flavoured with vanilla is then poured over the bread slices and nutmeg is sprinkled over the top. The pudding is baked in an oven until the custard is set and the bread slices are golden brown. Before serving, the surface of the pudding is dredged with icing sugar. Bread and Butter Pudding is served hot.

History

Bread and Butter Pudding is the descendant of an old English pudding called a Whitepot, which was popular in seventeenth-century England. Whitepots consisted of a mixture of cream, eggs, breadcrumbs, dried fruits and spices, and the mixture was boiled. The recipe for Bread and Butter Pudding came at a later date. In the middle of the nineteenth century, recipes for the popular pudding were appearing in cookery books. In the English cookery book *Household Management*, which was written by Isabella Beeton (1836–1865) and published in 1860, a recipe for the pudding is given, indicating that by that date the pudding was well established.

The Victorians were obsessed with being economical in the kitchen, and wastage was frowned upon. The cooks during that period were appalled by the extravagance of their French counterparts. Bread and Butter Pudding was substantial, nutritious and, most important to the Victorians, it was economical. Puddings such as Bread and Butter Pudding and Cabinet Pudding were created in order to use up left-over bread which otherwise would have been wasted.

The pudding remained popular right up until after the Second World War. It became a firm favourite with the working classes because it was so filling and it was also cheap and nutritious. However, it also appeared on the lunch menus of most hotels and restaurants, indicating that its popularity was not only restricted to the lower classes.

In the 1990s, Bread and Butter Pudding has taken a tumble in popularity with the British housewife. However, this classic traditional British pudding can still be found on the menus of some hotels and restaurants in Britain. For example, the renowned chef, Anton Mosimann, has created his own special recipe for this wonderful British pudding. I can think of no higher tribute!

∾ BRETON GÂTEAU ∾

Is a type of heavy sponge which is made with plain flour, butter, caster sugar, egg yolks and currants which have been soaked in rum. Sometimes mixed peel or chopped angelica are added to the mixture. The biscuit mixture is put into a well greased ovenproof dish or a flan ring and baked in a moderate oven. When cooked, the surface of the gâteau is scored with the point of a knife in a diagonal design and glazed. The gâteau is cut into wedges and can be eaten either hot or cold.

History

The gâteau was created in 1848 by a chef called Dubose who was working in the Seugnot family household in the district of *Finistère*, in the extreme west of Brittany. Translated into English, *Finistère* means land's end. Originally, the recipe for Breton Gâteau did not include currants and mixed peel; these ingredients were added to the recipe at a later date. Small biscuits called Galettes Bretonnes can also be made from the mixture.

∾ BRIOCHE – PÂTE A BRIOCHE ∾

Brioche is a rich fermented dough. It is made with bread flour, sugar, salt, eggs, yeast, butter and a little milk. The brioche can be moulded into a variety of designs, each design having a different name. For example, a brioche made in a fluted mould is called Brioche Parisienne or Brioche à Tète. If the brioche is made in a deep dariole mould, it then takes the name Brioche Mousseline. However, if it is made in a bread tin, it is known as a Brioche Nanterre. Brioche dough is also used in the production of Pain au Chocolat and Pain aux Raisins. This makes them richer than using the traditional croissant dough. When the sugar is omitted, brioche dough can be used for savoury dishes such as Beef Wellington or Pâté en Croûte.

History

Brioche is a French creation. In the seventeenth century it was known as Apostle or Prophet Cake. It originated in the Brie district of France north of Paris, a region famous for its cheese, which is also called Brie. Brie cheese dates back to the eighth century and was the favourite cheese of the Emperor Charlemagne (AD 742–AD 814), who was Emperor of France from AD 800. The original brioche was made with flour, salt and water, and the Brie cheese was added to the dough to flavour it. During that period brioche was leavened by one-day-old bread dough, which of course contained wild yeast. The approximate quantity of old bread used for this purpose was one quarter of the total brioche dough. Alexandre Dumas (1824–1895), the famous French writer who wrote *The Dictionary of Cookery*, informs us that the name Brioche was given to the pastry when Brie cheese was added to the basic dough.

At a later date, the water was replaced with milk, then eggs were introduced to the mixture, and finally butter was added to the recipe. At some point the Brie cheese was excluded from the recipe. Yeast was not used to leaven the dough until the end of the sixteenth century. In the book

Mémorial de la Pâtisserie (fourth edition), which was written by Pierre Lacam and published in 1898, he states that the Parisian bakers were the first to use fresh compound yeast.

In the eighteenth century, a patissier in Paris added 250 millilitres of eau-de-vie, which is an alcohol of 46 per cent proof, to four kilograms of flour, in order to make the flour stronger, thus increasing the elasticity of the dough. Strong flours were extremely difficult to obtain in France during that period – most strong flours were imported from Hungary and were outrageously expensive. Later, when white flour became available, it was used to make brioche. However, because of the high cost of the ingredients, it was eaten mainly by the rich. During this period bread was the staple diet of the French peasants, a rough, brown bread. Brioche was traditionally eaten by the peasants at Christmas and was regarded as a luxury food.

In the year 1788, the year before the French Revolution, the country's crop of wheat was virtually destroyed because of severe frost and extremely heavy rainfall, which rendered the wheat grain soft. Widespread famine followed the destruction of the crop. The French peasants were starving, and they marched through the streets of Paris in protest, demanding bread. Marie Antoinette, wife of Louis XVI, King of France from 1774, on hearing their cries, immortalized brioche forever by responding, 'Let them eat cake', referring, of course, to brioche. The peasants, infuriated by their Queen's indifference to their plight, rebelled against the monarchy. It was the start of the French Revolution!

∽ BUCKWHEAT ∽

Buckwheat is a grain plant of the family *Polygonaceae*. It grows to about one metre in height, in poor soil, and can tolerate poor summers. It is the seeds of the plant which are edible. Although it is an extremely nutritious grain, buckwheat is poor in gluten content and therefore it is necessary to mix it with wheat flour in order to make a successful bread dough. It is used throughout the world as an ingredient for speciality products: for example, it is used in the United States of America in the production of buckwheat pancakes, while in Russia it is the main ingredient in the traditional savoury dish, Blinis.

History

Buckwheat originated in Manchuria, a north-eastern region of China, and also in central Siberia. It was imported into Europe by the Slavs, an Indo-European people. Buckwheat bread was made in ancient times; then, of course, it was unleavened. It was made into girdle cakes or galettes. Its main ingredients were buckwheat flour, water, salt and sometimes animal fat. It was very hard and resembled a hard-shelled biscuit.

❧ BUTTER – BEURRE ❧

Butter is made from milk, usually cow's milk. It is a fat composition which is widely used by the patissier. The average cow's milk contains about 3.9 per cent of butterfat. Ten litres of milk are needed to make five hundred grams of butter. All butters are strictly controlled by legislation as to their fat, salt and moisture content. Butter provides energy as well as the fat-soluble vitamins A, D and E.

Butter is invaluable to the patissier in the production of butter creams, fermented doughs, sponge mixtures, pastry and biscuits. Its uses are too numerous to mention.

History

Butter dates back to ancient times. It originated in central Asia, where the nomadic herdsmen carried milk in small goatskin bags which swung on the sides of their horses. As the herdsmen rode along, the motion of the horse caused the small goatskin bags to act like little churns and produced the first type of butter. Butter was introduced into India and then gradually came into use in Europe.

Initially, the Romans used butter purely for medicinal purposes, preferring to use oil. The Ancient Greeks also were reluctant to use butter and preferred olive oil. However, eventually both Greeks and Romans relented, and the use of butter is well documented during the time of Ancient Greece.

In medieval England and France, as early as the thirteenth century, butter was recorded as being used by bakers and patissiers. It was also used for cooking purposes during that period. In the Middle Ages in England, butter was made in a wooden churn with a plunger. It became part of the daily diet and was used extensively for centuries.

In the seventeenth century in England, butter was extremely cheap. It was heavily salted in order to preserve it.

In the nineteenth century, cheaper butter substitutes were invented. They had an inferior flavour and not the same nutritional value; however, sales for the substitutes rose. Butter and the cheaper substitutes were to remain in competition up until the present day.

❧ BUTTER CREAM – CRÈME AU BEURRE ❧

There are many types of butter cream:

1 A solution of sugar and water is cooked to make a syrup. It is then poured slowly into a mixer containing whole eggs, and the mixture is whisked at medium speed and allowed to cool. The unsalted butter is then added and mixed until the mass becomes homogenous.
2 Unsalted soft butter is added to an egg custard and then whisked until a butter cream is obtained.

3 Unsalted butter and icing sugar are creamed together. Unsalted butter is usually made in Normandy in France, or in Holland.
4 Unsalted butter is creamed until soft and mixed with an Italian meringue or Swiss meringue. *See* Meringue.

Butter cream is used widely by the patissier as a filling for gâteaux, cakes, petits fours and for decoration. The butter cream can be flavoured according to the specific finished product. For example, Gâteau Moka is a Genoese sponge which is coffee-flavoured with a filling of coffee butter cream. Butter cream is much more popular in France for patisserie. In Britain, patissiers prefer to use fresh cream in the production of baked goods.

History

Butter cream was invented by a patissier called Quillet, in Paris, around the early nineteenth century. Originally the cream was known as Crème à Quillet; gradually it changed simply to Crème au Beurre.

C

∾ Cabinet Pudding ∾

The pudding is made in a Charlotte mould, which has been greased with butter and sprinkled with sugar. The bottom of the mould is layered with sultanas and currants. The mould is filled to the top with diced Genoese sponge. An egg custard is then made and strained over the diced sponges. The sponges are allowed to soak in the custard. The Cabinet Pudding is then placed in a tray of warm water and cooked in a moderate oven. The pudding is demoulded and served with a hot custard sauce.

History

This popular British pudding dates back to Victorian times. During that period, the thrifty Victorians were renowned for creating dishes from leftovers. The saying 'Waste not, want not', was a particular favourite of the Victorians. It was an era of grand houses and extravagant dinner parties which often resulted in large quantities of food being left over. Recipes such as Cabinet Pudding and Trifle were extremely popular during this period – both recipes were made with stale sponges, were economical and appealed to the Victorians, who regarded waste as a sin. The Trifle was served cold and Cabinet Pudding was steamed and served hot with a hot jam sauce. The Victorian recipe for Cabinet Pudding was made in a Charlotte mould, and the ingredients included stale sponge pieces, ratafias, macaroons, dried and glacé fruits, jelly or jam, and custard which was flavoured with brandy and vanilla.

∾ Candied Fruits – Fruits Confits ∾

Fresh fruits which are suitable for this process include, for example, apricots, figs, cherries, pears, melons, mangoes and pineapples. Ideally, the fruit should be of a high quality and should be uniform in size. It should be gathered before it is ripe. If necessary, depending on the fruit used, it should be peeled and cored.

The initial stage is to immerse the prepared fruit in a liquid solution to enhance its colour during the process. The next stage involves washing the fruit and blanching it to soften the flesh. The final stage involves immersing the fruit in a series of sugar solutions which have an increased density of sugar. This final stage can take several days in order to ensure that the fruit is saturated with the sugar solution. The total process can last up to twelve days, depending upon the fruit used. Candied fruit must be stored in airtight containers in order to prevent premature drying out.

History

Candied fruits were known to ancient civilizations in China, Asia and Greece. In ancient times, honey was used to preserve fruit, flowers and seeds. It was the Romans who introduced candied fruits to other parts of Europe.

In medieval France, candied fruits were served at banquets. In the sixteenth century, a French confectioner from the city of Apt, in the Côtes du Rhône district of France, supplied Pope Clement VII (1523–1534) with candied fruits. Oliver de Serres (1539–1619) wrote a book called *Théâtre d'Agriculture et Ménage des Champs*, which included a recipe on how to candy fruit. He stated that 'To achieve the perfect candied fruits, the syrup must reach the heart of the fruit'. The process used at that time by the French was a great deal more involved than the process which had previously been used by the Romans.

Candied fruits were a popular delicacy in Elizabethan England. They were often carried in the pockets of the nobility and were eaten throughout the day, just as we would carry a packet of sweets today. The process of candying fruits was regarded as a highly specialized task during this period. The fruits were often presented on the table at large banquets.

Today in France, after over four hundred years, the city of Apt still produces candied fruits, which are regarded as a speciality of the city. Each year, over fifteen thousand tons of candied fruits are exported abroad!

∾ CANNELÉ ∾

Is a gâteau which is made with a mixture of flour, eggs and sugar which is flavoured with rum and vanilla. The mixture is put into a serrated round mould and baked in the oven. The serrated edge of the gâteau is the main characteristic of Cannelé.

History

Over one hundred years ago in the city of Bordeaux, a port on the southwest coast of France, the local nuns, who cared for the poor in a hospice near the harbour, would often meet the ships docking in the busy port. Many of the ships were returning from voyages from the French colonies such as Tahiti. The ships were carrying cargoes of such luxuries as sugar, rum and vanilla. During that period these items were affordable only by the wealthy. However, as the cargoes were being unloaded they were often damaged. The nuns would beg for the damaged or spilt food to give to the poor in their care. With such exotic ingredients as rum, vanilla and sugar, they created, with the addition of eggs and flour, Cannelé, a delicious gâteau for their patients. The recipe for the gâteau spread throughout the Bordeaux region, where it is still popular today, and soon spread to other regions of France. Today in Paris, the Cannelé has become a speciality cake in the small fashionable patisserie called Ponjauron in the city.

∾ CAPE GOOSEBERRY – ALKEKENGE JAUNE DOUX ∾

The Cape gooseberry, *Physalis Peruviana,* is a plant which belongs to the *Solanaceae* family. It produces a small berry which is edible; the fruit is yellow in colour and is enclosed by thin, paper-like leaves. It will keep for several weeks and can be used in a variety of ways. To prepare the fruit, the outer leaves are removed.

The patissier uses the fruit in the production of petits fours; the small berry can be dipped in fondant, chocolate or boiled sugar. It is also an excellent fruit for making jam. Eaten raw, the fruit has a fragrant, sweet flavour which is quite delicious.

Cape gooseberries are a rich source of vitamins, especially vitamin C, potassium and beta carotene, which is needed to produce vitamin A. It remains an expensive fruit, but is usually available throughout the year in specialist shops or supermarkets.

History

The Cape gooseberry is native to South America. It was later introduced into Australia, India, Sri Lanka, China and Malaysia.

∾ CARÊME, ANTOINE ∾

Antoine Carême was a French chef who is regarded as the founder of the classical French Haute Cuisine.

History

He was born on 9 June 1784 in the Rue du Bac in Paris. His parents, Jean Gilbert Carême and Marie Jeanne Pascal, had a large family of fifteen children. His father was an alcoholic. The family lived in poverty, and Carême was encouraged by his father to leave home and earn money in order to become independent. He started working in a cabaret, which was a type of pub, where he worked for several years until he had finished his apprenticeship at the age of sixteen. He then found a job in the kitchen of a small restaurant in Paris. It was not long before the owner recognized how imaginative and talented the young boy was in the business and recommended him to the establishment of a Monsieur Bailly in the Rue Vivienne in Paris which was one of the first patisseries in the city, and was later to become the renowned La Maison Félix.

Carême was later employed by the French statesman, Talleyrand, working under the famous executive chef, Laguipière. Monsieur Laguipière was later to be made the executive chef to Marshal Murat, King of Naples (1767–1815). Laguipière froze to death retreating with the French army from Moscow; he was at that time executive chef to Napoleon.

In 1808 Carême married Henriette-Sophie Mahy de Chitenay. He was by this time acclaimed as one of the best chefs in France, and was responsible for organizing all the important functions for the Emperor Bonaparte.

Carême's greatest talent was in display work, and his reputation in this area has remained unsurpassed. They were works of art: palaces, temples and columns were made into display pieces using different types of sugar paste. One of his favourite hobbies was to spend his free time in the library sketching from books to give him new ideas for his display pieces.

However, as well as creating pastry recipes, Carême was becoming equally creative as a chef and was also responsible for many French classical cookery dishes. He became chef to Alexander I (1777–1825), who was Tsar of Russia from 1801. He was also employed by the Prince Regent in England as his executive chef. In 1823 he entered the service of James Rothschild, a financier.

Carême retired several years later in order to finish his book, *The Art of French Cookery in the Nineteenth Century* (1833). Other publications include *The Royal Patissier Parisian* (1815), *The Picturesque Pâtissier* (1815) and *The French Head Waiter* (1822). On 12 January 1833 he died at the age of forty-nine and was buried in the famous Montmartre Cemetery in Paris.

∾ CASSATA, SICILIAN ∾

A Cassata is a type of ice dessert. It can be made in an oblong mould or in a bombe glacée mould. The bombe is partially filled with vanilla ice cream and an orange sorbet, and a hole is left in the centre of the bombe which is filled with a special mixture consisting of whipped cream, macaroons, Italian meringue and candied fruit, such as angelica, orange peel and candied cherries which have been soaked in a liqueur. This Cassata is known as the Sicilian Cassata and is usually served on special occasions such as weddings and christenings.

History

The Cassata was invented by an Italian around 1860.

∾ CATO, MARCUS PORCIUS ∾

He was a Roman statesman (234 BC–149 BC).

History

He was reputed as saying, 'Carthage must be destroyed'. He wrote one of the first cookery books called *The Farming Manual*, which described in detail the everyday lives of Romans during that time, including how the bakers of that time made bread and pastries. It also revealed that as early as 168 BC they were regarded as having a profession and were called Pistores.

∾ CHARLOTTE ∾

This is a dessert which may be served hot or cold. Usually the Charlotte is sweet, but it may also be savoury. Often the Charlotte includes a bavarois mixture. There are numerous recipes for Charlottes, all with their own specific names. Originally they were made in dariole moulds, which were special metal bowls made of copper with brass handles. Today, for hygienic reasons the dariole moulds are made of plastic or stainless steel.

History

The name Charlotte dates back to the early nineteenth century. The Charlotte was inspired by a variety of English puddings during that period. It is probable that the Charlotte was named after Queen Charlotte, Princess of Mecklenburg-Strelitz, who was the wife of George III (1738–1820), King of Great Britain and Ireland from 1760. Mecklenburg is a district of Germany to be found on the Baltic coast. Since its creation in the nineteenth century the list of different types of Charlottes has extended, and today it remains just as popular as it was during that period.

∾ CHARLOTTE ANDALOUSE ∾

The same method as a Charlotte Russe (see below), but the bavarois mixture is flavoured with orange instead of vanilla. Alternatively, the mixture may be made with orange juice.

∾ CHARLOTTE AUX POMMES – APPLE CHARLOTTE ∾

Perhaps one of the most popular of all the Charlottes. The mould is lined with buttered bread slices which have been cut into fingers. The fingers are placed in the bottom of the mould and around the sides. A filling is added, consisting of apples which have been cooked in butter, breadcrumbs and sugar flavoured with cinnamon. Bread fingers are arranged neatly on the surface in order to cover the filling. The Charlotte is then baked in a hot oven. Breadcrumbs are added to the filling in order to absorb the excessive moisture from the apples, thus preventing the Charlotte from collapsing when it is turned out of the mould. Charlotte aux Pommes is served hot with a hot apricot sauce.

History

This hot Apple Charlotte was created by the French chef, Antoine Câreme, in 1820.

∾ CHARLOTTE POMPADOUR ∾

The dariole mould is lined with eclairs which have been filled with chocolate and coffee pastry cream. They are placed alternately around the mould. A chocolate or coffee bavarois mixture, or a combination of both, is then poured into the mould. The Charlotte is allowed to set in the refrigerator. Charlotte Pompadour is decorated with choux buns which are filled with coffee and chocolate pastry cream. The choux buns are arranged on top of the sweet and are glazed alternately with coffee and chocolate fondant. This is one of the most elaborate Charlottes.

History

The dessert was named after the mistress of Louis XV (1710–1774), who was King of France from 1715. His mistress was originally called Jeanne Antoinette Poisson, and later became the Marquise de Pompadour (1721–1764).

∾ CHARLOTTE ROYALE – CHARLOTTE ROYAL ∾

The same method as Charlotte Russe, but instead of finger biscuits the mould is lined with Swiss Roll. Once the bavarois mixture has set, the mould is then turned out and the Charlotte is glazed with hot apricot jam.

History

It was created in the eighteenth century.

∾ CHARLOTTE RUSSE ∾

The dariole mould is greased lightly with melted fat, usually unsalted butter, and the mould is lined with finger biscuits. A bavarois mixture, flavoured with vanilla, is poured inside the mould. The mixture is placed in a refrigerator and allowed to set for several hours. It is then turned out onto a dish and decorated with whipped cream.

History

Antoine Carême, the great French chef (1784–1833), created the Charlotte Parisienne, later known as the Charlotte Russe, as during that period everything Russian was considered extremely fashionable. Carême had also spent a great deal of time in Russia, where he was executive chef to

Alexander I (1777–1825), who was Tsar of Russia from 1801. Carême filled the base of the Charlotte Russe with a mixture called bavarois and the recipe remains much the same today. In 1820 Carême created Charlotte aux Pommes, which was a hot Charlotte.

✐ CHEESECAKE – GÂTEAU AU FROMAGE ✐

There are two main types of cheesecake. The first type, which is known as baked cheesecake, consists of a shortcrust pastry flan with a filling of cream cheese, eggs, sugar and flavouring. Other ingredients may be added to the basic filling mixture, such as almonds, dried fruit, fruit purée, nuts, fruit juices or zest of fruits. The cheesecake is baked in the oven. When cold, the baked cheesecake is decorated with freshly whipped cream and fruit. The second type is known as a gelatine set cheesecake and is uncooked. It has a base made with digestive biscuit crumbs and soft butter and the filling consists of soft cream cheese, sugar, cream (whisked egg whites or meringue may be added) and gelatine. A topping of a compote of fresh fruit such as strawberries, cherries or blackcurrants is added. The uncooked cheesecake can be put into a refrigerator to set or can be frozen for use at a later date.

History

A type of cheesecake dates as far back as 200 BC, during the Roman Empire. The small cakes (called Libums) were made with wheat flour, cheese and eggs and were baked in a type of oven. Another type of cheesecake which was very popular with the ancient Romans was the Savillum, which was made with wheat flour, ewe's cheese, honey and eggs. The mixture was baked in an earthenware dish and when it was cooked was brushed with hot honey and dredged with poppy seeds.

In thirteenth-century England, cheese tarts were extremely popular. The ruthless English king, Edward I (1239–1307), King of England from 1272, who was nicknamed Longshanks because he was so tall, reputedly adored cheese tarts. The type of cheese tart which was made at his court was made with a pastry case which had a filling of Brie cheese, cream, eggs, sugar and spices. The tarts were baked in the oven and served either hot or cold. Brie cheese was a French cheese which dates back to the twelfth century in France. King Edward I had a son, Prince Edward, who married Princess Isabella of France, daughter of Philip IV (1268–1314), who was King of France from 1285, and it is very likely that the young French princess brought this particular recipe from her homeland, as cheese tarts were also a popular speciality in France during that period. This type of old English cheesecake was on sale to the public as early as the fourteenth century, and cheesecake stalls were a familiar sight at annual country fairs.

The county of Yorkshire produced a speciality cheesecake which was made from local curd cheese, eggs and lemon, and baked in a pastry case. This recipe has survived up until the present day and is world-renowned.

However, it is generally accepted that the modern type of cheesecake originated before the seventeenth century in Russia and Poland, where a variety of speciality cheesecakes originated and have become classic recipes of these countries. The cheesecakes which were made in Russia and Poland were made with the curd of cheese, which was of a fairly hard consistency, egg yolks and cream. Fruit purée and lemon or orange juice were then added to the curd. This mixture was then sweetened with sugar and dried fruit, then poured into a pastry case and baked. It was in the seventeenth century that this type of cheesecake became popular in Britain. A recipe for a coconut cheesecake appeared in the English cookery book called *Modern Cookery*, by Elizabeth Acton, which was published in 1855. Recipes for a variety of cheesecakes appeared in other cookery books during this period.

The recipe for baked cheesecake was introduced to America by the early European immigrants. The uncooked, gelatine set cheesecake was created in America at a later date and was introduced into Britain in the twentieth century. The new convenience cheesecake became an outstanding success in this country and is probably one of the most popular desserts in Britain today.

∾ CHELSEA BUNS ∾

These are made from a basic bun dough which is rolled into an oblong shape. It is then brushed with melted butter and sprinkled with sugar, mixed spices and currants or sultanas. It is rolled out just like a Swiss Roll and cut into sections. The sections are placed on a baking tray and allowed to rise in a prover until they have at least doubled in size. The buns are then brushed with egg-wash and baked in a hot oven, approximately 225°C. When cooked, they are sprinkled with caster sugar. Chelsea buns are ideal for continental breakfast or afternoon tea.

History

The Chelsea Bun originated in Chelsea, a district of London, at the end of the seventeenth century. It is said that the Royal family and the nobility of that time visited the Chelsea Bun House in London each morning, to have coffee and to eat a Chelsea Bun. Such illustrious personages as George I (1660–1727), King of Great Britain and Ireland from 1714 was among the first to sample the new pastry. His son, George II (1683–1760), King from 1727, and his wife, Queen Caroline of Anspach carried on the tradition. Other continental pastries are similar to the Chelsea Bun, notably the French pastry called Pain aux Raisins and Danish pastries.

∾ CHERRY – CERISE ∾

The cherry is a tree of the genus *Prunus*, which also includes such fruits as peaches, plums, apricots and almonds, all belonging to the family *Rosaceae*.

There are two types of cherries, sweet and sour, both of which have been cultivated from the wild cherry tree. The sour cherry, *Prunus Cerasus*, and the sweet cherry, *Prunus Avila*, still grow wild in Britain. Cherry trees are grown not only for their fruit, but also because of their beauty. They produce beautiful white flowers and are often grown as ornamental trees. The cherry is rich in vitamin C and is a good source of potassium. It is widely available in this country.

The cherry, as a fruit, is used extensively by the patissier. It is quite beautiful in appearance, has a wonderful colour and the fruit is small and almost perfect in shape. Different varieties of cherries have quite distinctive flavours. The sweet variety can be eaten raw as a fruit or as a dessert. When used as a decoration, they enhance greatly a variety of desserts, gâteaux and pastry goods. Large black Morello cherries are used to make such classic desserts as Black Forest Gâteau and Cherry Strudel. The sour cherry can be used in the production of pies, jams and sorbets. Cherries are also used in the production of liqueurs and alcohol, such as Maraschino, which is the name of the particular type of cherry used in the production of the Italian liqueur. Kirsch is made with the kernels of the cherry and Cherry Brandy is also made with the fruit. This versatile little fruit is also used as an ingredient in many cookery dishes or used to make an accompanying sauce, for example, roast duck with black cherry sauce. It can also be conserved in alcohol and served after a meal, for example, Griottines.

History

The wild cherry tree from which the sweet cherry tree was grafted, originated in Persia and Armenia. The Romans were responsible for the cultivation of the fruit in France. Before they invaded the fruit grew in the wild throughout France. The Romans were responsible for introducing the tree to Great Britain. Pliny describes eight types of cherries, one of which was called after a member of his family. During Tudor times in England, the fruit was well documented in the making of tarts and pies and was extremely popular.

The fruit is now grown extensively in Britain, mainly in the south of England. Today, France is the largest producer of the fruit and the bulk of the production is used for the country's own consumption.

∾ CHINESE GOOSEBERRY, KIWI FRUIT – SOURIS VÉGÉTALE ∾

The Chinese gooseberry, or, as it is most commonly known, the kiwi fruit, belongs to the family *Actinidia Chinensis*. The fruit is oval in shape and has a rough greenish-brown skin. The skin is usually removed. The pulp of the fruit is pale green and has an abundance of little black seeds. It is understandable as to why this fruit was named the Chinese gooseberry, as it does taste a bit like the gooseberry; however, it is not as acidic and tastes slightly sweeter. It is extremely rich in vitamin C and is a good source of potassium. Eaten raw, the fruit is delicious.

The patissier uses the fruit mainly in the production of fresh fruit salads, tartlets, flans and iced sorbets, and because of its attractive appearance and colour it is used to decorate many desserts.

History

The fruit was named the kiwi by the New Zealanders, after their national emblem, the kiwi bird. The fruit was discovered in China in the late eighteenth century and was introduced to New Zealand shortly afterwards, where it was grown commercially. Today, kiwi fruits are grown in the USA and in Mediterranean countries such as France and Italy, where the production of kiwi fruit has surpassed that of New Zealand.

∾ CHOUX GLAND – ACORN BUN ∾

The Choux Gland is made from choux pastry and piped in the shape of a large acorn, approximately the size of a medium-sized choux bun. It is filled with Crème Chantilly which is flavoured with rum and it is then glazed with a green fondant and dipped in dark chocolate vermicelli on one side only.

History

It was invented after 1860, a short time after the large Gâteau Religieuse.

∾ CHOUX GRILLÉS ∾

These are choux buns filled with a pastry cream which is flavoured with rum. This type of pastry is usually served for afternoon tea.

History

Like Ramequins au Fromage, the Choux Grillés were invented in 1760 by a patissier called Avice.

∾ CHOUX PASTRY – PÂTE A CHOUX ∾

Choux pastry is made with cake margarine or butter, medium strength flour, whole eggs, salt, sugar and a liquid which can be water or milk, or a combination of both. The fat is placed in a pan with the liquid and allowed to melt and the liquid is then brought to the boil. The pan is removed from the heat and the flour is added to the liquid and mixed thoroughly into a panada. It is then returned to the heat until the pastry stops sticking to the pan and the spatula. The pastry is allowed to cool in a bowl before mixing in the eggs gradually until the correct piping consistency is obtained. The choux pastry is then piped into the required shapes onto a baking tray and baked until crisp and dry.

Choux pastry is one of the most versatile pastries and is used in the production of such classic savoury dishes as Pomme Dauphine, Gnocchi Parisienne, or as a garnish for soups such as Consommé aux Profiteroles. Classic sweet dishes include Gâteau Paris-Brest, Gâteau Saint-Honoré, Eclairs, Profiteroles and Croquembouche.

History

In 1533, when Catherine de Medici left Florence to marry the Duke of Orléans who was later to become Henry II (1519–1559), King of France from 1547, she brought with her to France her entire court, which included her chefs. Seven years later in 1540, her head chef, Panterelli, invented a hot, dried paste with which he made gâteaux. He christened the paste Pâte à Panterelli. The original recipe changed as the years passed, and so did the paste's name. It became known as Pâte à Popelini, which then became Pâte à Popelin. Popelins were a form of cake made in the Middle Ages and were made in the shape of a woman's breasts.

A patissier called Avice perfected the paste in the middle of the eighteenth century and created Choux Buns. The Pâte à Popelin became known as Pâte à Choux, since only Choux Buns were made from it. Antoine Carême in the nineteenth century perfected the recipe, and this is the same recipe for choux pastry as is used today.

∾ CHOUX PONT-NEUF – PONT-NEUF BUN ∾

This is a small tart made with short paste or puff paste trimmings, over which choux paste is piped into half-ball shapes. It is then baked and allowed to cool. It is filled with pastry cream, which has been flavoured with Kirsch or rum. The top of the bun is dredged on one half with icing sugar and brushed on the other half with raspberry or strawberry jam.

History

The Choux Pont-Neuf were being made in 1861 in a variety of cities in France – Lyon, Bordeaux and Nantes. In one particular day in a pastry shop in Nantes, the patissier used ten kilograms of cream to fill the Choux Pont-Neuf buns sold in his shop, highlighting the popularity of the buns during that period! The small pastry buns were called after the newly constructed Pont Neuf bridge over the River Seine in Paris.

∾ CHOUX SALAMBÔS – SALAMBÔ BUNS ∾

Small, oval-shaped choux paste buns which are filled with a pastry cream flavoured with Kirsch or rum, glazed with a light brown caramel and decorated with green nibbed almonds. Choux Salambôs are suitable as afternoon tea cakes.

History

They were invented by a Parisian patissier for the première of the opera *Salambô*, written and conducted by Reyer in 1890.

∽ CHRISTMAS LOG – BÛCHE DE NOËL ∽

The traditional Christmas Log is made with Genoese sponge in the shape of a log. It is coated with butter cream which is usually flavoured, and the sponge is usually also flavoured with alcohol or liqueurs complementing the flavour of the butter cream. The log is then decorated to resemble a real wooden log and adorned with holly, robins, Christmas trees, etc.

History

In France, the meal after midnight to celebrate Christmas will always end with the Christmas Log as a dessert. It will either be a Christmas Log biscuit or an iced log. In England, Christmas lunch, which takes place on Christmas Day, will usually end with Christmas Pudding as a dessert or Christmas Cake. Bûche de Noël is the French equivalent of the British Christmas Pudding or Christmas Cake.

The tradition of the Christmas Log in France dates back to the warlords of the tenth century. During this period the peasants had to pay a tax to their lord. Usually it was wheat, hay, straw, wood, poultry or wine. On Christmas Day they brought a large wooden log, often the main trunk of a tree, since chimneys in the castles were so large. Depending upon the province, peasants laid fruit or wine over the logs as a sign of prosperity for the New Year. The idea of the Christmas Log originated from this period.

∽ CHRISTMAS PUDDING – POUDING DE NOËL ∽

Christmas Pudding is a mixture of flour, eggs, breadcrumbs and suet which contains a variety of dried fruits, spices and nuts, flavoured with alcohol such as rum or brandy. Traditionally the mixture was enclosed in muslin and steamed for several hours. Today, however, the pudding is usually put into tin foil containers and steamed. The Christmas Pudding is made months before the festive season in order to allow the flavour and aroma to develop. The traditional accompaniment to the pudding is brandy butter.

History

Christmas Pudding or Plum Pudding was created in 1675. In Scotland it is often referred to as a Clootie Dumpling. The invention of the pudding bag or pudding cloth in the seventeenth century heralded new recipes for steamed suet puddings. Before 1675, the pudding was known as Plum Broth, which in fact was savoury pudding thickened with breadcrumbs and was not served as a dessert but at the beginning of the meal.

According to the French catering magazine *Hippocrate* (Ref.: *November issue*, 1947), the original recipe for a sweet steamed pudding with fruits was brought back from Spain to England in the middle of the seventeenth century by the Duke of Buckingham. The Duke had been sent on a mission to Spain to arrange a marriage for the young Prince of Wales (1600–1649), who later became King Charles I of Great Britain and Ireland in 1625. The Duke failed to arrange a marriage, but he brought back the recipe for a type of Plum Pudding, so his mission was not a complete failure!

The custom of pouring brandy over the Christmas Pudding and setting it alight before serving originated in Britain hundreds of years ago, a custom which is still practised today. Another custom which has survived is the tradition of putting small trinkets or coins into the pudding mixture before steaming; this dates back to the eighteenth century. In the nineteenth century the Duke of Wellington introduced the Christmas Pudding to the Parisians during a stay in Paris at Christmas in 1815. In June of that year he had defeated Napoleon at the Battle of Waterloo. The French were not impressed by the heavy steamed pudding, and since that date the recipe has largely been ignored by the French.

Today, hundreds of years after its creation, Plum Pudding remains the English national dish and is the traditional dessert served at the end of the British Christmas dinner. Christmas would not be complete without Christmas Pudding served with lashings of brandy butter.

∽ CINNAMON – CANNELLE ∽

Cinnamon, *Cinnamomum Zeylanicum*, is a sweet spice with a wonderful flavour. It comes from a small evergreen tree which flourishes in hot, wet, tropical countries throughout the world. The spice is extracted from the bark of very young trees. It is used a great deal by the patissier to flavour pastry goods and puddings. Usually the cinnamon is ground, but cinnamon sticks can also be used to flavour certain recipes. In the Middle East, this sweet spice is used to flavour a variety of savoury dishes.

History

The English word 'cinnamon' is a derivative of the Latin botanical name for the tree, *Cinnamomum*. The modern French name for the spice, *cannelle*, comes from the old French word *canne* (Ref.: *Le Petit Robert 1*, 1972). The tree is native to Sri Lanka, but today is grown in other parts of the world, for example, Indonesia, Madagascar, Mauritius and Brazil.

Cinnamon is a very old spice, perhaps one of the oldest spices known to man: it was mentioned in manuscripts during biblical times. It was the Chinese who were the first to use the spice as a flavouring in cookery. They had knowledge of spices such as cinnamon and cloves long before the Europeans. It was brought back and introduced into Portugal by the Portuguese explorer, Vasco da Gama (1469–1525), on his return from one of his voyages of exploration to the East Indies. The French and Portuguese were responsible for introducing the spice to the rest of Europe, brought back from their colonies in the East.

In medieval England, cinnamon was used to flavour an endless variety of cakes and puddings. Originally the English used the spice to flavour sweet as well as savoury dishes. At that time spices were very expensive, and dishes tended to be heavily spiced.

⟟ CLAFOUTIS ⟟

Clafoutis is a mixture of plain flour, eggs, sugar, milk and, of course, cherries, which are the main ingredient. The curiosity of the dish is that the stones of the cherries are not removed. The dessert can be served hot. The mixture is baked in an earthenware dish, then dredged with sugar before serving. It can also be used as a filling for a tart or flan and can be served hot or cold and then dredged with sugar.

History

The name Clafoutis comes from the French verb *clafir* (Ref.: *Le Petit Robert 1,* 1972), which comes from a particular dialect which is spoken in the centre of France. *Clafir*, in English, means to fill. Two French provinces are claiming that the Clafoutis originated from their area. The Berry, which is now divided into two districts, Le Cher and L'Indre, is an area situated in the middle of France. These two districts are well known for their massive production of cherries. The other province claiming the recipe as theirs is Le Limousin, which also produces a large quantity of cherries between the end of May and the end of July.

⟟ CLEMENTINE ⟟

Is simply a small orange. It is a hybrid between a mandarin and an orange. These hybrids are called tangers and include not only the clementine, but also the king mandarin. The clementine is associated with Christmas in Britain because it is a winter fruit. It is grown extensively in North Africa and Spain. The small fruit, which is rich in vitamin C, has a lovely flowery smell which is quite distinctive and is very sweet to eat. As a fruit, it is very popular with the patissier and is used in the production of petits fours déguisés, tartlets, flans and fruit salads. Its small, orange-coloured segments are ideal for decoration purposes.

History

The clementine was created in 1902 in Algeria by Father Clement, who grafted a mandarin tree onto a bitter orange tree called Bigaradier.

∾ CLOVE – CLOU DE GIROFLE ∾

The clove tree, *Eugenia Aromatica*, belongs to the *Eucalyptus* family. The tree, which needs a tropical climate in which to grow, reaches a height of seven metres. Today, it is well established in such places as Madagascar, Sri Lanka and Indonesia. The clove is the dried, unopened bud of the evergreen tree. It is widely used as a flavouring in savoury as well as sweet dishes. Many pastry dishes are flavoured with cloves. For example, Rum Babas and Savarins are soaked in a syrup which has been flavoured with cloves. Cloves are also used extensively in cookery to flavour sauces.

History

The English word 'clove' is a derivative of the Latin word *clavus*. The French word for the clove is *clou de girofle*, which translated into English means nail of the unopened flower. The small, dried bud does indeed resemble a small brown nail. The tree is native to the Moluccas Islands in South-East Asia.

The Chinese were the first to use the clove as a spice in their cookery thousands of years ago. It was not until the Middle Ages that the spice was introduced into Europe. The Portuguese explorer, Vasco da Gama (1469–1525), brought the spice back to Portugal from the East Indies at the end of the fifteenth century. The Portuguese then introduced it into other parts of Europe.

∾ COCOA – CACAO ∾

Cocoa is a powder produced from the beans of the *theobroma cacoa* tree. The cacoa tree grows in tropical countries in Central America, Oceania, Equatorial Africa and South Africa. The fruit or pod contains the cocoa beans which are allowed to ferment at a temperature of between 45°C and 47°C. The fermentation is allowed in order to kill the sprouts of the beans and to remove the pulp. The beans become a deep shade of red to brown in colour, allowing the aroma to develop. They are then dried. Under the sun this can take up to two weeks; however, in cocoa production today, special-ized machinery is used for this process as it is more efficient. The dried beans are then packed and exported to factories. A bean contains 55 per cent of fatty matter known as cocoa butter, 10 per cent of albumin, 1.5 per cent of theobromine, which is a type of caffeine, and minerals.

In the factory the beans are soaked, then heated to a temperature of between 100°C and 150°C to intensify their aroma and to eradicate any humidity which remains. The beans are then pounded in machines at a temperature of between 50 °C and 70 °C, allowing the fat content or cocoa butter to mix with the solid mass to obtain the cocoa paste. As well as cocoa powder, cocoa butter is also obtained from the bean. Cocoa butter is filtered, tempered, moulded and finally stacked. It melts at 37 °C, does not go rancid and keeps extremely well. It is used in confectionery to produce chocolate sweets. Cocoa powder is used as a flavouring for cakes, pastries, confectionery and ice creams.

Chocolate – Chocolat

To know what chocolate is, one has to understand the structure of the cocoa bean. The bean consists of cocoa butter and cocoa powder. Good quality chocolate is referred to as converture and consists of crushed cocoa beans, cocoa butter and a syrup solution. Poorer quality chocolate is referred to as baker's chocolate. The cocoa butter is replaced with vegetable oil. Good quality white chocolate consists of cocoa butter, refined sugar and flavouring, for example, orange or lemon.

History

In Central America, thousands of years ago, the *theobroma cacoa* tree, which means food of the gods, grew in the wild. The tree reaches a height of five to seven metres and produces large pods which can measure anything between fifteen and thirty centimetres. The pod is shaped like a rugby ball and weighs between three hundred and five hundred grams. An established tree will produce up to one hundred and sixty fruits, which is approximately six kilograms of cocoa. The cocoa pod may contain between thirty and seventy beans, each bean measuring approximately twenty-five millimetres in length. The life-span of a cacoa tree is about thirty years, and the tree will produce fruit five years after being planted.

The Indians who lived in the tropical forests used the pod as a source of food. Initially, they ate the pulp from the pod and discarded the beans inside. The discarded beans were a source of food for the parrots and squirrels in the forest. However, the Indians eventually realized that the beans were a valuable source of food, which could be used for their own consumption.

The Mayan Indians who originated in the Yucatán peninsula in Central America in 2600 BC, and had sites in Mexico, Guatemala and Belize, ate the flesh and the beans of the cocoa pod. By the tenth to twelfth centuries, the Mayan Indian civilization had declined and Mayan Central Mexico was then ruled by the Toltec Indians. They followed the tradition of eating the flesh and the beans of the cocoa pod.

In the thirteenth century, the Aztec Indians, who had migrated from the north, cultivated the cacoa tree. The cocoa beans became, for them, a source of food and money. A rabbit was worth ten beans and a slave was worth over one hundred beans! The beans were then pounded, grilled, mixed with water and used as a drink. The drink was reputed to be the cure for a variety of diseases. The cocoa butter which formed on the surface of the liquid was used as a beauty cream.

In the sixteenth century, a voyage to the New World was financed by the Spanish King. On 30 July 1502, Christopher Columbus landed in South America. The Aztec Indians greeted him at Guanaga and made a gift to him of the cocoa beans. To them it meant a source of wealth. In 1519, when the Spanish Conquistador, Hernando Cortés, landed in South America, the Aztec Emperor, Montezuma II (1466–1520), Emperor from 1502, attempted to stop him. However, no great struggle resulted and no battle was ever recorded. Later, Cortés wrote: 'after you have drunk this beverage, it is possible to travel a whole day without feeling tired'. No wonder the Indians referred to the cocoa beans as the 'food of the gods'. The cocoa bean was then taken back to Spain. The Spanish, who did not like the bitter taste of the drink, added honey to sweeten it. Later, cane sugar was used to sweeten cocoa when the Spanish cultivated sugar cane in South America.

In 1568, the cocoa beans were imported to countries in Europe commercially. Aware of the fashion of the time and the quantity of cocoa beans in demand, the Dutch took the lead in the shipment of the new commodity between Central America and Europe. In 1585, the first shipment of cocoa beans arrived in Spain from Vera-Cruz in Mexico. Cocoa was introduced to the Italians in 1594, but it was not until 1657 that the British introduced cocoa to the nation.

When Anne of Austria, daughter of Philip III of Spain, married the French King Louis XIII in 1615, cocoa was introduced to the French nation. On the 25 May 1659, Louis gave to David Chaillon, who was an officer of the Queen, the exclusive privilege to sell a beverage called chocolate to his clientèle in his Parisian café in the Rue de L'Arbre-Sec. In 1679, the first shipment of cocoa, which was produced by a French colony, arrived in the port of Brest, in Brittany in France.

During the reign of Louis XV (1710–1774), who was King of France from 1715, it was fashionable for the aristocracy to carry little purses which contained pastilles made of cocoa and sugar. In 1770 the first chocolate company was opened in France, called Thé's Pelletier. At the Faculty of Medicine in Paris, the first machine to pound cocoa beans was invented by a Frenchman called Doret. The French Revolution in 1789 temporarily halted progress in production as the International Blockade practically stopped the consumption of cocoa and chocolate. In 1819, Pelletier built the first factory in Paris, which used steam as a method of production. Around the same time, François-Louis Cailler founded in Switzerland, the first Chocolaterie, which was a shop specializing uniquely in the production of chocolates on a commercial scale.

Nine years later, in Amsterdam, a Dutchman called Conrad Johannes Van Heuton invented a new technique in the manfacture of cocoa. The machinery removed a great deal of the cocoa butter from the beans and pounded the residue into a very fine powder. The product was patented by the

Dutchman, and cocoa powder in the form we know it today was born.

Antoine Brutus Meunier, in 1824, opened at Noisiel-sur-Marne, east of Paris, the first industrial chocolate factory in the world, and in the same year Philip Suchard founded at Neuchatel in Switzerland the famous Suchard chocolate factory, the first of its kind in Switzerland. This heralded the beginning of chocolate production in Switzerland, and in 1831 Amedee Kobler opened the second chocolate factory. This was followed by a procession of chocolate manufacturers such as Daniel Peter, Lindt and Tobler, resulting in Switzerland becoming one of the leading countries in the production of quality chocolate.

Industrialization brought more efficient and sophisticated machinery, and in 1841 a new machine was invented by Hermann, which was to replace the one invented by Doret sixty years earlier. In 1850 François-Jules Devinck invented a new machine which roasted, mixed and scaled the cocoa beans.

Chocolate which was manufactured at this time was dark chocolate, known to us today as plain chocolate. In 1870, at the Tobler factory in Switzerland, a new chocolate was invented after eight years of research, and it was christened milk chocolate.

∾ COCONUT – NOIX DE COCO ∾

The coconut tree belongs to the *Palmae* family, *Cocos Nucifera*. The tree grows to a height of thirty-five metres. When the tree reaches maturity, it yields over a hundred coconuts in a single year. The nut is enclosed within a hard, brown shell which has a rough, hairy texture. The inside of the nut has hard, white, flesh and the nut contains a white, pleasantly flavoured milk. The coconut is a poor source of vitamins and minerals in comparison to other nuts. The flesh is usually used when dried in desiccated or flaked form and is used extensively in the production of confectionery, sponge mixes, petits fours, or to decorate a variety of cakes and pastries. Coconut is used in cookery by countries in the East, and many classic traditional Eastern dishes contain coconut as a flavouring. The flesh, when eaten raw, is quite pleasant and has a very delicate flavour.

History

The name 'coconut' comes from its Latin name, *Cocos Nucifera*. The coconut tree is native to Malaysia. It is recorded that the natives of the Indus region of Asia ate coconuts five thousand years ago. The Persians brought the coconut back from their military expeditions in the Indus region, which is in the north-west of India. In AD 750, Baghdad became the trading capital of the Arabian world. The coconuts were imported from India to be sold in countries in the West, thus introducing the coconut throughout Europe.

It was not until the sixteenth century that the nut was introduced into Britain, and it was commonly known as the Indian nut because it had been imported from India. It was nearly a hundred years before the name coconut was used by the English. However, the coconut has never really been appreciated by the British, in comparison with other imported nuts. It has remained something of a novelty, and is mostly associated with the coconut shy, a familiar stall at the British fairground today. Across the Channel in France, the coconut is sold in slices from coconut stalls at fairgrounds. However, desiccated coconut has been highly valued since Victorian times as an ingredient in Western cookery, as a flavouring and also for decoration purposes.

Today, coconuts are cultivated throughout the world in countries such as Sri Lanka, India, Malaysia, Kenya, the Ivory Coast and the Philippines.

❧ COFFEE – CAFÉ ❧

Exactly where the coffee plant originated from remains unclear; however, it is thought to have been growing for thousands of years in the tropical forests of the world. The coffee shrub, which grows up to fifteen metres in height, belongs to the botanical family *Rubiaceae*, which consists of over five hundred different types. There are three main species, *Arabica*, *Canephora* and *Liberica*, which are used for the production of coffee. The two most important species of coffee are *Arabica*, which accounts for 70 per cent of the world's production, and *Canephora Robusta*. Two other species are grown on a smaller scale; *Liberica* and *Dewevrei*. *Arabica* consists of numerous varieties, among which there are Typica and Bourbon, which have in turn been developed into different strains. *Arabica* grows well in a temperature between 15 and 24 °C and *Robusta* in a temperature between 22 and 30 °C. Generally speaking, the *Arabica* species grows well at a high altitude; however, it could be damaged by frost at an altitude of two thousand metres. This happened to a crop in Brazil in 1994, resulting in the price of coffee soaring in the world market. *Robusta* grows well at an altitude of up to eight hundred metres. The coffee plant cannot tolerate frost.

History

Over a thousand years ago in Abyssinia, which is known as Ethiopia today, a goat herder called Kaldi reported that his goats, after eating some red berries from bushes in the mountains, seemed to be full of energy and began leaping about wildly. The abbot in charge of the local monastery was intrigued by the reports, and decided to gather the berries. He mixed them with hot water to produce an infusion of clouded liquid. The infusion was pleasant to taste and resulted in the abbot having an increased energy level. The liquid became the accepted drink within the monastery, and thus coffee as a beverage was born! In the Arabian states, coffee as a drink remained almost a state secret for over five hundred years. It was the traditional drink because alcohol was forbidden for religious reasons.

In the middle of the sixteenth century, coffee had spread to the Yemen, Egypt, Syria and Turkey, where it became known as the 'wine of Araby'.

In the seventeenth century, it was the Venetians who brought coffee in large quantities to mainland Europe. Coffee reached Vienna in 1683 from Turkey. By the end of the seventeenth century, Austria, Germany, France, Britain and Holland had coffee houses which were open to the public. The first coffee house was opened in Oxford in 1600 and the first coffee house in London was opened in 1652. Coffee was introduced into Virginia in the United States of America by the European settlers in the New World.

In 1714, Pancras Bourgmastre, who was the Mayor of Amsterdam, presented a young coffee plant to Louis XIV (1638–1715), King of France from 1643. The coffee plant was planted at Versailles in one of the conservatories. It was then transplanted to the Jardin des Plantes in Paris. In 1720, a Monsieur de Jussieu gave a cutting of the young coffee plant to a young French naval officer called Captain des Clieux who was sailing from France to his estate in the French colony of Martinique in the Caribbean. The voyage was delayed by storms and attacks by pirate ships, and the young captain sacrificed his water ration in order to keep the coffee plant alive. Eventually he reached the colony and planted the first coffee plant on the island. Des Clieux died in 1726, by which time there were over two hundred coffee plants in Martinique. By 1777, over twenty million coffee plants were growing on the island. By the end of the eighteenth century, coffee was grown in tropical and sub-tropical areas, East and West, around the world.

An exotic, but expensive way to brew coffee was created by Frederick the Great (1712–1786), King of Prussia from 1740. He substituted champagne for water and reputedly drank fifteen cups of the mixture every day!

Today, coffee is a popular drink worldwide. Coffee is grown all over the world, for example, Brazil, Bolivia, Costa Rica, Ecuador, Haiti, Jamaica, Panama, the Congo, Ethiopia, Kenya and India. *Canephora Robusta* is grown in Central and West Africa. The tallest coffee plant, which grows to a height of twenty metres, is called *Liberica* and can be found in Malaysia and West Africa, although world demand for this coffee is low. The inter-breeding of coffee plants is so widespread that it is extremely unlikely that we will ever know the exact number of different species. Every plantation wants its plants to resist disease and obtain the maximum yield over a minimum period of time.

∼ COFFEE, DECAFFEINATED ∼

A process in which the caffeine is removed from the coffee.

History

The process was started by a German chemist called Runge in 1820. His friend, the poet Johann Wolfgang von Goethe (1749–1832), suffered from insomnia, reputedly caused by drinking large quantities of coffee. Runge, intrigued by this, worked on the idea of removing the caffeine from the coffee. The method started by Runge was perfected by Ludwig Roselius at the turn of the century.

✍ COLOURINGS, FOOD ✍

Colouring is an artificial or natural substance which is used to enhance the presentation of food. Natural food colourings are extracted from a variety of sources and may have additives included during the manufacturing process. Artificial food colourings are also used in foods produced for human consumption. However, there is EEC legislation controlling the use of food colourings. In Britain, the Ministry of Health controls the amount of food colouring which is permissible in food produced for human consumption. A recent creation are food colourings which are flavoured, for example, yellow colouring is flavoured with lemon. The main natural food colourings which are used today are listed below:

Cochineal: Is a bright red food colouring which is extracted from an insect native to Mexico and South America. The colouring is obtainable in a liquid or powdered form.

Sodium Chlorophylin: Is a green colouring extracted from a variety of plants and grasses. It is obtainable in a liquid or powdered form.

Caramel: Is a brown food colouring obtained from a caramelized solution. It is obtainable in a liquid or powdered form.

Saffron: Is a bright yellow food colouring obtained from the crocus plant, which is native to Asia. The yellow stigmas of the crocus are dried and used to manufacture this natural yellow colouring.

Carbonization of vegetables: Black food colouring is obtained by burning a selection of vegetables until a black powder is obtained.

Carrots: A bright orange colouring is obtained from the vegetable. It is available in a liquid or powdered form.

Natural fruits: A violet colouring is obtained from the juice of raspberries and blueberries.

History

The practice of colouring foods dates back to medieval times in Britain. An array of natural colourings was obtained from vegetables, dried fruits, nuts and spices such as saffron. Dishes during that period were often gilded with gold or silver. Natural food colourings were also being imported from as far afield as India during this period; sandalwood, for instance, was commonly used to enhance the colour of food. In 1590, a Franciscan monk from Pisa in Italy created the bright red colouring called Carmine. Sixty years later, a chemist called Homberg gave a detailed description of how Carmine was obtained. Hundreds of years ago, some food colourings were obtained by quite disgusting methods. For example, in 1740 a brown colouring was obtained by mixing powdered coal with boiling milk.

∽ CONVERSATION GÂTEAU ∽

The Conversation Gâteau can either be made as a large gâteau inside a flan ring or as individual gâteaux in small pastry tins. The base is made of a thin layer of shortcrust pastry or puff pastry trimmings. It is then filled with almond cream which is flavoured with rum. A second layer of pastry is laid over the cream mixture, over which a thin layer of royal icing is spread with a pallet knife. Finally, thin strips of pastry are laid across the surface of the gâteau to make a criss-cross pattern. It is then baked in an oven at 200 °C until light golden brown in colour.

History

The Conversation Gâteau originated from the city of Lyon, in the south-west of France. It was created by a patissier called Boinon in 1796 and was introduced to the Parisians in 1863.

∽ COQUE DE CAHORS ∽

This is a type of country bread, very much like a French torte, but as rich as a brioche dough. It is flavoured with lemon and orange essence, vanilla and rum.

History

Eaten since the Middle Ages, it is a large cake eaten at Easter time and very much in fashion at picnic time.

∽ CORNELIAN CHERRY – CORNOUILLE ∽

Is a small tree which grows up to a height of six metres. The colour of the fruit ranges from a deep red to a rich purple. Although sweet, they have a slight acidic edge to their taste. The fruit ripens in late summer. It is a good source of vitamin C.

History

It grows in the temperate parts of the northern hemisphere. In the region of Périgord and Lot, in the south-west of France, Cornelian cherries are still to be found growing wild. It has been grown in orchards in France for centuries, and was grown among other fruit trees such as apple and pear. In the Périgord district in the south-west of France, the cherries are used to make a sweet fruit tart which is a speciality of the district.

∾ CORNFLOUR – FARINE DE MAÏS ∾

This is the flour milled from corn. It is the inner part of the kernel which is milled from the cornmeal. It is mostly used by the patissier as a thickening agent and in desserts such as Blanc-mange. Corn oil is also extracted from the cereal, and the solution of glucose syrup, which is used in cookery, is also made from cornflour.

History

Cornflour dates back to the middle of the nineteenth century.

∾ CORNISH PASTY ∾

This is a type of savoury pie which is made of shortcrust pastry enclosing a savoury filling of diced lamb or beef, potatoes, swedes, onions and butter, which is salted and highly seasoned with pepper. The pastry is then baked in the oven.

History

The pasty originated in Cornwall hundreds of years ago, when the area's main industry was tin mining. Tin miners working at sites such as Zennor, Penzance and St. Agnes would spend long periods of time underground in the mines. The pasty became their main meal of the day. It was filling, nutritious and extremely practical as it could be carried easily by the miners in their pockets. The popularity of the pasty as a convenience meal has survived until today.

∾ COULIS ∾

A Coulis can be sweet or savoury. As a dessert, it consists of a composition of fruit juice or fruit purée or wine and sweet syrup. It comprises about one-third of syrup to about two-thirds of fruit juice or fruit purée or wine, depending upon the sweetness of the particular fruit which is used. A savoury Coulis consists of vegetables, either raw or cooked, which have been liquidized and cooked to a pouring consistency. The sweet or savoury Coulis are used to accompany desserts or savoury dishes in order to enhance their flavour and also to add a splash of colour to the final presentation of the dish. Coulis have become extremely popular with the arrival of Nouvelle Cuisine.

History

The word *coulis* comes from the French verb *couler*, which means to pour. The verb originated in the twelfth century (Ref.: *Le Petit Robert 1*, 1972). Although the sauce can be traced back to Roman times, it was not until a much later date that it was called a coulis. The story goes that a Roman statesman, Marcus Tullius Cicero (106–143 BC), was eating in the house of a friend who was called Lentilus. He was served mallow leaves which were accompanied by a rich fruit compote which we today know as a coulis. Cicero was reputed to have enjoyed the compote so much that he over-indulged himself and suffered from acute indigestion for a period of ten days.

It is interesting to note how names such as Lentilus were derived during Roman times. The inhabitants of Latium or Lazio, in the west of central Italy, were mostly farmers or soldiers, and were self-sufficient, growing their own food and vegetables. Their names were taken from the type of vegetable which they grew. For example, the farmer who grew lentils became Lentilus, the farmer who grew peas became Piso, and so on.

∽ CRANACHAN ∽

Cranachan is a traditional Scottish dessert which is also known as Cream Crowdie. It is a mixture of beaten double cream, toasted oatmeal, sugar or honey, fruits of the season such as raspberries, bilberries or blackberries and it is sometimes flavoured with rum. It is served in cups and accompanied by shortbread fingers.

History

Cranachan is a classic Scottish dessert and has a long history. It was originally made in a large pan at Hallowe'en, when charms were mixed through it to ward off the evil spirits. Revellers consumed it by the spoonful, eager to find a charm which would bring them good luck. It remains a popular dessert in Scotland today; however, the custom of putting charms into the mixture has disappeared and it is no longer associated with Hallowe'en.

∽ CREAM CARAMEL – CRÈME RENVERSÉE AU CARAMEL ∽

Is an egg custard which can either be made in a large dariole mould or small individual moulds. The bottoms of the moulds are coated with a layer of caramel before the custard is poured into them. They are placed in a tray which is filled with warm water and baked in the oven. When cooked, they are allowed to cool before being turned out of the moulds, upside down onto a serving dish, revealing the caramel topping. The baked custards are served cold, often with a caramel syrup. It is probably one of the most popular cold desserts today in Britain.

History

The French name for the dessert, Crème Renversée au Caramel, translated into English means upside down caramel cream – a perfect description of this cold sweet because it is literally turned upside down and then served.

∾ CREAM HORNS – CORNETS FEUILLETÉS ∾

Cream horns are made with strips of puff pastry of approximately two centimetres in diameter which are rolled over a greased horn mould shape and are then baked in the oven. When cooked, the cream horns are filled with either sweet or savoury fillings depending upon the type of cornet.

Sweet Cream Horns: The rolled pastry is brushed with water, egg-wash or egg white, then rolled in caster sugar and baked. The filling is often flavoured pastry cream or fresh whipped cream.

Savoury Cream Horns: The rolled pastry is brushed with water or egg-wash and is then rolled in grated cheese and baked. The fillings are endless, and may be anything from cheese sauce to a savoury mousse.

History

The name *cornet* is derived from the French word *corne*, dating back to the thirteenth century (Ref.: *Le Petit Robert 1*, 1972). Translated into English, *corne* means horn. In his book, *Mémorial de la Pâtisserie*, Pierre Lacam described how Cornets Feuilletés were made in the nineteenth century. Since then, the recipe and method has not changed a great deal. However, the cornets at that time were filled with Crème Chantilly or Crème Chiboust. Today, they are filled with a wide variety of sweet or savoury fillings.

∾ CRÈME BOURDALOUE ∾

Crème Bourdaloue is a special cream which consists of ground almonds, egg yolks, beaten egg whites, whole eggs, caster sugar and cornflour, and is flavoured with Kirsch. Originally the cream was used as a filling for tarts, which were then baked and glazed with chocolate. Today, the cream is still used, but the tarts are not glazed with chocolate, instead fruit is used as a finish.

History

Pierre Lacam, author of the *Mémorial de la Pâtisserie* (fourth edition), which was published in 1898, stated that the Crème Bourdaloue tarts were created by a French patissier called Lesserter, in the Rue Bourdaloue in Paris.

∾ CRÈME BRÛLÉE ∾

Is a very rich custard made with double cream, egg yolks and sugar, and is flavoured with vanilla. The mixture is put into individual ramekin or soufflé dishes and baked in an oven until set. When cooked, it is allowed to cool before the surface of the custard is dredged with sugar. The Crème Brûlée is then placed under a grill or salamander in order to caramelize the sugar – some patissiers use a blowtorch or a hot poker. The dessert is served cold, and it has a wonderful rich, buttery flavour which is quite distinctive.

History

Crème Brûlée, translated into English, simply means burnt cream. The recipe is well known in Scotland and dates back to the late eighteenth century, by which time it was a well established dessert in the east of Scotland. The original recipe was most probably created at an earlier date in France. Scottish cookery had been greatly influenced by the French during the 'Auld Alliance' in the sixteenth century. French chefs were employed in wealthy households during that period, bringing with them a selection of recipes which were to influence Scottish cuisine forever. The old Scottish recipe for Crème Brûlée at that time was flavoured with cinnamon and orange, the cream mixture was covered with a type of spun sugar or a thick layer of sugar and then browned in the oven. Spun sugar had been invented by a French chef called Sabatier in the middle of the eighteenth century in France. Although the link between the two countries was severed by the Act of Union between Scotland and England in 1707, many aspects of Scottish life were to remain strongly influenced by the French.

∾ CRÈME CHANTILLY – WHIPPED CREAM ∾

In France, the minimum fat content authorized by law for Crème Chantilly is 30 per cent, whilst in Great Britain it is 35 per cent. However, it may rise to 38 per cent. The cream is whisked, entrapping air bubbles, thus making it light and eventually thicker. A Crème Chantilly should always be whipped at the coldest temperature possible; 2 °C is the correct tempera-ture. It is usually flavoured with vanilla essence and sweetened with caster or icing sugar, for example, to each litre of cream, 120–200 grams of sugar is added. During the summer months, or in an environment which is too warm, melted gelatine may be added to the cream to enable it to hold better; for example, approximately 10 grams of melted gelatine to each litre.

History

Crème Chantilly was created by a Frenchman called Vatel in 1660. He worked as a head waiter within the Château de Chantilly for the Prince of Condé.

∾ CRÈME D'AMANDE – ALMOND CREAM ∾

Is a cream which consists of an equal quantity of unsalted butter and caster sugar which is beaten until it is light in texture. A mixture of eggs and rum is added, then finally ground almonds and a little flour are mixed in. The cream is used as a filling in a variety of cakes and pastries such as Gâteau Pithivier, Conversation Gâteau, Croissants, etc.

History

It was created in 1506 by a patissier called Provenchère, who had a patisserie situated in the Rue du Cygne in Pithivier in France. The family patented the cream until the reign of Louis Philippe (1773–1850), King of France from 1830 to 1848.

∾ CRÈME DE CHÂTEIGNE – CHESTNUT CREAM ∾

Chestnut Cream evolved from the basic butter cream. It is simply made with cooked chestnuts pounded into a purée and mixed with butter cream, then flavoured with Kirsch.

History

It was created at the turn of the nineteenth century by a French confectioner.

∾ CRÈME PÂTISSIÈRE – CONFECTIONER'S CUSTARD, PASTRY CREAM ∾

This consists of milk, eggs, sugar and starch as a thickening agent with vanilla as a flavour. The amount of eggs and sugar used will basically determine what the cream will be used for and the quality of the cream required. The standard recipe for a Crème Patissière consists of a litre of milk, 250 grams of caster sugar, two whole eggs, two egg yolks, 100 grams of unsweetened custard powder and vanilla essence. This mixture would be used as a filling for Eclairs or Choux Buns, for example.

A Crème Mousseline is a much richer mixture, and would be used as a filling for a Gâteau Paris-Brest. The Crème Mousseline consists of 500 millilitres of milk, 500 millilitres of cream, up to 16 egg yolks, up to 500 grams of caster sugar and 75 grams of unsweetened custard powder and vanilla to flavour.

History

Crème comes from the old French word *craime* dating back to the twelfth century, which then became *cresome* in the thirteenth century (Ref.: *Le Petit Robert 1*, 1972). During the time of the great French chef, Antoine Carême (1784–1833), the crème was called A l'Ancienne which means the old way, indicating that the crème dated before that period. It is interesting to note that the old method had more eggs and a great deal more butter added to it. By today's standards the mixture would be regarded as a Crème Mousseline. Carême used the crème extensively in his newly created vol-au-vents.

∾ CRÈME PRALINE – PRALINE CREAM ∾

Praline cream consists of a caramel to which whole hazelnuts or almonds are added. It is then pounded into a thick mass and mixed with butter cream, then flavoured with Kirsch.

History

The praline cream was created at the turn of the nineteenth century. With the creation of butter cream it heralded an endless stream of different and exotic flavoured creams using butter cream as their base.

∾ CRÊPES – PANCAKES ∾

Crêpes are made with a batter of pouring consistency made from wheat, barley or buckwheat flour, eggs, salt and milk or water. Butter or lard and sugar are also added. Crêpes can be sweet or savoury. The batter is allowed to rest for half a day. They are made in a special pancake frying pan, similar to a conventional frying pan but much smaller, with a thicker base and lower sides. The batter is poured into the pan which has previously been oiled and the excess oil poured out. The oil should be at flash point and the crêpes are cooked for a minute or so on both sides. They may be tossed or turned with a palette knife.

History

The French word *crêpe* is a derivative of the Latin word *crespus* (Ref.: *Le Petit Robert 1*, 1972). The English word 'pancake', comes from the old word *pannequet*, which means cakes from the pan. Crêpes were eaten by the Jews and Romans. There have been centuries of religious significance, tradition and pagan custom behind the modern Shrove Tuesday celebration, when we traditionally eat pancakes. At one time it was preceded by 'Collop' or Shrove Monday, when a traditional dish of meat was served. It was the final day of holidaying before the 'Pancake Bell' was rung and Lent began. The day following Shrove Tuesday is Ash Wednesday, the beginning of Lent which lasts for six weeks. Ash Wednesday dates back to Anglo Saxon times, when St. Augustine arrived to convert the Britons. It was his idea to smear the ashes of palms burnt after the previous Palm Sunday on the heads of penitents.

It was Pope Gelasse I (AD 492–6) who instituted Shrove Tuesday as a day of religious rejoicing to replace the 'Lupercales' festival, which was a Roman festival in honour of the god Pan. On Shrove Tuesday crêpes were made from foods which were forbidden during Lent and they would then be eaten by those going to be 'shriven' or absolved of their sins.

∞ CRÊPE SUZETTE ∞

Crêpe Suzette is a hot sweet dish. Loaf sugar is crushed and added to melted butter, the mixture is allowed to caramelize over heat, orange and lemon juice are then added and it is cooked very quickly for a minute or so. The sauce should remain oily. The already prepared crêpes are then placed in the hot sauce and are allowed to soak. Liqueur such as Grand Marnier, Curaçao or Cognac is added and the dish is then flambéed. The crêpes should be served immediately.

History

This recipe for crêpes was created in 1901, by a chef working in the Café de Paris in Monaco, in honour of a beautiful young lady who accompanied Edward, Prince of Wales. The young lady was called Suzette. It is said that whilst eating the delicious crêpes the Prince of Wales heard of his father's death and of his succession to the throne, thus becoming King Edward VII of Great Britain and Ireland.

∞ CROISSANTS ∞

Croissants are made from an enriched bread dough in which pastry margarine or butter is enclosed and then rolled in order to form layers of dough and fat. The croissant dough is rolled into an oblong shape and cut into strips, then into triangles, which are then rolled into the crescent shape which is so familiar. The crescent-shaped dough is then allowed to prove until it triples in size. The croissants are then brushed with egg and baked in a hot oven until golden brown. In France, the quality of croissants is instantly recognized by the shape. The crescent-shaped croissant is made with margarine, whilst the straight-shaped croissant is made with butter. Croissants may also have a sweet filling; for example, pastry cream, jam or almond cream may be added to the croissant dough before rolling them. They are then called 'Pain au', meaning bread with a specific filling; for example, some croissants are filled with chocolate before rolling. They are then called Pain au Chocolat.

History

The croissant was invented in 1683 by a Pole called Kulyeski who lived in Vienna. The word 'croissant' comes from the Austrian word *Hönchen*, meaning little moon. At that time the city was besieged by a huge Turkish army commanded by Kara Mustafa. A small force of the Turkish army decided to dig a tunnel beneath the walls of the city and to invade during the night. Apparently some bakers working underground heard the noise and raised the alarm. Dying of hunger, the people of Vienna called for help. Charles de Lorraine and a Polish noble called John Sobieski (1624–1696), King John III of Poland from 1674, crushed the Turkish army with the help of a valiant officer named Kulyeski. As a reward for his bravery the Polish king gave him a large stock of coffee beans which were abandoned by the defeated Turkish army and also gave him authorization to open a coffee shop. Kulyeski opened the shop and ordered the bakers who raised the alarm to bake small individual portions of bread in the shape of a crescent to commemorate their victory over the Turks, as the emblem on the Turkish flag was a crescent. The crescent bread shapes became known as croissants and were an immediate success.

～ CROISSANT AU LARD – BACON CROISSANT ～

This is a savoury croissant, although it can also be made with puff pastry, especially if it is to be served at a buffet. Croissants au Lard are simply bacon rashers rolled inside the shapes before they are baked.

History

The French word *lard* dates back to the Middle Ages. Translated into English it means bacon. In Germany, bacon was called *Bakko*. During the Middle Ages bacon was also used as a part payment instead of money by the clergy.

～ CROQUEMBOUCHE ～

The Croquembouche consists of choux paste buns filled with a pastry cream flavoured with Kirsch or rum which are then glazed with a light caramel solution. The well known and familiar tower shape of the cake is obtained by placing glazed choux buns which have been dipped in a caramel solution around a conical mould. The base of the Croquembouche consists of nougatine, which is known in Britain as croquant. When the conical mould is completely covered in choux buns, it is decorated with royal icing which is piped around the nougatine. The rest of the cake is decorated with sugared almonds, pulled sugar flowers, leaves and ribbons.

In France, the Croquembouche is the traditional celebration cake served at special occasions such as weddings and christenings. It is the equivalent of the British celebration cake which is made with fruit and covered with marzipan and decorated with royal icing. Both countries decorate their celebration cakes according to the occasion. For example, a wedding cake usually has a replica of the bride and groom placed on top of the cake and a christening cake usually has a replica of a baby in a cradle. The custom of decorating the celebration cakes with small favours, which are then presented to the guests as keepsakes, is another custom shared by both countries.

History

Croquembouche is a derivative of the old French word *crôque-en-bouche*, which translated into English means to crunch in your mouth. The spelling of the word changed in the middle of the nineteenth century and it was no longer hyphenated. The Croquembouche was created in France. Originally the gâteau consisted of fruits which were dipped in a cooked sugar solution and built carefully on top of each other.

In the nineteenth century the renowned French chef Antoine Carême (1784–1833) totally transformed the original gâteau by using filled choux buns which he built around a conical shape to achieve the form of a tower, decorating the Croquembouche elaborately with pastillage flowers and leaves on a pastillage base.

In the early twentieth century the Croquembouche was presented on a nougatine base and decorated with piped royal icing and pulled sugar flowers, leaves and ribbons.

∾ CRÔQUE MONSIEUR AND CRÔQUE MADAME ∾

This is a very popular French snack which is served hot. It consists of bread, mornay sauce, cooked ham, grated cheese and butter. Two slices of bread are toasted, on one side only, and then buttered. The cold sauce is spread over one slice, then a slice of cooked ham is placed on top, the sauce is then spread over the ham and the second piece of bread is placed on top. A final coating of sauce is spread over the bread and sprinkled generously with cheese and a few knobs of butter. It is then cooked until golden brown in a hot oven. When served with a fried egg on top, the savoury is called a Crôque Madame.

History

The Crôque Monsieur was created in 1919, in Paris, and the Crôque Madame was created shortly afterwards.

✎ Croûte aux Fruits – Fruit Crust ✎

This consists of dry Savarin slices which are dusted on both sides with icing sugar and caramelized under a grill or salamander. The slices are then topped with either fresh or tinned fruit, glazed with jam and decorated with whipped cream.

History

The sweet was invented shortly after the Savarin. It is very similar to the sweet which is made at Easter in France called the Golden Crust of Savoy. The Golden Crust of Savoy is shallow fried like a Pain Perdu, but is served without fruit or cream.

✎ Crystallized Flowers – Pétales de Fleurs Cristallisées ✎

Flowers are crystallized by immersing the petals in a gum solution, then coating them in caster sugar. The petals are then allowed to dry. Crystallized mimosa, rose and violet petals are used to decorate an array of classic desserts, for example, Coupe Bébé, Coupe Malmaison, Croquembouche and Coupe Glacée Rose Chéri.

History

Before the birth of Christ, flowers such as orange blossoms were used in the Middle East to flavour cookery dishes. The Romans used gladioli in some recipes, not only the flowers, but the bulbs as well! In Elizabethan England, flowers were used in abundance in salads, as flavourings in recipes, or crystallized to eat as a sweet. The favourite flowers used in cookery during that period were roses, violets, primroses, cowslips and broom.

✎ Currant, black – Cassis ✎

The blackcurrant *Ribes Nigrum* is a small, round, attractive berry. It is extremely rich in vitamin C and also contains minerals. It is excellent eaten raw, or used as a filling for pies, tarts, fools, cheesecakes, bombes glacées and sorbets. Because of its pectin content, it is excellent for jam and jelly making and the fruit freezes well. The fruit is also used to make a famous French liqueur known as Crème de Cassis, which is made in the city of Dijon. Another very popular aperitif, known as Kir, is made with white wine and Cassis. There are numerous varieties of the fruit, for example, Tor Cross, Laxton's Giant and Seabrook's Black.

History

Blackcurrants have grown in the wild for thousands of years in northern countries with temperate climates. However, it was not cultivated in Europe until the seventeenth century. Throughout history, the fruit has always been recognized for its medicinal properties. Today, blackcurrants, because of their high content of vitamin C, are used by pharmaceutical companies in the preparation of syrups, lozenges and health food drinks.

∾ CURRANTS, RED AND WHITE – GROSEILLES ROUGES ET BLANCHES ∾

The redcurrant is bright red in colour and much smaller than the blackcurrant. It is popular in this country to make redcurrant jelly, which is used to accompany meat dishes. It is also used in the production of the popular British sweet, Summer Pudding. In France, the redcurrant is used in the making of a highly renowned redcurrant jelly. Eaten raw, the berries are excellent in flavour, but do need to be eaten with sugar as they are acidic in taste. The fruit is rich in vitamin C and contains minerals.

History

The redcurrant, like the blackcurrant, has grown wild for thousands of years. However, the redcurrant was cultivated before the blackcurrant, almost a hundred or so years earlier. The whitecurrant is a variety of the redcurrant.

∾ CUSTARD POWDER – POUDRE A CRÈME ∾

Custard powder is made with cornflour which is flavoured with vanilla and coloured artificially to produce a mixture which acts as a substitute for real custard, which is made with egg yolks, sugar and milk.

History

It was invented by Alfred Bird (1813–1879), a chemist. He also invented the chemical raising agent, baking powder, as his wife was allergic to eggs and yeast, which were the natural raising agents commonly used in cookery.

D

~ DARIOLES: TARTLETS, DARIOLE MOULDS ~

These are a type of egg custard tartlet. The small, deep, pastry tartlets have a filling consisting of caster sugar, wheat flour, eggs, milk and butter. Other ingredients such as fruit, nuts and spices may be added to the filling. There are a variety of different recipes for this pastry. The deep pastry cases are baked blind and the fruit, nuts and spices are placed at the bottom of the tartlets. The custard is cooked until it thickens, then strained into the pastry cases which are then baked in the oven. When cooked, the small tartlets are dredged with icing sugar. A large dariole tart can also be made which is then cut into individual slices.

History

The French word *dariole* is a derivative of the old French word *daryol*. The small pastry tartlets date back to medieval times in France, probably to the beginning of the thirteenth century. They were introduced into England by the French shortly afterwards. They were popular in England during the reign of Edward II (1284–1327), who became the first Prince of Wales in 1301 and was King of England from 1307.

At a later date, special moulds were designed in France for a variety of puddings and were named dariole moulds. The deep individual moulds and single large deep mould were modelled on the deep pastry cases used in the medieval recipe, hence the name.

~ DATE – DATTE ~

The date palm, *Phoenix Dactylifera*, grows to a height of between twenty and twenty-five metres. The life-span of the tree can be anything up to sixty years, and the tree may produce fifty to sixty kilos of dates each year. The dates grow in large bunches. The fruits are extremely nutritious and contain protein, vitamins and minerals, but it is their high sugar content which makes them a high energy food which is of particular value to the diet.

Dates can be divided into three main types: 'soft', 'hard', and 'semi-dry'. They are delicious when eaten fresh, or they can be candied or dried. They are extremely versatile and can be used in cookery dishes and a variety of baked goods. They are used extensively by the patissier in the production of petits fours. Today, dates are grown commercially in the Middle East,

Northern Africa, and more recently they have been introduced as a commercial crop to Mexico, Arizona, Southern California and South Carolina.

History

The date palm is native to the Middle East. It is an ancient fruit and dates back to 50,000 BC. The trees flourish in hot, dry climates, but need to be near water. They grow wild along the banks of the River Nile. The use of the fruit was widely documented during the early Egyptian and Mesopotamian civilizations; because of its high nutritional value it was used extensively in the diet. The fruit provided a rich food source for the nomadic tribes travelling in the deserts of Arabia, sustaining them on long journeys. The early Roman civilization also appreciated this highly nutritious fruit, and valued it primarily for its high sugar content. Dates were used by the Romans to sweeten dishes. Often the juice was pressed out from the dates and the syrup was used instead of honey. Sugar was not known to the Romans at that time.

In the fourteenth century, Britain's trading with southern Europe had escalated. Great spice ships belonging to Spain, Portugal and Italy arrived in British ports with cargoes of exotic fruits and spices. It was during this time that dates were first introduced to the British.

∽ DIPLOMATE GÂTEAU ∽

This is a flan which is made with shortcrust pastry. The bottom of the pastry flan is covered with diced stale sponge, currants and mixed peel. A mixture consisting of eggs, sugar and milk is then poured over the sponge pieces and fruit. The gâteau is then baked in a warm oven. When cooked, it is allowed to cool before being glazed with boiling apricot jam and decorated with glacé cherries and angelica. It is very similar to the English recipe for Cabinet Pudding.

History

The Diplomate Gâteau was created by a French chef called Montmirrel, in honour of the French writer and diplomat, François René Chateaubriand (1768–1848). He was posted as French Ambassador to London from 1822 to 1824. The gâteau was initially called Gâteau à la Chateaubriand during this period. At a later date, the name of the gâteau changed to Diplomate Gâteau.

∽ DOUGHNUTS ∽

Doughnuts are made with an enriched fermented dough consisting of strong flour, which is rich in gluten, milk, caster sugar, salt, vegetable oil, eggs and yeast or baking powder. The doughnuts can be made in a variety of shapes such as rings, fingers or buns. Buns are shaped by hand, but doughnut rings are obtained by rolling out the dough and cutting the rings with pastry cutters. The doughnuts are deep fried in hot oil, drained and then coated with icing sugar or caster sugar. The bun and finger-shaped doughnuts are often filled with jam or whipped cream.

History

A type of doughnut was created in Austria in the seventeenth century. It was small and round in shape and was called a Faschingskrapfen. Initially, the pastry could only be made by the bakers employed in the Austrian royal household. A similar type of pastry was made by the Dutch during that period. It was when permission was granted by the Austrian royal household for the recipe to be made outside the royal court that the pastry spread to Germany, France and eventually to England. It was taken across the Atlantic to America by immigrants at the beginning of the nineteenth century. It is thought that it was the Americans who changed the shape of the small, round pastry to the now popular ring shape.

There is a great deal of controversy as to where this pastry actually originated. Some professionals argue that the Dutch pastry was, in fact, the original doughnut whereas other professionals believe that the true ancestor of the doughnut of today is the Austrian Faschingskrapfen. Another school of thought is that the doughnut actually originated in Britain, many pointing to the fact that a recipe for the doughnut appeared in an English cookery book called *Modern Cookery*, published in 1855 by Woodfall and Hinder, indicating that the doughnut was well established in some parts of Britain by that date. It is indeed true that doughnuts at that time were a speciality on the Isle of Wight, an island lying off the south coast of England. However, the ingredients used in the recipe differ considerably from the original Austrian recipe, even the method of cooking is completely different, as the doughnuts in the English recipe are shallow fried.

∾ DUNDEE CAKE ∾

Is a light fruit cake which is made with butter, brown sugar, eggs, self-raising flour, sultanas, ground almonds and orange peel. Recipes for this speciality cake vary, and a variety of ingredients are sometimes added to the original recipe, for example, mixed peel, lemon zest, currants and raisins. The cake is made using the creaming method. The mixture is put into a round cake tin which has been lined with greaseproof paper. The surface of the cake is decorated with blanched almonds which are arranged in concentric circles. It is then baked in a moderate oven for approximately two and a half hours. Dundee Cake is easily distinguishable from other fruit cakes by its roasted almond topping.

History

The town of Dundee on the east coast of Scotland is famous for not one, but two local specialities, Dundee Cake and Dundee Marmalade. The world-renowned Dundee Marmalade was created by a local grocer in the town at the beginning of the eighteenth century. Such was the success of the new preserve that towards the end of the eighteenth century the first marmalade factory was built in the town in order to produce the famous preserve on a commercial basis.

The commercial production of the marmalade resulted in a by-product of orange peel. This is where Scottish ingenuity came into force. Instead of wasting the surplus orange peel, the canny Scots created the recipe for Dundee Cake, using the orange peel as a flavouring, giving this speciality cake its distinctive and unique flavour.

E

∽ ECCLES CAKES ∽

Are small round cakes which are made with puff pastry and have a filling consisting of butter, brown sugar, mixed peel and currants. The puff pastry is rolled out and then cut into rounds with a pastry cutter. The filling is placed in the centre of the pastry round and the edges are then drawn up into the centre. The rounds are then turned upside down and rolled slightly with a rolling pin until the dried fruit shows through the pastry. The surface of the cakes is then scored with the point of a sharp knife to make a lattice pattern and brushed with egg-wash before baking. When cooked, the Eccles Cakes are dredged liberally with caster sugar.

History

Eccles Cakes are named after the town of Eccles in Lancashire from where they originated. The little town is not only famous for its speciality pastry cakes, but also for the ancient religious annual service called the Eccles Wakes, which were held in the small Norman church in the centre of the town. The church dates back as early as the twelfth century and was built after the Norman invasion of England which started in 1066.

∽ ÉCHAUDÉ ∽

Is a pastry which is made with wheat flour, salt, ammonia, eggs and butter. The ingredients are mixed into a firm dough which is allowed to rest for three hours in a warm place. The pastry is then divided into pieces and rolled into strips which are then cut into squares. The pastry squares are cooked in simmering water until they are light in colour. The squares are then drained in a colander, baked in an oven for twenty minutes and served hot. Although Échaudés are not as popular today as they were in the past, they are still regarded as a classic French patisserie.

History

This old French pastry dates back to the twelfth century. The original pastry was made with flour and water which was mixed to a firm paste. The paste was flavoured with aniseed. It was then moulded into a circular shape by hand, and to achieve the shape of a crown the points of the crown were cut out with a pair of scissors. The crown of pastry was free-standing, and was poached in simmering water. When cooked, it was allowed to soak overnight in cold water. The pastry was then removed from the water, drained and allowed to dry before it was baked in the oven. The Échaudé was created by a patissier called Caribous, in the town of Albi, which is in the Tarn region of France. After the religious wars in Europe during the eleventh and twelfth centuries, the Échaudé disappeared from the French table and was forgotten for over a hundred years.

In 1440, Taillevent, a renowned French chef, revived the old recipe. He changed the recipe by adding half an ounce of potassium to one and a half kilograms of flour, in an attempt to improve the original recipe. The new recipe resulted in the reappearance of the Échaudé at the French table.

In the sixteenth century, during the time of Catherine de' Medici, the Échaudé was to undergo another transformation. The patissiers employed in the royal household of Catherine de' Medici changed the original round shape of the pastry into a square. From that date onwards, the traditional shape of the Échaudé was square.

In 1702, the recipe for Échaudé was perfected by a French patissier called Favart. He added a chemical raising agent consisting of potassium carbonate and ammoniac acid to enable the pastry to rise during baking. This was not the only change to the recipe; he also added butter, eggs and salt to enrich the paste. Favart also designed special moulds in which to bake Échaudé. Before, the pastry shape was free-standing because the pastry was so firm that it did not need a mould to support it. The addition of eggs and butter resulted in a softer pastry, which needed to be supported by a mould.

In 1898, the fourth edition of a book called *Le Mémorial Historique et Géographique de la Pâtisserie*, written by Pierre Lacam, was published. It contained a recipe for Échaudé which is very similar to the recipe used today. In the nineteenth century, such was the popularity of the pastry that they were made by specialist patissiers. During this period, a speciality of the city of Paris was the Échaudé which was made with puff pastry.

～ ÉCLAIR ～

This is made with choux pastry which is piped into the shape of a sausage. The pastry shapes are then baked in the oven. Once cooked, the shapes are split through the middle and are usually filled with either whipped cream or pastry cream. In Britain, the traditional filling used is whipped cream; the pastries are then glazed with melted chocolate. However, in France the traditional filling is a flavoured pastry cream of chocolate or coffee and the pastry is glazed with either a chocolate or coffee fondant, depending upon the flavour of the filling. Alas, the difference between the traditional recipes of each country does not end there! Éclairs in Britain tend to be larger than the Éclairs made in continental Europe.

History

The French word *éclair*, translated into English, means lightning. The pastries were given the name by the French because they could be eaten 'in a flash', hence the name Éclair. The small pastry was created by Antoine Carême (1784–1833), the renowned French chef. Although choux pastry had first been created in the sixteenth century, the pastry had always been piped in the shape of a bun. Antoine Carême created a new recipe for choux pastry and also introduced a new shape. The first Éclairs made were smaller in size and were glazed with caramel. The traditional chocolate and coffee glaze came at a later date. Éclairs were not known in England until the nineteenth century.

∾ EGG – OEUF ∾

An average hen's egg weighs sixty grams. It consists of seven grams of shell, thirty-five grams of white and eighteen grams of yolk. It is a highly nutritious food and contains fat, protein, vitamins and minerals such as calcium and iron. A variety of birds' eggs are consumed by humans, the most popular ones being duck, goose and quail eggs. It is, however, the egg of the domestic chicken which today reigns supreme in popularity.

Eggs are extremely versatile, and can be cooked in a variety of ways. For example, they can be poached, scrambled, boiled and fried and must surely be one of the most popular breakfast or supper dishes of today! Eggs are an essential ingredient used by the patissier and the chef in the production of an endless variety of cakes, puddings, sauces, pastries and cookery dishes. They are usually used when fresh, but they can be frozen and can also be dried.

History

In the year 2000 BC, fowls were already domesticated in India. They were introduced into Greece by the Persians and eventually spread throughout Europe. In 500 BC, the ancient Romans regarded hens as religious birds and their eggs were sacred. The Romans, however, were extremely partial at this time to peacocks' eggs! At a later date they used hens' eggs extensively in their cooking, and it was they who were responsible for introducing eggs into Britain during the Roman invasion in AD 43.

In medieval Britain, the eggs of hens, ducks, geese, peacocks and pheasants could be bought in the market. However, eggs remained of religious significance. Lent eggs were painted with a red dye and were forbidden to be eaten during that period. The decorated eggs were blessed by the church.

In 1493 Christopher Columbus, the great Italian explorer and navigator, on one of his great sea voyages of discovery, made a port of call in the West Indies and introduced hens to the islands and the New World.

During the reign of Louis XV (1710–1774), King of France from 1715, eggs remained part of religious celebrations. After Easter Sunday Mass, it was the custom for his subjects to present eggs to the King. The eggs were elaborately decorated and were painted with blue, green and red dyes; they were often finished with gold leaf. The eggs were then distributed by the King to his courtiers. In 1787 in France, eggs were still forbidden to be eaten during religious festivities.

Today, eggs are still of religious significance throughout the Christian world during Easter festivities. They are still hard boiled and then decorated. In Britain, children roll the decorated boiled eggs down a hill until they crack, and they are traditionally eaten on Easter Sunday. This ritual signifies the resurrection of Christ on Easter Sunday, when the stone which covered the entrance to his tomb was rolled back and he arose. The egg, and rolling the egg, signifies the rolling of the stone and Christ's rising from the dead.

The popularity of eating eggs throughout Easter celebrations has grown through the ages. Not only are natural eggs painted and decorated, but chocolate, croquant, sugar paste and nougat are used to shape eggs which are then elaborately decorated and presented to children as an Easter gift.

∽ EGG CUSTARD – CRÈME ANGLAISE ∽

Is a composition of egg yolks, sugar and milk. The mixture is cooked in a pan slowly over a gentle heat, or in a bain-marie. It can also be baked. A variety of flavourings can be used to flavour the basic Egg Custard; however, the mixture is usually flavoured with vanilla. Egg Custard can also be used as an accompanying sauce to a variety of sweets, such as fruit pies and steamed fruit puddings. It is also the basis of many desserts, such as bavarois, mousses and ice creams.

History

The French call Egg Custard Crème Anglaise, which translated means English Cream. Custard is an English creation. In the Middle Ages, custard was simply a mixture of eggs and milk which was used as a topping for meat and fish pies which were then baked in an oven. Eventually pies were made which contained only the egg mixture with the addition of sugar, thus creating a sweet rather than a savoury pie; however, this was not until several hundred years later, in the nineteenth century. Custard eventually referred simply to the egg mixture which filled the pie. The mixture of eggs, sugar and milk was served as a dessert or as an accompaniment to puddings.

In the middle of the nineteenth century, custard powder was invented by an Englishman called Bird. It contained cornflour as a thickening agent instead of eggs, and the yellow powder was simply added to milk, boiled and then served. It was to become one of Britain's most popular convenience desserts!

∾ ESCOFFIER, AUGUSTE ∾

A world-renowned French chef and gastronome, founder of classical French cuisine.

History

Auguste Escoffier was born in 1846, in a small village called Villeneuve-Loubet, in the south of France. He started training to become a chef at the tender age of thirteen in his uncle's restaurant in the elegant city of Nice. He spent the next six years learning his craft in the restaurant before going to Paris in order to further his career. He eventually found a position in the extremely fashionable and exclusive restaurant called Le Petit Moulin.

In 1870 he was drafted as a Chef de Cuisine during the Franco-Prussian conflict and was based at army headquarters, which was located in the city of Metz in the north-east of France.

After his demob from the army, he returned to work in Le Petit Moulin where he stayed for another three years. His next two positions in the Grand Hotel de Monte-Carlo and the Hotel National de Lucerne secured his reputation as one of the finest chefs in France.

In 1880 he met the hotelier, César Ritz. The meeting was to change his life forever. Ritz was greatly impressed by the work of Escoffier. They joined forces and together made a worldwide reputation for themselves and a string of exclusive hotels in which they worked together, such as the Savoy and the Carlton hotels in London. Together they catered for royalty and the élite of society, and their partnership gained a worldwide reputation.

It was during this period that Escoffier was to transform the art of cooking. His predecessor, the renowned French gastronome and chef Antoine Carême, had transformed the cooking of medieval times. Escoffier, in turn, transformed the heavy and elaborate displays of Carême and laid the foundation of classical cuisine. He created such classic French dishes as Pêche Melba, Soufflé Rothschild, Fraise Sarah Bernhardt, Filets de Sole Coquelin and Salade Réjane. He was also responsible for creating the Party System within the kitchen. The new structure of the kitchen included specialized chefs such as the Patissier, the Entremetier, the Saucier, the Garde Manger and the Rôtisseur. This structure has survived, and still exists within the kitchen today.

In 1902, at the age of fifty-six, he published his first book, *Le Guide Culinaire*, which was well received by the public. His second book, *Le Livre des Menus*, was published ten years later.

In 1919 Escoffier retired. He was seventy-three years old. Undeterred by his age, he started to write his third and final book, *Ma Cuisine*, which was published in 1935. Auguste Escoffier died in 1935 at the grand old age of eighty-nine.

F

∽ FAR BRETON ∽

The Far Breton is made in a Genoese tin. The tin is well greased with butter and a mixture consisting of plain flour, sugar, eggs and milk which has been flavoured with vanilla essence is poured into it. Dried raisins or prunes which have been soaked in rum may be placed on the bottom of the tin before the mixture is poured in, if desired. It is then baked in a hot oven for three-quarters of an hour.

History

The Far Breton is a speciality of the Brittany region in the north-west of France. This patisserie was created over a hundred years ago. Originally it could be either sweet or savoury. The savoury Far Breton was similar to a quiche and the sweet Far Breton resembled a clafoutis. In the Brittany region in the past, it was a patisserie which was traditionally served at weddings. Each district in Brittany boasts of its own speciality. For example, in the Brest district raisins are used in the recipe, in Quiberon dried prunes are added, and in Saint Pol de Léon the recipe contains no fruit at all. However, although the Far Breton is regarded as a speciality of Brittany, its popularity has spread throughout France.

∽ FIG – FIGUE ∽

The fig tree belongs to the family *Moraceae Ficuscarica*. The tree bears edible fruit. The fig contains vitamins, minerals and is a good source of potassium. It is high in fibre when dried and has laxative properties. Fresh ripe figs contain as much as 25 cent of their weight in sugar. There are three main types of figs: green, brown and purple-coloured fruits. The fruits are found on the branches of the tree between the leaf and the branch itself. The structure is complex; it is a multiple fruit, containing hundreds of tiny fruits which in fact are often thought of as seeds. The tree reaches a height of ten metres and grows in warm to sub-tropical regions of the world.

The patissier uses the fruit in fruit salads or in the production of some tarts and flans. However, when dried they are used extensively in recipes for cakes and puddings. They are also delicious eaten raw.

History

The fig tree is native to western Asia. The fig has been known to man since the time of Adam and Eve, when the leaves of the tree were used to hide their nudity. The trees were grown in ancient Egypt and were cultivated in ancient Greece. In Egypt, baskets of figs were buried with the Pharaohs in their tombs.

During the Roman conquest, the fig was introduced to the countries along the Mediterranean coast. In Rome, the trees were grown in the main public square where Romulus and Remus were suckled by a she-wolf. The fruit was also used in Roman times to force-feed geese, in order to fatten them and make them more succulent for the table. The Romans sent the fruit as gifts to their friends at the beginning of each New Year, much the same as we would send chocolates today! They also attempted to introduce the tree into southern Britain, but failed miserably because of the cool climate.

The fig was reintroduced to Britain in the middle of the sixteenth century, around the same time that it was introduced to North America. Today, the fig grows extensively in warm countries throughout the world.

⚥ FINANCIERS ⚥

This is a mixture of ground almonds, caster sugar, whisked egg whites, flour and melted butter which is flavoured with vanilla essence. The mixture, which is of a very soft consistency, is poured into well greased Barquet moulds and baked in a moderate oven. The small cakes are usually served for afternoon tea.

History

Financiers were created in a small patisserie in La Rue Saint-Denis in Paris by a patissier called Lasne. The patisserie was situated near the Paris Stock Exchange, or, as it is called in France, La Bourse. Each day the stockbrokers or financiers would buy patiseries as a snack to eat on the floors of the Stock Exchange, as often their work was so pressurized that a lunch hour was impossible. Many of the patiseries sold in the shop were made with butter cream and decorated elaborately. They were extremely difficult to eat without cutlery and a serviette. Lasne created these small, dry cakes specifically for the financiers to enable them to eat their lunchtime snack without getting their fingers sticky. So the cakes were christened Financiers.

⚥ FLAN DE JEAN COCTEAU ⚥

Is a flan which is made with shortcrust pastry and has a filling made with milk, eggs, sugar, vanilla essence and unsweetened custard powder. The cooked custard is poured into the pastry flan, stoneless dried prunes are dropped into the custard and the filling is allowed to cool. The flan is then baked in the oven for thirty minutes. It is served cold.

History

Jean Cocteau (1889–1963) was a well known French poet, dramatist and film director. He adored the custard flan. His close friend Jean Marais, who was a well known French film star, often visited Cocteau at his apartment in Milly-La-Porêt on the outskirts of Paris. He often stopped at a nearby patisserie to buy his friend a custard flan. Cocteau was a frequent and valued customer, and the owner of the patisserie knew him well and was a great admirer of his work. In his honour he created a new recipe, which was a custard flan with the additional ingredient of prunes, Cocteau's favourite fruit. He christened it Flan de Jean Cocteau in his honour.

❧ FLAN MERINGUÉ ❧

This is a flan which is filled with a cooked cream made with flour, eggs, salt and milk. When the cream is cooked, butter is beaten into the mixture and the cream is sweetened with sugar. The flan is then baked in the oven. When cooked, the surface of the flan is covered with piped meringue and icing sugar is dredged over the meringue topping. The flan is then put back into a hot oven to allow the meringue's surface to caramelize.

History

The Flan Meringué was created in 1840 by a young French patissier called Chaumette whilst working in a fashionable patisserie in Paris. Like many other recipes, this one was created by accident. There was a surplus of the sweetened cream filling, and to avoid wastage the owner of the patissier, Monsieur Quillet, decided to use the extra cream as a filling for a pastry flan. Once cooked, it did not look at all appetizing. The young patissier suggested to his employer to pipe meringue over the filling and then bake in the oven until the meringue was golden in colour. Once cooked, he decorated the flan with piped jam and redcurrant jelly. The new creation was an overnight success.

Chaumette opened his own patisserie in Paris a few years later, and it was to become one of the biggest patisseries in the French capital. Within a decade the Flan Meringué was made in the majority of patisseries in Paris, and reached the height of its popularity in the middle of the nineteenth century. Each patisserie had its own particular decoration for the flan.

❧ FLAN RINGS – CERCLES À FLAN ❧

Are steel rings which are used to support pastry in the production of flans and tarts.

History

Originally flan rings were made out of copper. In 1840 a French patissier called Trottier invented the steel flan rings which are still used today.

∾ FLUMMERY ∾

Is a mixture of fruit, semolina pudding, jam and fresh cream – this, of course, is the modern version. Although a dish of yesteryear, as recently as 1969 a type of Flummery was on the menu of the famous Turnberry Hotel in Scotland. The dish Flamberry of Semolina consisted of raspberry fruit and jam which were placed in the bottom of a fluted glass. A mixture of cool, sweetened semolina was poured into the glass; it was then decorated with whipped dairy cream and sprinkled with roasted oatmeal.

History

The recipe dates back to the seventeenth century. Originally it was a mixture of oatmeal which was soaked in water and then boiled to a thick mixture of jelly-like consistency. It was often seasoned with salt and pepper and served as an accompaniment to meat dishes, or the mixture was sweetened with honey and served as a dessert. In England, the dish was particularly popular in Cheshire and Lancashire.

In the middle of the eighteenth century, a variety of different recipes for Flummery were published by English cookery writers. The original recipe had changed a great deal, with other ingredients being added, such as cream and sherry.

At the beginning of the nineteenth century in Britain, a popular recipe for Flummery consisted of oatmeal, water and sugar which was boiled and then flavoured with orange-water. During that period another recipe for Flummery was created in Cornwall in the south-west of England. This was a Rice Flummery, which was made with ground rice instead of oatmeal, milk, lemon peel, cinnamon, sugar, butter and was flavoured with almond essence.

Across the Channel in mainland Europe, the dessert was popular in several countries. In Holland, for example, it was made with gelatine or isinglass, a type of gelatine which is extracted from the bladder of the sturgeon. The isinglass was used to set a type of egg custard which was then flavoured with a fortified wine such as sherry. However, in Spain, the Flummery was made with rice flour, sugar and cream which was then flavoured with cinnamon.

By the early twentieth century, it was well established as a dessert in Britain. Today, however, the popularity of the Flummery as a dessert has greatly diminished, the nearest substitute for the Flummery being the Bavarois. In France, the Flummery is still made to produce the patisserie called Gâteau Flamri. This is a pastry flan with a filling which consists of semolina which has been cooked in white wine and sweetened with sugar. The Flummery is also still made in the United States of America.

∼ FONDANT ∼

Is a mixture of sugar loaves, water and glucose syrup which is boiled to a temperature of 117°C until it thickens. The mixture is then kneaded on a moistened marbled surface until it crystallizes into a malleable white mass which is smooth and creamy. By using cubes or loaves of sugar in the process this results in a whiter fondant being achieved. The fondant can be stored in an airtight container and covered. Fondant is used in the production of confectionery and is also used as the basis for icing traditional celebration cakes such as the British wedding cake.

History

The recipe for fondant icing is French. It was created by a French patissier called Gillet in 1824 whilst working in a patisserie called Le-Moine in Rue Lombard in Paris. It was then called sucre glacé or, translated into English, iced sugar. Originally the fondant was not made with glucose syrup, as this was not created until later in the nineteenth century. The resulting fondant was grey in colour and, of course, of a much inferior quality. The quality of the sugar used in the original recipe was also poor by today's standards.

∼ FRANGIPANE ∼

Frangipane is a cream which is made with almond cream and pastry cream. The percentage of almond cream to pastry cream varies, but it is generally accepted that the correct ratio is two-thirds of pastry cream to one-third of almond cream. Frangipane is flavoured with vanilla essence and rum. Starch is usually added to the cream before baking, and when cooked it should have the consistency of a rich pastry cream. It is used extensively by the patissier in the production of a variety of cakes and pastries. For example, it is used as a filling in Gâteau Jalousie, Conversation Gâteau and in the production of petits fours.

History

When Catherine de' Medici, a young Italian noblewoman, married King Henry of France in 1533, she was only fourteen years of age. Her new homeland was strange to her, and she was homesick for her native Italy. She did not like French food or French customs. To enable her to settle in her new country, she brought with her from Italy her own chefs and servants. Her personal chef, who was called Popelini, introduced many Italian recipes to the French court, an influence which was to affect French cuisine forever.

One of the young Queen's favourite dishes was the Italian classic dish called Polenta, which was a cornflour-based dish. Popelini was unable to obtain all the necessary ingredients in France to make the dish, so he decided to adapt the Italian recipe. The new recipe he created contained brown sugar, wheat flour, guinea-fowl eggs, salt, bitter almonds, powdered roots and milk. He baked the ingredients and finally beat some butter into the cooked mixture. Catherine adored the new highly flavoured and scented cream. The smell of it reminded her of a very fashionable French perfume of that time which had been created by a fellow Italian nobleman called Le Marquis Frangipani who lived in Paris. She decided to christen the cream delicacy Frangipane cream in his honour.

The Parisian patissiers, aware of the popularity of the perfume and realizing the potential of the new cream called Frangipane which had the royal stamp of approval, decided to use the cream as a filling for a variety of patisseries. The Frangipane-based patisseries and desserts became extremely popular and highly fashionable, and their popularity has lasted until the present day.

❧ FRITTER – BEIGNET ❧

Is a portion of sweet or savoury food which is coated in batter made of flour, eggs and milk and then deep fried in fat.

History

The French word *beignet* is derived from the thirteenth-century French word *buignet*, which came from an earlier French word *buyne* (Ref.: *Le Petit Robert 1*, 1972), which translated into English means a lump. The English word 'fritter' comes from the method of cooking the portion of food, which in old French is *friture*, meaning deep frying. The term is still in use today.

Fritters originated in North Africa and the Middle East as long ago as 400 BC. The Moors introduced them into Spain and the fritters spread into France. The Crusaders brought the recipe back to Britain on their return from the Holy Wars. However, the recipe was slightly different from that of today's fritters. The portions of food were not coated in batter, but were sandwiched between two pieces of pastry and then deep fried in hot oil. Sweet fritters at that time were sweetened with honey and savoury fritters were made with meat, fish or vegetables.

❧ FRUIT CAKE – CAKE AUX FRUITS: TRADITIONAL BRITISH WEDDING CAKE ❧

Cakes have been made with the addition of fruit for centuries in England. The English plum cake is the ancestor of today's modern fruit cakes. Originally the plum cake was made with a fermented dough to which fat, sugar, eggs, spices and dried fruits were added.

History

During the reign of Elizabeth I (1533–1603), who was Queen of England from 1558, small plum cakes were made especially for weddings. Probably this was the start of the fruit cake being accepted as a celebration cake for weddings in England. The small individual cakes were thrown at the bride and groom to bring them health and prosperity. Another custom was to throw rice over the heads of the newly married couple; this was said to aid fertility. This is an ancient Chinese custom dating back thousands of years.

In Scotland, however, the ancient wedding cake was not made of fruit, but was a large round oatcake which was decorated. At a later date, the Scottish wedding cake was made of shortbread which was decorated with favours. The favours were presented to guests after the wedding meal as keepsakes, another custom which has withstood the passage of time. The wedding guests simply broke off a piece of shortbread from the large short-bread round, which was traditionally eaten at the end of the meal. Another ancient ritual was the breaking of shortbread over the bride's head as she was carried across the threshold of her new home. It is not clear as to the exact date when the shortbread wedding cake was replaced with the tradi-tional fruit cake as the accepted celebration cake in Scotland.

Across other countries in Europe symbolism was a part of life, especially at special celebrations such as christenings and weddings, each country having its own customs and traditions. For example, in the Brittany region of France, the ancient wedding cake was made with brioche dough. In neighbouring Italy, there is a tradition of breaking a piece of the wedding cake over the head of the bride as she enters her new home with her husband; this is very similar to the Scottish custom. Friends and relations in Italy throw corn instead of rice over the heads of the newly-weds as a symbol of health and prosperity. The Romanians' traditional wedding cake is a honey cake. The honey cake is made in small rounds. Each cake is sep-arately decorated and one is given to each guest; they are similar to the British favours and are kept as a keepsake. One custom which seems to be common in all European countries is the use of tiny replicas of the bride and groom to decorate the traditional wedding cake. These ancient customs and rituals seem to be ingrained in the culture of all European countries, and many have survived until the present day.

However, in the seventeenth century the English plum cake was trans-formed. The recipe for the plum cake was made with enormous quantities of dried fruits and was heavily laced with rum. The cake was made to keep for long periods of time in order for it to be carried to far-off English colonies. Initially, the cake mixture was not supported in a mould, but was placed on sheets of buttered paper and then simply lifted into the oven. The result, of course, was a large, uneven and misshapen cake. The decoration of these huge fruit cakes was very crude, as at that time royal icing had not been created. The cakes were simply iced with a mixture of beaten egg whites, rose-water and sugar.

Over a period of time, the plum cake was to improve beyond recognition. For example, at the beginning of the eighteenth century the tin hoop was invented. The hoop was used as a support for the cake mixture and ensured that an even and perfectly shaped round cake was achieved. These plum cakes were made for special occasions and celebrations. They were so highly valued that it was not unusual during that period for a plum cake to be presented as a gift to members of the royal family.

The descendant of the plum cake is the modern fruit cake of today. The fruit cake is still regarded in Britain as the traditional celebration cake and is made for special occasions such as weddings and christenings. The traditional British wedding cake usually consists of several elaborately iced and decorated fruit cakes. The cakes are placed on top of each other according to size and are separated and supported by pillars between each tier. Favours are arranged around the cake and distributed to guests as keepsakes. Small replicas of the bride and groom are placed on the top of the wedding cake. The custom of throwing rice over the bride and groom is still prevalent throughout Britain today; however, confetti has become popular and is often used as a substitute for the traditional rice.

G

∽ GALETTE DES ROIS ∽

The Galette des Rois is made with puff pastry or brioche. The pastry or brioche is usually made with butter. This type of galette can be served plain, or can have a filling of almond cream or apple purée. The plain galette is called Galette Nature and the galette with a filling is called Galette Fourrée. Galette des Rois is a pastry which is traditionally made and eaten during the period after Christmas.

However, there are many different types of galettes which are made and eaten throughout the year in France. For example, in the district of Limousin in the south-west of France, a galette is made which is the speciality of the region and is called Galette de Plomb, which translated into English means Lead Girdle Cake. The name is quite appropriate because it is made with a very rich paste which makes the galette very heavy in texture.

In Brittany, a galette can also refer to a type of crêpe. The large Breton crêpe is made with buckwheat flour, eggs, salt, sugar, butter, cinnamon, milk and is usually flavoured with alcohol, for example, Calvados. The galette is cooked very quickly over a girdle and is paper-thin. It is eaten while hot. The galette is eaten as a snack and is sold in restaurants and cafés. A familiar sight in markets in France is the galette stall, where the galettes are cooked in the open and are sold as a hot snack.

For weddings, christenings and any large celebration, galettes are made as large as one metre in diameter. This huge crêpe is made from wheat flour, butter, eggs and sugar, with the addition of candied angelica. Each guest receives a piece.

It is interesting to note that the Kouign-Aman galette or gâteau is not only a speciality of Brittany, in the north-west of France, but also of southern Cornwall, in the south-west of England. *Kouign* in Celtic means gâteau or galette and *Aman* is the Celtic word for butter. This type of galette is made with rich puff pastry and is high in sugar content. It also contains yeast and is flavoured with rum and vanilla.

History

The word 'galette' is derived from a thirteenth-century French word *galet*, which means a round, flat pebble (Ref.: *Le Petit Robert 1*, 1972). Presumably, the pastry got its name because of its round shape and its colour, which resembles that of a flat pebble.

The galette originated in Italy during the might of the Roman Empire. The ancient pastry even then had a religious significance and was made in honour of the Roman god, Saturn. As the centuries passed, the recipe for the galette changed, as did the religious significance of the pastry. Today in France, the Galette des Rois is baked on Twelfth Night to celebrate the Twelfth Day after Christmas, or the day of Epiphany. The day of Epiphany became a recognized religious day by a church decree, a day on which the nations in the Western world celebrate the manifestation of Christ to the Magi. However, in the Orient, the day was commemorated long before, to celebrate the journey of the Three Kings who travelled from the East to worship the baby Jesus. Perhaps this is why in France the galette is called Galette des Rois, which translated means King's Cake, referring to the Three Kings who travelled so far bearing gifts.

Today in France, the Galette des Rois remains extremely popular, and the tradition which is centuries old lives on. Before the galette is baked, an object made of porcelain is inserted into the raw pastry. The object usually represents the baby Jesus or the Virgin Mary. Centuries ago, it was a simple dried bean which was inserted into the pastry. The shape of the dried bean resembled that of a foetus – a symbol of life and of the baby Jesus.

The Galette des Rois is eaten at the end of the celebration meal during the period of Epiphany. It is always served with a glass of champagne. The galette is placed in the centre of the table and a golden paper crown is placed on top of it. It is then cut into sections like a cake and each person sitting at the table is served a piece of the pastry. The person who receives the portion which contains the porcelain object is crowned King or Queen for the day and must wear the crown. The lucky recipient must then choose a member of the opposite sex to become his/her partner for the day, and places the small object into his or her chosen partner's glass of champagne. There is a great deal of anticipation, fun and laughter around the table, and the tradition hopefully will survive into the future.

∽ GANACHE ∽

This is a mixture of chocolate converture, which is the best quality of chocolate, and sterilized or pasteurized cream. The mixture is flavoured with a vanilla pod and liqueur or alcohol. The type of liqueur or alcohol used depends upon the type of converture used in the recipe. For example, if dark converture is used, the ganache will be flavoured with rum. If coffee-flavoured converture is used, the ganache will be flavoured with either rum or Tia Maria. This recipe for ganache produces a very high quality product. However, there are many different types of ganache, and recipes vary, as does the quality of the ingredients.

The method to make ganache is very simple. Cut the chocolate into pieces and allow it to melt over a bain-marie. In the meantime, pour the cream into a pan, flavour it with the vanilla pod and heat. Do not allow it to boil. When the chocolate has melted, add the warm cream, beating all the time until a smooth, piping consistency is achieved. It is then flavoured with liqueur or alcohol.

The ganache is widely used by the patissier as a filling for gâteaux, in the production of confectionery, petits fours and for the flavouring of butter creams. Ganache is the main ingredient in the production of Rum Truffles.

History

The recipe for ganache was created by a French patissier in the middle of the nineteenth century.

∽ GASTRONOMIE – GASTRONOMY ∽

The word *gastronomie* is of French origin and dates back to the year 1800 (Ref.: *Le Petit Robert 1*, 1972). The word first appeared in print in France in 1801, in a book called *Gastronomie ou l'Homme des Champs à Table*, which translated into English literally means *The Peasant at the Table*. The book was written by a French magistrate called Berchoux who was born in 1765. The book was translated into English in 1810 and into Spanish in 1820.

∽ GÂTEAU ∽

In Britain today, the word 'gâteau' is used to describe Genoese sponge cakes which are sandwiched together in a series of layers with fresh whipped cream, butter cream or ganache. The Genoese sponge can be made with a variety of flavourings. The gâteau is then elaborately decorated with piped fresh cream or a flavoured butter cream, fruits and nuts. Classic examples are Black Forest Gâteau, Chocolate Gâteau or Mocha Gâteau.

The term 'gâteau' in France is used to describe a much wider variety of pastry goods or cakes which are not necessarily made with Genoese sponge. For example, the renowned Gâteau Pavlova is made with a meringue base, the Gâteau Mille Feuille is made with puff pastry and the Gâteau Saint-Honoré is made with choux pastry.

History

The word 'gâteau' dates back to the twelfth century, and is a derivative of the old French word *gastel* and the old German word *Wastel* meaning food (Ref.: *Le Petit Robert 1*, 1972). However, it was not until the nineteenth century that the word was adopted by the British. Initially, the French word was used to describe a variety of different baked pastry goods, and it was not until the early twentieth century that the word was used by the British to describe an elaborately decorated layered Genoese sponge cake.

∽ GENOA CAKE – PAIN DE GÊNE ∽

This is a type of sponge which is made with whole eggs, egg yolks, caster sugar, flour, cornflour, butter and candied peel, and flavoured with vanilla essence and orange-flavoured liqueur such as Curaçao.

History

In the year 1800, a French marshal called Masséna (1758–1817) lay siege to the Italian port of Genoa. The besieged people of the city were starving, their only food being rice and almonds. During the siege they consumed more than fifty tons of almonds. Several years later, in Paris, in a patisserie called Chiboust, the head patissier, who was called Fauvel, created the recipe for Genoa Cake and named it after the Italian port in remembrance of the besieged Italian people.

∽ GENOESE SPONGE – GÉNOISE ∽

This is a mixture of eggs, sugar, flour and butter. The butter is optional. There are two main methods of making the sponge. These are known as the hot and cold methods. The main difference between the two methods is that when making a hot Genoese sponge the eggs and sugar are heated together in a bowl over a bain-marie before being whisked. Genoese sponge is used extensively by the patissier in the production of a variety of gâteaux and cakes.

History

This type of sponge was created by a patissier who was born in the Italian city of Genoa. He created the sponge while working in a patisserie in the French city of Bordeaux. He was observed by a Parisian patissier called Auguste Julien, who took the recipe for the sponge back to the establishment in Paris where he worked, called Chiboust, and named it after the Genoese patissier who created it.

∽ GIANDUJA ∽

This is a combination of hazelnuts, icing sugar, chocolate converture and cocoa butter. It is used by the patissier to flavour butter cream, pastry cream, confectionery and iced products.

History

This mixture is an Italian creation of the twentieth century. It has been known in France only in the last decade. It was named after a famous Italian comedian called Gianduja.

∾ GINGER – GINGEMBRE ∾

Ginger is a pungent spice which is obtained from a plant belonging to the family *Zingiberaceae*. The perennial plant grows to approximately one metre in height. It is from the root of the plant that the spice is obtained.

Today, the spice is used by the patissier in its powdered form as a flavouring in the production of cakes and pastries. The root can also be crystallized, and is commonly referred to as stem ginger. Stem ginger is a speciality used during the Christmas festive season in the making of Christmas puddings and fruit cakes. Ginger root can also be purchased when fresh. It is mostly used in cookery recipes as a flavouring. The root is peeled then grated and added to the dish.

History

The word 'ginger' is a derivative of *gingembre*, an old French word dating back to the eleventh century. It is a derivative of the Latin word *zingeber*.

The plant is native to tropical Asia. It has been known to man for thousands of years, and was used by the Ancient Greeks and Romans as a flavouring in their cooking, especially for savoury dishes.

In the Middle Ages, the spice was used extensively throughout Europe and was regarded as a common spice. Guillaume Tirel (known as Taillevent), who was the executive chef to the French monarch Charles V (1338–1380), King of France from 1364, used the spice in a variety of recipes which he created during that period.

In the sixteenth century, the Portuguese introduced the plant to Africa during one of their great seafaring expeditions. The famous Portuguese navigator, Vasco da Gama (1469–1525) carried the plant from India on his return journey to Portugal, making a port of call in South Africa. The plant was not introduced into Britain until the late sixteenth century.

∾ GINGERBREAD – PAIN D'ÉPICE ∾

This is a moist, dark brown cake which has a heavy texture. It consists of wheat and rye flour, caster and inverted sugar (added to the mixture in order to produce a moist and well-flavoured Gingerbread), honey, whole eggs and spices, and bicarbonate of soda used as a raising agent. If inverted sugar is not used in the recipe, treacle is used instead. The spices which are usually used in the making of Gingerbread are ginger, cinnamon, vanilla, liquorice, anise, coriander, pepper and the zest of lemons.

History

Gingerbread was introduced to France, Britain and Germany when the first Crusaders returned from the Holy Wars. The recipe for the rich cake included a variety of spices from the Middle East.

During the Middle Ages in England, knights in tournaments would present a piece of Gingerbread to their ladies. The Gingerbread pieces were made in the shape of a shield which was studded with cloves and brushed with egg white, to give the surface of the shield a shiny appearance. Gingerbread at that time was also used as payment to workers; it was in fact a form of money.

In France and Belgium, the spiced cake was known as Pain d'Épice, which translated into English means Spiced Bread. In 1380, Marguerite of Flanders spoke highly of the leavened cake mixture made with wheat flour, honey and spices. It was not until a much later date that treacle would replace the honey. Some years later, Philip the Good (1396–1467), Duke of Burgundy from 1419, sampled the Pain d'Épice in Courtrai in Belgium. He brought the recipe back to the French province, and from Burgundy its popularity spread throughout France. For the first time in France, it became available to the public and was sold in pieces at fairgrounds throughout France. Reims, a city in the north-east of France, became the largest producer of Gingerbread.

In the sixteenth century, bakers specialized in the making of Gingerbread. To become a qualified Gingerbread baker, an apprentice would have to be able to make a cake of three kilograms in weight, observed by a panel of Master Craftsmen Bakers of Gingerbread.

In the late seventeenth century, special moulds for Gingerbread were produced in a variety of different shapes, representing kings, queens, legendary heroes or animals. In 1827 in France, the first giraffe arrived from Africa to be housed in the Parisian zoo, called Le Jardin des Plantes. The bakers of Gingerbread in the city seized upon this opportunity and started to make the Gingerbread biscuits in the shape of a giraffe. The Parisians loved the idea, and Gingerbread made in the shape of a giraffe remained popular for a long time.

⮞ GLASSE, HANNAH ⮜

Hannah Glasse (1708–1770) was an English cookery writer. Her first cookery book, *The Art of Cookery*, was published in 1747. It was the most popular book of that period and had no less than twenty editions. Her second book, *The Servant's Directory*, was published thirteen years later in 1760. *The Compleat Confectioner*, her third and last book, was published in 1770. This is of particular interest to the patissier, as it contains an abundance of recipes for puddings, confectionery, cakes and pastries, including the first recipe for ice cream to be published in Britain.

During this period, the English were renowned for the quality of their puddings, cakes and pastries. It was the time of the English phenomenon, afternoon tea, when tea was served with wafer-thin sandwiches and an abundance of sweet baked goods. The British Empire was at its strongest, and included numerous far-off colonies from which endless supplies of cheap sugar could be imported, an essential ingredient in the production of these goods.

Hannah Glasse's books were written mainly for larger households with servants, unlike the French cookery books written at that time, which contained recipes that could only be described as Haute Cuisine. During the sixteenth and seventeenth centuries the majority of cooks and cookery writers in England were female. However, in France during this period males dominated this field, and it was not until the twentieth century in France that females entered the profession. Hannah Glasse's immortality is assured, as many of her recipes have taken their place in the British repertoire and she is still regarded as one of the most important cookery writers of that period.

∽ GLOBUS ∽

This is a type of fritter made with wheat flour and curd cheese which was rolled into individual balls, fried and then dredged with poppy seeds and brushed with honey.

History

The globus was a speciality of the Romans and was very popular during that period. It no longer exists, but was probably the first type of fritter to be made.

∽ GNOCCHI ∽

Gnocchi is a type of dumpling. It can be made with semolina, choux pastry, savoury short paste or potatoes. There are a variety of different types, all with different names. The most popular recipes are the following:

Gnocchi à la Romaine

These are semolina and cheese dumplings which are coated with a mixture of milk, breadcrumbs and melted butter. The dumplings are then browned under a grill and served with a tomato sauce.

Gnocchi à la Parisienne

These are savoury short pastry tartlets, which have been baked blind and are then filled with a cheese sauce mixture, to which choux pastry quenelles have been added. The filling should be heaped into the small individual tartlets and dredged with grated Gruyère or Cheddar cheese, and allowed to brown in a very hot oven before being served. Another variation is to place the choux pastry quenelles in an earthenware dish, cover with a cheese sauce, top with grated cheese and bake. The dumplings are very popular in France, especially in the south of France. They are usually eaten at lunchtime as a snack.

History

The recipe for Gnocchi was created in Italy. The word Gnocchi is the plural of the word *gnoccho*, which belongs to the dialect of the Piedmont district in the north-west of Italy. The word dates back to the late nineteenth century. Translated into English, *gnoccho* means a small piece or a small mouthful, which described perfectly the original mouth-sized dumplings. However, today the dumplings are made in a variety of sizes.

∾ GOOSEBERRY – GROSEILLE A MAQUEREAU ∾

The gooseberry belongs to the family *Saxifragaceae*. The gooseberry bush flourishes in the wild, in cool and moist conditions in the northern hemisphere. The bush produces a small, round, green fruit which has a rough skin. The fruit is sour to the taste. It is a good source of vitamin C and fibre. The gooseberry is a summer fruit, and is used in the production of fools, pies, sorbets and jams.

History

The gooseberry probably originated in the northern regions of Europe. The word 'gooseberry' was possibly derived from the French name for the fruit, *groseille*, as it was first cultivated in France. However, the fruit never enjoyed the same popularity there as it did in Britain. The only classic recipe created in France using the fruit was the savoury dish Groseille à Maquereau, a mackerel dish accompanied by a gooseberry sauce. Such was the popularity of the dish that the French refer to the fruit as groseille à maquereau. However, the fruit has made little impact on French cuisine.

In Britain, on the other hand, the fruit gained in popularity. In Elizabethan and Tudor England the fruit was used to a great extent to stuff geese. The acidic taste of the gooseberry counteracted the fatty taste of the bird. It has also been suggested by some that this is in fact how the gooseberry got its name – simply meaning the berries used to stuff the goose.

By the beginning of the eighteenth century, the fruit was being used in the production of pies and puddings. A favourite pudding during that period was Gooseberry Fool.

The fruit reached the height of its popularity in the nineteenth century in England. It was cultivated by private growers throughout the northern regions of England. Clubs were formed and annual shows organized to give prizes for the largest and best flavoured gooseberries.

∾ GOUFFÉ, JULES ∾

Gouffé was a French cookery writer. He was born in Paris in 1807. As a young man, he trained to be a patissier and eventually opened his own patisserie in Paris which became a great success, employing twenty-eight patissiers. Due to ill-health, probably caused by heavy physical work and long hours, he retired and left the running of the patisserie to his younger brother.

He became extremely bored in retirement, and under pressure from two of his friends, Alexandre Dumas, the famous French novelist, and Baron Brisse, he accepted a position as Executive Chef Patissier at the renowned Jockey Club in Paris.

In 1867 his first book was published, called *The Book of Cookery*. Five years later his second book was published, called *The Book of Pastry*. His third book, *How to Preserve Food*, was very innovative and explained how to can a variety of foods using a new method of preservation invented by Nicholas Appert, which involved sealing food in glass bottles and subjecting them to heat. He died on 28 February 1877, in the city of Neuilly on the outskirts of Paris.

ᴥ GOUGÈRE ᴥ

A Gougère is a savoury bun which is made with choux pastry and cheese. The cheese used in the recipe is usually Gruyère. The cheese is added to the pastry in a variety of different ways: for example, it may be diced and mixed into the choux pastry, or the cheese can be grated and added to the pastry. Sometimes a piece of cheese is simply inserted into the choux bun before baking. The choux pastry can be piped into a large ring for several persons or a small ring for one person only. It can also be piped into small individual buns.

History

Originally the bun was known as Tarte au Fromage, which translated into English simply means a cheese tart. It was not until the thirteenth century that it was called Gocere, from which the present name of Gougère was derived. The cheese used during that period was Gruyère cheese, which originated in Switzerland in the twelfth century. Burgundy, a region in the south-east of France, was renowned for the quality of its Gougères.

By the nineteenth century, the savoury was extremely popular throughout France and was usually eaten as an entrée at lunchtime. In the Champagne district of France, it is a speciality which is eaten during the Christmas season.

ᴥ GRANITÉ ᴥ

A Granité is a water ice which is made with fruit juice and syrup. The mixture is not too sweet, and the amount of sugar used in making this ice preparation is minimal. The Granité is so called because of its rough texture, caused by the tiny particles of ice in the mixture, which resemble the coarse-grained texture of granite. During the freezing process the mixture is not beaten, thus causing the ice particles to form.

A Granité can be served between the fish course and the meat course in a meal. The main reason for doing so is to remove the taste of fish and freshen the diner's palate before eating the next course. A Granité served at this stage of a meal is usually made with orange or lemon juice. It can also be served as a dessert, and can be made with a variety of fruits, such as guava, papaya, strawberries and kiwi fruit.

History

The first type of Granité was made thousands of years ago by the Chinese, with snow, fruit juice and honey. The Ancient Greeks and then the Romans inherited the knowledge, and the water ice was extremely popular during ancient times. It has remained popular throughout the centuries, and today it can be found on the menus of the world's most reputable hotels and restaurants.

∾ GRAPE – RAISIN ∾

The grape belongs to the family *Vitaceae*. The fruit is covered by a thick skin which can be green, golden or dark red in colour. The central pulp of the fruit has no colour. The skin contains tannin and the pulp contains sugar, fruit acids, water and pectin. The grape is used mainly in the production of wine throughout the world. However, eaten raw as a fruit it is delicious and is one of the most popular fruits on the market today. There are thousands of varieties of *Vitis Vinifera*. The grapes used in the production of wine are bitter to taste, and only ten or so varieties can be used raw, as a fruit to be eaten.

The patissier uses black and green grapes a great deal because of their small, round, almost perfect shape and their attractive colour. They are excellent for decoration purposes, especially for gâteaux. They are also used in the production of small tartlets and petits fours.

History

The fruit originated in Asia and dates back to antiquity. The vines need plenty of sunshine to ripen in summer and a cool enough winter to enable them to rest. The cultivation of grapes for wine making began in ancient Persia, and the art of wine making spread to other countries. During biblical times, wine making was well documented.

The early Greek and Roman civilizations cultivated the vine not only for wine making, but also for the fruit, which they ate raw. The Greeks and the Romans valued wine so highly that it was considered sacred by both civilizations. The Romans were responsible for introducing the vine into the interior of Europe, as far north as England and as far east as Hungary.

During the twelfth century, wine became in great demand throughout Europe. Henry II of England (1133–1189), King of England from 1154, married Eleanor of Aquitaine, thus strengthening the trading links between the two countries. During that period, wine was imported to England from France in great quantities.

In the fourteenth century, Britain became an ally of Portugal and opened the port wine trade. Port wine, which was much cheaper than French wine, became the favourite British tipple. Over the centuries, the taxes imposed on wine imports grew to such an extent that wine became so expensive that it was affordable only by the very wealthy.

In the seventeenth century, the vine was introduced into America, South Africa and to the other side of the world, into Australia.

Today, the major producing countries of wine are Italy, Spain, France, the United States of America, Australia and South Africa.

∽ GRAPEFRUIT – PAMPLEMOUSSE ∽

The grapefruit belongs to the family *Citrus Paradisi*. It is a descendant of the pomelo. The grapefruit is rich in vitamin C and pectin and is available throughout the year.

It is not used widely by the patissier, but may be used in flavouring some desserts. The fruit is usually eaten raw as an appetizer at the beginning of a meal, for breakfast, lunch or dinner. It is also used in the production of marmalade. About 50 per cent of the world's grapefruit crop is used for the production of grapefruit juice.

History

The grapefruit originated in Asia. It was first introduced into Florida by a Frenchman in the early part of the nineteenth century, and by the end of the century the fruit was being cultivated there on a commercial scale. It then spread to other states in the south of the United States. Today, Israel, Argentina and Africa are among the main producers.

∽ GUAVA – GOYAVE ∽

The tree which produces the fruit belongs to the family *Psidium Guajava* of *Myrtaceae*. It grows to a height of ten metres. The guava fruit varies in its shape, size and colour, and is a rich source of vitamin C, potassium and fibre. The fruit is highly flavoured and aromatic and, although sweet, it is also slightly acidic. There are many varieties. It is delicious when eaten raw, and is used by the patissier in the production of fresh fruit salads, custards, sorbets and mousses. Although a comparatively new fruit to the patissier, it is gaining in popularity.

History

The tree originated in South America in Peru. It was cultivated there during the time of the Incas, around 1000 BC. The Indians had an excellent knowledge of agriculture. From Peru, the fruit spread northwards. Spanish and Portuguese sailors, on expeditions to the New World, were the first Europeans to taste the exotic fruit. They introduced it to other regions.

The guava was introduced into Great Britain in the seventeenth century. By that time the fruit was well established in India and Asia, where it is still widely cultivated. Today, the fruit is also cultivated in Hawaii, Southern Florida and Southern California.

H

∽ HAZELNUT – NOISETTE ∽

Is a small, round, brown nut with a smooth, hard shell which is the fruit of the hazel tree, belonging to the genus *Corylus*. The trees grow wild in northern countries. The nuts are rich in fat and protein and have a lovely sweet flavour which complements a wide variety of pastries and sweets. They can be used whole as a decoration for sweets and cakes and can also be ground or chopped and added as a flavouring to mixtures for cakes, biscuits and pastries.

A richly flavoured oil is extracted from the nut which is used mainly in salad dressings. Hazelnut oil is very expensive, and because of this is not used a great deal by the patissier. Another by-product of hazelnuts is praline paste.

History

Nuts have been a source of food for man since ancient times, and hazelnuts are no exception. The hazel tree probably dates as far back as prehistoric times.

∽ HIPPOCRATE ∽

A French magazine which was first published in 1947. It provided a wealth of information on the history of food, dating as far back as the Egyptian civilization up to the twentieth century.

∽ HONEY – MIEL ∽

Honey is a sweet substance which is made by honey bees from the nectar of flowers. It consists of two sugars, fructose and glucose. It also contains enzymes, colouring matter, acids and pollen grains. Honey has anti-bacterial properties and is widely used in medicines today. The flavour, colour and texture of honey is determined by a variety of factors, such as the plant, the type of soil, the particular season and the climate. It is regarded as one of the most nutritious of natural foods and contains all the necessary vitamins which are essential to good health. The vitamins present in honey can only be destroyed if the honey is overheated. Honey is also extremely rich in mineral content.

When honey is used as a sweetener it is much sweeter than sugar. Bakery goods which are made with honey will stay fresh and moist for much longer periods of time than goods which are made with sugar. It does not require refrigeration and can be stored at room temperature, but it must be stored in a dry area as it absorbs and retains moisture.

History

Honey has existed since the coming of bees to the planet, long before mankind. Neolithic man gathered honey from trees in the wild. Armed with long wooden poles, they protected themselves with smoke in order to ward off the bees.

In ancient times, the main sweetening agents used by man were wild honey, sugar cane, which was known as 'honey from the weeds', and early morning dewdrops which had fallen on the leaves of plants and trees, producing a sweet, sticky substance which was collected by man.

The early Egyptians used honey widely, not only as a sweetener and a delicacy, but also as a healing agent. They were the first to discover honey's anti-bacterial properties and they used it for medicinal purposes such as healing wounds. It was also used in the production of cosmetics during this period. By the year 3500 BC, bees had become domesticated, and the method used by the Egyptians was quite advanced.

Honey was sacred to the Egyptians and was used in religious ceremonies. They believed in the afterlife, and mummified their Pharaohs and buried them in magnificent tombs. Such was the value of honey, that it was buried with their rulers in order to sustain them in the afterlife.

During the Roman civilization, honey was highly regarded and valued. The use of honey as a sweetener in cookery is well documented in the ancient manuscripts written by Marcus Apicius, a reputable Roman gastronome and historian. It was also added to wine, and this became a favourite tipple of the ancient Romans. The Romans, like the Egyptians, were aware that honey was highly valuable as a medicine and health food. Such was the popularity of honey during the Roman Empire that it became scarce, and the price of honey escalated until it became a food available only to the wealthy. When the Romans invaded Britain in 55–54 BC, bee-keeping was widespread throughout the island, an industry which grew as time passed.

In the thirteenth century, honey was ousted as the main sweetening agent by sugar, which was extracted from sugar cane. However, during this period sugar was available only to the wealthy. More than five hundred years passed before sugar which was extracted from sugar beet became available. Large refineries were built, and ensured that sugar was inexpensive and available to everyone.

Today, honey is produced commercially on a massive scale and sold worldwide to be eaten in its natural state. The varieties of honey available to the consumer are extensive, and many regions of the world produce honey. It is still regarded as a valuable health food and is highly valued for its anti-bacterial properties. It is widely used in medicines produced by pharmaceutical companies: for example, it is used as a soothing agent in a variety of cough mixtures. It is also used in the production of cosmetics, such as soaps and hand and body lotions. Honey is also widely used as a flavouring in bakery.

Recently, honey has been found in sealed containers in the tombs of Pharaohs in Egypt. The honey was over five thousand years old and was still edible. Little wonder that it was used as a preserving agent!

∾ HOT CROSS BUNS – PETITS PAINS CHAUDS DE PÂQUES ∾

Are small buns which are made with a fermented yeast dough which is very similar to a basic bread dough. The dough is flavoured with spices such as cinnamon, nutmeg and mixed spices. Currants and mixed peel are added to the dough. It is then divided into small round balls and a process of fermentation is allowed to take place before baking. The buns are decorated with small crosses which are made from rice paper, or the crosses can also be made from a paste of flour and water. They are then brushed with eggwash and baked. When cooked, they are glazed with a mixture of milk and sugar.

History

The cross, as a symbol, has been used to decorate cakes as far back as four thousand years ago. Throughout the ages, special cakes and pastries have been made to celebrate religious occasions. For example, the ancient Babylonians, who worshipped the sun, made cakes in the shape of the sun and placed a cross in the middle of the cake. In Ancient Greece and Rome, cakes and pastries were decorated with the symbol of the cross.

However, the symbol of the cross took on a new significance with the coming of Christianity. For Christians worldwide, the cross signifies the crucifixion of Jesus Christ and his sacrifice. Originally the symbol of the cross was achieved by pressing a small wooden crucifix into the bun before baking to leave the imprint of a cross. At a later date, the cross was made separately with water pastry dough which was placed on the surface of the bun before baking. More recently, the cross has been made with rice paper. It is unclear as to the precise date when the symbol of the cross first appeared on the bun.

Today, the Hot Cross Bun is made throughout the Christian world during Easter celebrations. The small buns are made and sold on Good Friday, which in the Christian church is the Friday before Easter, a special day in the Christian calendar, kept to commemorate the crucifixion of Christ. Several hundred years ago, a by-law in England decreed that the buns could only be sold on Good Friday.

An interesting statistic to note is that in the year 1890 in Paris over ten thousand Hot Cross Buns were sold between Good Friday and Easter Sunday, highlighting their popularity during that period. In France during that period, the buns were sold hot, explaining the name Hot Cross Bun.

Today, Hot Cross Buns are still part of Easter celebrations throughout the Christian world. Such is their popularity that they are now made all year round and sold in great quantities, somewhat diminishing their religious significance.

I

∾ ICE COUPE – COUPE GLACÉE ∾

A Coupe Glacée simply means an iced dessert which is served in a coupe, which is a type of glass with a stem. There are endless varieties of Coupes Glacées and each has a different name.

History

A *coupe* is an old French word which dates back to the twelfth century. *Coupe* translated into English means a type of drinking glass which is usually quite wide and shallow and stands on a short stem. The idea for the iced dessert called Coupe Glacée is attributed to the famous French gastronome, Auguste Escoffier (1846–1935). Listed below are some of the most popular coupes.

Alexandra

Consists of strawberry ice cream which is covered with a macédoine of fruit, flavoured with Kirsch. Coupe Alexandra is decorated with piped Chantilly Cream, glacé cherries and candied angelica.

History

It was named after the last Tsarina of Russia, Alexandra Feodorovna (1872–1918), who became the wife of Tsar Nicholas II of Russia in 1894. The whole royal family were shot by the Bolsheviks at the end of the Russian Revolution.

Andalusia – Andalouse

Consists of lemon sorbet and orange segments, flavoured with Maraschino or Curaçao and decorated with Chantilly Cream.

History

It was named after the province of Andalusia, which is in southern Spain. The province is a large producer of citrus fruits such as lemons and oranges, which are the main ingredients used in this coupe.

Brazilian – Brésilienne

Consists of Maraschino or pineapple-flavoured ice cream and diced pineapple which is then decorated with glacé cherries and pieces of angelica.

History

It was named after the South American country of Brazil where the pineapple originated, which is the main ingredient used to make this coupe.

Chateaubriand

Consists of vanilla and apricot ice cream which can be flavoured with either Cognac or apricot brandy. The coupe is decorated with fresh strawberries and piped Chantilly Cream.

History

It was named after the French writer and diplomat, François René, Vicomte de Chateaubriand (1768–1848). He wrote *Atala* in 1801 and *The Genius of Christianity* in 1802. Chateaubriand spent many years living in exile in America during the French Revolution.

Joséphine Baker

Consists of chocolate ice cream, fresh pineapple, Cointreau liqueur and pistachio nuts. The coupe is decorated with piped Chantilly Cream and dark flaked chocolate.

History

It was named after the French comedienne Joséphine Baker, who was extremely popular in France at the beginning of the twentieth century.

Longchamp

Consists of vanilla ice cream and Biscuits à la Cuillère which have been soaked in Benedictine liqueur. The biscuits and ice cream are then coated with Melba sauce and decorated with piped Chantilly Cream.

History

It is named after the famous French racecourse Longchamp, which is situated on the outskirts of Paris.

Montmorency

Consists of vanilla ice cream and stoned cherries which are coated with Melba sauce. The coupe is decorated with glacé cherries, pieces of angelica and piped Chantilly Cream.

History

It was named after the French city of Montmorency. The city is famous for producing cherries of the finest quality.

Mozart

Consists of vanilla ice cream on top of which half a fresh peach which has been poached is placed. It is flavoured with peach brandy. The ice cream and peach are coated with Melba sauce. The coupe is decorated with flaked almonds and piped Chantilly Cream.

History

It was named after the famous Austrian composer, Wolfgang Amadeus Mozart (1756–1791).

Pêche Alexandra – Peach Alexandra

Consists of vanilla ice cream, half a fresh peach which has been poached, and strawberry purée. It is then sprinkled with crystallized rose petals and covered with spun sugar.

History

It was created by the French chef and gastronome, Auguste Escoffier (1846–1935), in honour of Queen Alexandra (1844–1925), who was the Queen Consort of Edward VII (1841–1910), King of Great Britain and Ireland from 1901. She undertook a great deal of charitable work, and in Britain, Alexandra Rose Day was so named to commemorate her work.

Pêche Cardinal – Peach Cardinal

Consists of strawberry ice cream and half a fresh peach which has been poached. The ice cream and peach are coated in Melba sauce. The coupe is decorated with piped Chantilly Cream and flaked roasted almonds.

History

It was named after Cardinal Armand Jean Duplessis, Duc de Richelieu (1585–1642), who became a Cardinal in 1622. He became Chief Minister of France in 1624.

Pêche l'Aiglon

Consists of vanilla ice cream and half a fresh peach which has been poached. The ice cream and peach are then glazed with a cream which has been flavoured with a Maraschino liqueur. The coupe is decorated with crystallized violets and a veil of spun sugar.

History

The French word *aiglon*, translated into English, means young eagle. It was the nickname given to Napoleon II (1811–1832) by the Bonapartists who were the followers of his father, Napoleon I (1769–1821), Emperor of France from 1804. This coupe was named after Napoleon II.

Pêche Melba – Peach Melba

Consists of vanilla ice cream and half a fresh peach which has been poached. The ice cream and peach are coated with a Melba sauce made with raspberry purée, sugar and lemon juice. It is decorated with piped Chantilly

Cream and roasted flaked almonds. Peach Melba is usually served with petits fours secs which are called Langues de Chat.

History

It was created in 1889 by the famous French gastronome and chef, Auguste Escoffier (1846–1935). The coupe was named after the Australian opera singer, Helen Porter Mitchell, who was affectionately nicknamed Nellie Melba. Pêche Melba was first made by Auguste Escoffier whilst he was working as the Executive Chef at the world-renowned Savoy Hotel in London where the opera singer was staying.

Pêche Sarah Bernhardt

Consists of strawberry ice cream and half a fresh peach which has been poached. The ice cream and peach are decorated with piped Chantilly Cream which has been flavoured with Curaçao liqueur. Chopped pistachio nuts are sprinkled on top of the cream.

History

It was named after the famous French actress Henriette Rosine Bernard (1844–1923), whose stage name was Sarah Bernhardt. She was adored not only by the French, but was world famous and regarded as one of the finest actresses of her time. She frequently appeared in Paris at the renowned Comédie Française; however, she also excelled as an actress in leading roles in Shakespearian tragedies.

Poire Belle Hélène – Pear Belle Hélène

Consists of vanilla ice cream and half a fresh pear which has been poached. The ice cream and pear are coated with hot chocolate sauce and decorated with piped Chantilly Cream and crushed crystal violets.

History

It was named after the famous opera *La Belle Hélène*, which was composed in 1864 by the French composer, Jacques Offenbach (1819–1880). He wrote light operas which he presented at the famous Bouffes Parisiens.

Victoria

Consists of strawberry and pistachio ice cream and fresh fruit salad, to which champagne or fine champagne is added. The coupe is decorated with piped Chantilly Cream. Often the pistachio ice cream is omitted.

History

It is highly likely that Coupe Victoria was named after Victoria (1819–1901), who became Queen of Great Britain and Ireland in 1837.

⤳ ICE CREAM – GLACE ⤳

Is a pasteurized preparation which is brought to a semi-hard state through a freezing process. The four main methods of making ice cream are:

1 **Ice Cream made with eggs**   This is made with powdered or pasteurized milk, caster sugar, inverted sugar, egg yolks, a stabilizer and is flavoured with vanilla. This type of ice cream can be made in a variety of flavours and colours.
2 **Ice Cream made with cream**   This is made with pasteurized milk, cream, caster sugar, inverted sugar, a stabilizer and is flavoured with vanilla. This type of ice cream can also be made in a variety of flavours and colours.
3 **Ice Cream made with syrup of natural flavourings**   This is made with pasteurized milk, butter, sugar, inverted sugar, a stabilizer and is flavoured with natural flavourings such as chocolate, praline or coffee.
4 **Ice Cream made with syrup and fresh fruits**   This is made with spring water, sugar, inverted sugar, fruit juice or fruit pulp, powdered milk and a stabilizer. This type of ice cream is flavoured with the natural fruit juice or fruit pulp which is used in the recipe.

There are strict laws which govern the manufacture of ice cream. Commercially, ice cream is made in a special ice cream machine which pasteurizes the mixture automatically. As a general rule, hygiene is critical when making this product. When the ice cream comes out of the machine, it will be approximately at a temperature of below 6°C to 8°C. The ideal temperature at which ice cream should be served is below 12°C to 14°C.

History

The use of ice cream in the composition of a drink or dessert dates as far back as 4000 BC. One thousand years later, according to Egyptian hieroglyphics, drinks were cooled in earthenware amphoras which were buried in the ground.

The Chinese were the first to make a type of sorbet around 3000 BC. They drank an iced dessert which was made with snow, fruit juice and honey. Eventually milk was added to the composition – the birth of the first type of ice cream!

The ancient Greeks also used ice. A Greek historian and soldier called Xenophon (430 BC–354 BC) recorded in manuscripts that the Greek soldiers during that period were very fond of cold drinks made with ice, honey and fruit juices. During the reign of Alexander the Great (356 BC–323 BC), the Greek people buried drinks deep in the ground in earthenware amphoras surrounded with ice which was then covered with oak leaves.

The early Romans dug holes in the ground which had interior stone walls, like a well, and placed charcoal in the bottom of the well in order to preserve the ice which they gathered from neighbouring glaciers. The Romans valued ice and appreciated its preserving qualities. Nero (AD 37–AD 68), who was Emperor of Rome from AD 54, had a type of ice sorbet served at his table. The sorbet was made with a composition of crushed fruit, rose-water, snow and honey. The Roman nobles made the sorbets the fashion of the day during that period. Their houses were constructed with special cellars which were used to keep ice and also to preserve and keep their food cold.

During the third Crusade, Richard the Lionheart (1157–1199), King of England from 1189, was offered between battles an ice sorbet by his adversary, Saladin (1138–1193), who was the Sultan of Egypt from 1174. The ice sorbet was made with ice which was gathered from the mountains of Libya. It was, in fact, the ancestor of the Sherbet. The Arabs introduced the Sherbet into Italy, and it later became known as Sorbetto.

In the thirteenth century, the Venetian merchant and explorer Marco Polo (1254–1324), on one of his great voyages of exploration, visited China. He discovered that the Chinese had found a way to harden their drinks by using a mixture of potassium nitrate and water. The explorer, on his return to his native Italy, introduced the iced dessert to the Italians and gradually it spread throughout Europe, even as far north as Russia.

In sixteenth-century Europe, iced desserts had become extremely popular. In 1533, Catherine de' Medici (1519–1589), an Italian noblewoman, married King Henry II of France. She brought to her new homeland from her native Italy a personal retinue of chefs and courtiers. The new French Queen introduced to the French court several types of iced desserts. One of her chefs, who was called Buentalenti, had created an iced dessert which consisted of a composition of fruit juice, sugar and liqueur. Another Italian, called Cassati, introduced a type of ice cream to the French in the city of Lyon. During this period, Italy had taken the lead in making iced desserts. All iced desserts at that time were known as Italian Ice.

The seventeenth century was going to see a further transformation in ice production. The famous head waiter, Jean-François Vatel (1631–1671), who worked for the Prince of Condé, surprised the guests during a banquet by serving an iced dessert made with ice, fruit juice and sugar which had a marble effect. It was, in fact, the first Granité. During the reign of the Sun King, Louis XIV (1638–1715), King of France from 1643, ice creams which were made with milk, eggs, sugar and flavoured with vanilla or chocolate were served at the Château de Versailles near Paris.

In England in 1644, at the court of Charles I (1600–1649), who was King of Great Britain and Ireland from 1625, an iced dessert was made for the first time by adding cream as well as milk to the mixture. The recipe was created by a young French chef called Gérard Tirsain, who was employed in the kitchens of the royal household (Ref.: *Le Pâtissier Moderne*, October–December issue, 1984). In 1649 the young French chef returned to Paris and sold his ice cream to a Parisian patisserie under the name of

Neapolitan Ice. However, it was not until the eighteenth century that the term 'ice cream' was used to describe the iced dessert. It is uniquely an English term: in France, for example, ice cream is referred to as *la glace*, which translated into English simply means ice.

In 1660, a Sicilian called Francesco Procopio dei Coltelli opened the famous Café Procope in Paris. It was the first café in France which sold ice cream, or, as the French called it, *la glace*. However, even then its consistency was more like that of a Granité. The new dessert available to the public for the first time was an overnight sensation! The Parisians adored the new iced dessert, and no fewer than eighty different flavours of ice cream were offered to the public. Italian chefs who specialized in making ice cream flocked to Paris to open small businesses.

The craft of making ice cream was considered a profession on the continent at that time, and chefs specializing in making the iced dessert were called Limonadiers. In 1673 a royal decree was imposed and a tax was levied on all the products. This tax proved to be extremely unpopular. It also decreed that the Limonadiers could only make ice cream with fruit and flowers. By the year 1700, in Paris alone there were two hundred and fifty Limonadiers.

The first recipe for ice cream appeared in Britain in a cookery book called *The Compleat Confectioner*, which was written by the famous English Victorian cookery writer, Hannah Glasse (1708–1770). The recipe was quite vague and highlighted how the English had not yet mastered the art of making the dessert in comparison with their European neighbours.

At the end of the eighteenth century, in 1798, a Neapolitan called Tortini invented the Biscuit Glacé and the Bombe Glacée. The renowned French chef, Antoine Carême (1784–1833), created the first iced mousse which was flavoured with caramel. More elaborate desserts followed, using a variety of flavoured ice creams and mousses. For example, such classic desserts as Omelette Norvégienne and a selection of Bombes Glacées were created.

Across the Channel in Britain, during the nineteenth century, ice cream, which had previously been regarded as a dessert for the élite, had become widely available to the British public. During this period, Britain had become a haven for Italian immigrants, and many utilized their specialist knowledge of making ice cream by starting small businesses. Ice creams which were nicknamed 'Penny Licks' were sold by ice cream vendors on street corners in most of the major cities in Britain.

The popularity of ice cream had also spread across the Atlantic to the United States of America. In 1846 an American housewife called Nancy Johnson invented the first manual ice cream machine. Eleven years later, the first factory to produce ice cream on a massive commercial scale opened in the city of Baltimore. Ice cream became a mechanized industry in America, and Britain followed suit shortly afterwards.

Inventions such as the first mechanical domestic refrigerator, which was developed using ammonia compression by the German inventor, Karl von

Linde, in 1879, meant that ice cream could be stored in the home. A few years later, the domestic freezer was invented. These inventions helped to increase the popularity of ice cream in the home.

In the twentieth century, ice cream has become one of the world's most popular desserts and it is made on a massive commercial scale. It is the century of ice cream cones, chocolate bars and ice lollies. Today, the consumption of ice cream per head of population in France is six litres per year, in Britain it is eight litres per year, but in the United States of America it is sixteen litres per year. That's a lot of ice cream!

ᔆ ICED DRINKS – BOISSONS GLACÉES ᔆ

An iced drink is an ice dessert which has been partially thickened by the freezing process.

History

The iced drink became popular in France in the eighteenth century. In 1779, in a fashionable café in Paris called Des Caveaux, iced liqueurs were in vogue.

ᔆ ILES FLOTTANTES – FLOATING ISLANDS ᔆ

A cold dessert which consists of meringues served in an egg custard. The egg whites are whisked until stiff and the sugar is folded in to make the meringue mixture. Spoonfuls of meringue are then poached in simmering milk until the meringue is cooked. The small meringues are then removed from the milk and the egg yolks are added to make a custard which is sweetened with sugar and flavoured with vanilla. The custard is then poured into serving dishes and allowed to cool before the small meringues are placed on top. This dessert is a great favourite not only in France, but also in Britain.

History

The French name Iles Flottantes, when translated into English, simply means Floating Islands. The name is quite appropriate, as the small spoonfuls of meringue resemble tiny white islands floating on a sea of yellow custard. The recipe in France dates back to the early seventeenth century and was mentioned in *Le Cuisinier Français*, which was written by the distinguished French chef, La Varenne (1615–1678).

It is very interesting to note that a similar recipe called Floating Islands dates back to the eighteenth century in Scotland. The Scottish recipe originated from the north-east of Scotland. This is another example of the French influence on Scottish cuisine, and it is highly likely that the Scottish recipe was taken from the original French recipe Iles Flottantes, which may have been brought over by the French at an earlier date. The old Scottish recipe, although similar to the French recipe, differs slightly; it included redcurrant jelly, cream, eggs, white wine and lemon peel. The egg whites were whisked until stiff and sugar was added to make a meringue mixture which was then flavoured with redcurrant jelly. Instead of custard, the Scottish recipe contained cream which was beaten together with white wine and sugar. Lemon peel was then added. The cream mixture was placed in serving dishes and spoonfuls of meringue were placed on top.

J

∾ JALOUSIE GÂTEAU ∾

The gâteau is made with puff pastry and is oblong in shape. The puff pastry is rolled into two oblong shapes, one of which is used for the base and the other for the top of the gâteau. The base is usually covered with raspberry or strawberry jam. However, apple purée or almond cream can also be used as a filling. The pastry top is folded in half lengthwise and using a knife a series of slits are cut along the fold. It is then placed on top of the base and the filling is enclosed by sealing the edges. The gâteau is then brushed with egg wash and baked in the oven. It is removed from the oven five minutes before it has finished cooking, dredged with icing sugar and returned to the oven to allow the sugar to caramelize.

History

Jalousie is a French word, and translated into English simply means 'jealous'. It was created in France well over a hundred years ago. The gâteau is still a popular dessert in Britain and France today.

∾ JAM – CONFITURE ∾

Is a conserve of fruit made by boiling fruit with sugar for a period of time until it reaches a thick consistency. The fruit used to make jam must be fresh: for example, ideal fruits are blackberries, redcurrants, blackcurrants, strawberries and apples. In jam making, the amount of sugar used to the amount of fruit is quite high – usually approximately 750 grams of sugar to one kilogram of fruit. However, the amount of sugar used can vary, and it depends upon the length of time for which the jam is going to be kept. The higher the sugar content used in the preparation, the longer the keeping period of the jam. Therefore the amount of sugar used can vary between 750 grams and 1500 grams to each kilogram of fruit. The whole fruits and sugar are cooked at a high temperature of around 105°C to 107°C, until the mixture reaches setting point. It is a long cooking process and can take several hours. The jam mixture is then poured while still warm into specially prepared sterilized glass jars and sealed.

History

The exact date as to when the word 'jam' first entered the English language is unknown. However, recipes for jam were published in cookery books in

Plate 1   *Scones and Teabread*

Plate 2   *Croquembouche*

Plate 3 *Pavlova*

Plate 4   *Charlotte*

Plate 5   *Petits Fours*

Plate 6 *Sugar display – flowered harp*

Plate 7 *Sugar display – yellow rose with ribbons*

Plate 8 *Key Lime Pie*

Plate 9 *Gâteau St Honeré*

Plate 10   *Gâteau Sacher*

Plate 11   *Black Forest Gâteau*

Britain in the eighteenth century. Prior to that date, the process of preserving fruit by this method was referred to as a conserve or a preserve of fruit. The French word for jam is *confiture* and dates back to the middle of the sixteenth century.

This method of preserving fruits, however, is an ancient one. In Roman times, Gaius Plinius Secundus, Pliny the Elder, who was a Roman scientist and historian, wrote about a preparation of quinces which were candied in honey; this was probably the ancestor of jam. Pliny the Elder was killed in the city of Pompeii, which was destroyed when the volcano of Mount Vesuvius erupted in AD 79. So the process of preserving fruit was known to the Romans before that date. At a later date, they made a type of preserve with fruits and sugar cane syrup which could be kept for several months.

It was from the East that the Europeans were to gain the knowledge of jam making as we know it today. During the Crusades, the Crusaders brought back to Europe Arabian recipes on how to preserve fruits. By the fourteenth century, jam was highly valued in France. For example, in 1350 it was recorded that a solicitor who won a court case on behalf of a family was not paid in money, but with containers of jam! During the fourteenth century, the first recipes for jam were published in France. These recipes included such ingredients as quinces, peaches, pears, parsnips, carrots, marrows and nuts such as walnuts and fresh almonds. The main sweetening agent used in these recipes was honey, and not sugar. These jams were reputed to cure minor ailments and diseases. Francis I (1494–1547), King of France from 1515, swore by the healing properties of jam. The French city of Bar-le-Duc, which is approximately a hundred miles east of Paris, became renowned during this period for its quality jams. The jams were exported to every corner of France, even to neighbouring Belgium. The jams became so exclusive and were in such great demand that they were only served at the tables of the French aristocracy.

In the sixteenth century, Michael of Nostradamus (1503–1566), the famous French physician and astrologer, wrote a small book on the method of jam making. The recipes in his book were heavily influenced by Arabian recipes, which the French believed produced better quality jams. The ingredients included wine, fruits and water and used sugar or honey as a sweetener.

In Britain by the nineteenth century, a variety of recipes for jams appeared in a selection of cookery books written by Victorian writers. It was the first time that the process of preserving fruit was called jam. However, jam was to remain a luxury in Britain up until the beginning of the nineteenth century, because sugar was extremely expensive until that period. It was with the introduction of sugar beet as a crop that sugar prices tumbled. Sugar which was extracted from beet was much cheaper, and became affordable to the mass of the population. It also meant that jam could be produced on a commercial scale in factories.

Today, jams are as popular as ever, and with the introduction of new and exotic fruits to the market the varieties of jams are endless. The majority of jams are made in bulk in factories, but over 30 per cent of jams which are made in Europe are still made in the home. Jam making has now become a quick and simple process. For example, there are special jam sugars available on the market today which enable jams to be made with a boiling time of only four minutes.

∽ JELLY ∽

Is a preparation which is made with the juice of fruits and sugar. The fruits used in jelly making are high in pectin content.

Pectin is a jellying substance present in many fruits which, when combined with heat, allows the mass to set. Fruits which are particularly rich in pectin and ideal for jelly making are apples, redcurrants, blackcurrants, citrus fruit, gooseberries and quinces. Powder and liquid pectin are now readily available and can be used in jelly making.

∽ JELLY DESSERT ∽

A sweet jelly is a composition of water with a fruit flavouring or fruit juice, gelatine and sugar. The gelatine is used as a setting agent in the dessert. It can be purchased in powdered form or in gelatine sheets. The gelatine is softened in cold water, and then heated with the fruit juice or flavoured water until it dissolves. Sugar is then added. The mixture is then poured into a jelly mould and allowed to set in a refrigerator.

Convenience jellies in the form of crystals and concentrated set jelly cubes, known as table jelly, became available in the early twentieth century and are now commonly used by the patissier in the production of desserts.

Classic desserts which include fruit jellies are Charlotte Andalouse, Charlotte Moscovite and, of course, Trifle.

Types of jelly

A *Liqueur jelly* is a jelly which has been mixed just before it sets with a chosen liqueur.

A *Russian jelly* is a jelly which has been beaten cold before it is put into the mould.

A *Ribboned jelly* is a jelly dessert which consists of two or three different coloured and flavoured jellies.

History

The first jellies which were made were savoury, not sweet. They were meat jellies which were obtained by boiling various parts of animals in order to extract the gelatine. These savoury jellies are still used today, especially in the production of patés and pies. Aspic jelly is used extensively in the decoration and presentation of cold buffet dishes such as Salmon in Aspic.

Aspic jelly was introduced to the British by the French at the end of the eighteenth century.

Jelly which was flavoured with fruits came at a much later date than these original savoury jellies such as Calf's Foot Jelly. The first mention of fruit-flavoured jelly in cookery books was not until the seventeenth century. However, they did not become widely known until the nineteenth century.

In the early to the mid-twentieth century, fruit jellies reached their height of popularity in Britain. Convenience jellies had arrived, and were made in a variety of flavours and colours. Special moulds were made in abundance. These jellies were often served with fresh cream and custard. It became one of the most popular desserts in Britain during this period, especially with children.

Today, the popularity of jelly as a dessert has greatly diminished, caused by more exciting ready-made desserts becoming available on the market.

∾ JUNKET ∾

Consists of milk which has been sweetened with sugar to which rennet is added. Rennet is an extract obtained from the stomach of calves. It contains an enzyme which is called rennin. It is usually used in the process of cheese making in order to coagulate the milk. When the rennet is added to the sweetened milk it curdles, and the mixture is then allowed to set. The junket is traditionally served with clotted cream.

History

The dessert dates back to medieval times in England. In Elizabethan England, junkets were a popular dessert; more sugar was added, and a popular flavouring used for the junket during this period was rose-water.

K

∾ KUGELHOPH ∾

The Kugelhoph is a type of cake which is made from a yeast dough. The dough consists of baker's flour, yeast, salt, sugar, milk, butter and Malaga dried raisins. The dough is made like a brioche dough, using the French method. The distinctive shape of the Kugelhoph is obtained by using a special aluminium mould which is round and fluted, with a hole in the centre. The mould is heavily greased with butter and then liberally sprinkled with flaked almonds. The dough is shaped by hand in the shape of a crown and then placed into the mould. The Kugelhoph is then placed in a prover, in order for the dough to rise. It is then baked. When cooked, the cake is turned onto a cooling tray. It is allowed to cool and is then dredged with icing sugar. The Kugelhoph is usually served at breakfast or with afternoon tea. The cake is cut into slices and can be spread with either butter or jam.

History

The Kugelhoph was created in the city of Lemberg in Poland in 1609. In 1770, Lemberg fell into Austrian hands, and remained so until 1919. It then reverted once again to Polish rule until 1939, when it finally became part of the USSR and was renamed Lnon or Lvov.

The cake was brought to France by Stanislas Augustus Poniatowski (1732–1798), King Stanislas II of Poland from 1764 to 1795. When he lost his kingdom, his son-in-law, Louis XV (1710–1774), King of France from 1715, gave to him the Duchy of Alsace-Lorraine, a province in the north-east of France. Stanislas moved to Alsace-Lorraine and brought with him his entire royal household, which included his executive chef, Chevriot. The Polish King was a fine gourmet, and one of his favourite sweets was the Kugelhoph, which Chevriot always served sweetened with Malaga wine or rum.

However, it was Marie Antoinette, the wife of Louis XVI (1754–1793), King from 1774, who was ultimately responsible for making the Polish sweet fashionable in France. The Queen adored the Kugelhoph served each morning with her coffee. At that time it was appreciated by the élite of French society.

Pierre Lacam, in his book, *Mémorial de la Pâtisserie*, states that the Kugelhoph was brought to Paris from Strasbourg in Alsace in 1840 by a French confectioner called George, who opened a patisserie in the Rue de Coq. Such was the popularity of the Kugelhoph that the shop was producing hundreds each day, and the small establishment had to employ twenty-five bakers and confectioners to meet the demand.

The name 'Kugelhoph' is Alsacian and is of Germanic origin. Simply translated, it means *Kugel* – ball, *hop* – dough, the dough which rises from yeast made from the hops.

Originally the specialized moulds to make the cake were made from copper and varnished earthenware. Today, aluminium is used to make the moulds.

∞ KUMQUAT ∞

Is the fruit of the kumquat tree, belonging to the *Rutaceae* family. *Fortunella Japonica* and *Margarita* are the species which are cultivated for their edible fruits. The kumquat measures only about four centimetres across and it looks like a tiny orange. However, it is not a true citrus fruit. The tiny fruit is eaten whole and, unlike the orange, it does not need to be peeled. It is rich in vitamins and minerals.

History

Kumquat trees originated from south-east China. In the past, the tiny fruits were preserved in honey and eaten as a delicacy by the Chinese. Later, the fruits were preserved in sugar. The plants were not introduced to Western countries until the late seventeenth century.

L

∽ LACAM, PIERRE ∽

A renowned French patissier and writer.

History

Pierre Lacam was born on 27 December 1836 at Saint-Armand-de-Belvés, a small village not far from the city of Sarlat in the Dordogne district in the south-west of France.

His early career was spent working as a patissier, and he was employed in the households of the French aristocracy; for example, he worked for such illustrious personages as Charles III, Prince of Monaco. His creations in patisserie included petits fours made with butter and almonds and he was responsible for creating a series of specialized gâteaux with Italian meringue toppings, which at that time was a completely new idea.

Later in his career he devoted a great deal of his time to writing about the art of patisserie. He was also appointed as Chief Editor of a popular French gastronomic magazine which was published in Paris. In 1865 his first book on patisserie, *Le Pâtissier-Glacier* was published in France. Fifteen years later, his second book was published, *Le Mémorial Historique et Géographique de la Pâtisserie* (first edition). Like his predecessor, Antoine Carême, he devoted his life to the promotion of the specialized art of patisserie in his work and in his writings. Lacam was made a member of the French Academy of Gastronomy in honour of his life's work. He died in Paris at the age of sixty-six.

∽ LARDY CAKE ∽

This cake is made with white bread dough. The method of making the cake is very similar to making puff pastry and involves rolling the fat into the bread dough in a series of folds and turns. The bread dough is rolled out and then pieces of lard, sugar, mixed fruit, mixed peel and spices are sprinkled on top of the dough. The dough is folded and rolled out once again, and the process is then repeated. The cake is baked in the oven.

History

The traditional Lardy Cake is always made with lard, hence the name. This quintessentially English recipe dates back hundreds of years. The cake has long been associated with the old English village fair, when they were made by the villagers and sold along with other village produce on a variety of stalls. Each region in England can boast of its own special recipe, from as far south as Sussex to as far north as Northumberland. In the north, small villages straddling on either side of the Roman Wall from Newcastle in the east to Carlisle in the west have their own delicious recipes known locally as Lardy Rolls or Lardy Cakes.

✑ LEMON – CITRON ✑

The lemon, *Citrus Limon*, belongs to the family *Rutaceae*. It is the fruit of a small evergreen tree which grows to a height of approximately six metres. The lemon is a citrus fruit which is very rich in vitamin C and also contains minerals and pectin. There are three main varieties of lemons, known as Verna, Verdelli and Real.

The lemon is an extremely versatile fruit. For example, the skin may be candied, or the zest used as a flavouring in a variety of baked goods and cookery dishes. The juice of the lemon is also known to have medicinal value and is often used in the manufacture of medicines such as cough syrups. It can also be used to make preserves. Lemon slices and segments are used a great deal by the patissier as a decoration for a variety of desserts and pastries. The immensely popular drink called Lemonade is made with the juice of lemons. Some of the most popular desserts use lemon as the main flavouring, for example, Lemon Meringue Pie, Lemon Soufflé and Soufflé Glace Milanaise.

History

The English word 'lemon' is a derivative of the old French word *limon*, which in modern French means lime. The French word for lemon is *citron*, which is a derivative of the Latin words *citrus* and *citrium*, meaning citrus fruit. Thousands of years ago, lemons grew wild in the Himalayan mountains. At a later date, the tree was introduced into Mesopotamia and then into Babylon. It was the Jews who introduced the fruit into Palestine.

The lemon tree was known to the early Roman civilization. However, the Romans valued the tree more than the actual fruit. Lemon trees were grown extensively in Roman gardens as a shrub and were highly valued because of their visual beauty.

In the eleventh century, it was the first Crusaders who introduced the fruit into Europe on their return from the Holy Wars in the Middle East. However, lemons at that time were regarded as a rarity and were outrageously expensive. By the thirteenth century, cargoes of exotic fruit such as oranges, lemons and pomegranates began to arrive in Britain from southern European countries, such as Italy, Portugal and Spain. Over the next few hundred years, the trading between Britain and southern Europe increased, resulting in exotic fruits becoming much cheaper and therefore more readily available to the majority of people. Lemons began to be used extensively in kitchens throughout the land. The lemon also began to be highly valued by the British for its medicinal value, especially in the fight against a common disease which was widespread at that time, known as scurvy. Scurvy was a particularly unpleasant disease caused by vitamin deficiency in the diet.

In the late sixteenth century, it became extremely fashionable to erect glasshouses in which to grow exotic fruit trees such as oranges, lemons and pineapples. Glasshouses built to house orange trees were known as orangeries and those built to house pineapple plants were called pineries. The British, just like the Romans thousands of years previously, not only appreciated the fruit, but also appreciated the visual beauty of the trees.

∾ LEMON MERINGUE PIE ∾

Lemon Meringue Pie is a pastry flan which is made with sugar paste and has a filling consisting of water, sugar, custard powder, lemon juice, lemon zest, butter and egg yolks. The custard filling is cooked until it thickens and is then poured into the baked pastry case and allowed to cool. A meringue is then piped over the surface of the custard and it is placed in a hot oven until the meringue topping is golden brown.

History

It was probably created in the nineteenth century. A recipe for Lemon Meringue Pie appeared in an edition of the English cookery book *Household Management*, written by the Victorian writer Isabella Beeton, which was published in 1893. An American speciality called Key Lime Pie, which is very similar to Lemon Meringue Pie, was created in the state of Florida in the late nineteenth century. Limes instead of lemons are used as a flavouring. The pie takes its name from the small town of Key West where the pie was first created. Key Lime Pie has now become a Floridian speciality of some renown.

∾ LIÉGEOIS CAFÉ ∾

Is a drink which is served in a fluted wine glass or a champagne glass. Approximately one-fifth of the glass is filled with hot, freshly ground coffee, into which a small scoop of coffee ice cream is placed. It is then topped with freshly whipped cream and decorated with roasted almond flakes. Liégeois Café is usually served with petits fours secs or shortbread fingers. It does not necessarily need to be flavoured with coffee, as other flavourings such as vanilla, chocolate or strawberry are sometimes used.

History

The iced drink was created in 1860 in the city of Liège in Belgium.

∽ LIQUORICE – RÉGLISSE ∽

Liquorice is a perennial plant belonging to the pea family *Leguminosae*. The plant grows up to two metres in height. It is the root of the plant, with its highly distinctive perfume, which when dried or powdered is used as a flavouring agent. It is also valued for its medicinal properties. The plant grows wild in southern Europe, Asia, the Middle East, Afghanistan and North America. In countries such as France, Spain, Russia and Germany, it is now grown on a commercial scale.

History

The plant is native to southern Europe. The English word 'liquorice' is of Greek origin and translated into English means sweet root. The French word *réglisse* dates back to 1393 (Ref.: *Le Petit Robert 1*, 1972).

Liquorice has been used as a flavouring and for medicinal purposes since ancient times. Around 5000 BC in ancient Babylon, the root of the plant was prescribed by chemists and doctors to heal ulcers and sore throats.

Thousands of years ago in India, the Buddhists considered the liquorice plant sacred. To celebrate the anniversary of Buddha, the priests submerged images of their god in a liquorice-flavoured liquid.

During the time of Christ, children were given whole dried roots of liquorice to suck on, in much the same way as children today eat sweets.

In Europe during the Middle Ages, the root of the plant was ground into a fine powder and used to flavour puddings, cakes and drinks. Napoleon I (1769–1821), Emperor of France from 1804 to 1815, was extremely partial to a special drink which was flavoured with powdered liquorice.

In England towards the end of the seventeenth century, a Yorkshireman named Dunhill opened a sweet factory to produce the first liquorice sweets in the town of Pontefract. He called his new creation Pontefract Cakes, and they became one of the most popular sweets in Britain.

During the Victorian period in England, liquorice was eaten in many households after an evening meal as it was reputed to aid digestion, a custom which has long since died out.

Today, liquorice is used as a flavouring in a myriad of confectionery, perhaps the most popular being Pontefract Cakes, Bootlace Liquorice and Liquorice Allsorts. In powdered form it is used as a flavouring in pastry and bakery goods as well as in cookery. Its medicinal properties are still recognized worldwide and it is used to treat minor ailments. It can be purchased in a variety of forms in chemists and health food shops. The famous Italian liqueur Sambuco is flavoured with liquorice.

∽ LOGANBERRY ∽

The loganberry, *Rubus Specie*, belongs to the family *Rosaceae*. It is a true hybrid, the result of grafting the blackberry and raspberry plants. The plant produces an oblong fruit berry which is deep red in colour and resembles the raspberry, but is much larger. It is a prickly plant and produces white blossoms. The fruit is rich in vitamin C. Its culinary uses are wide: it is excellent for jelly and jam making and is also used in the production of sorbets, fruit coulis, tarts and pies.

History

The loganberry was first grown in Britain towards the end of the nineteenth century. Today, it is widely cultivated throughout Britain in private gardens and on a commercial scale. It is also grown on the west coast of America.

≈ LYCHEE – LITCHI ≈

The lychee, *Litchi Chinensis*, belongs to the *Sapindaceae* family. The tree grows to a height of approximately fifteen metres and produces an edible small round fruit, which has a hard, pink-coloured skin with a rough texture. When the skin is removed, it reveals the white, translucent flesh of the fruit. The fruit's flavour is subtle but quite distinctive and has a slightly acidic taste. The flesh of the fruit encloses a brown seed. There are about half a dozen varieties of lychees which are cultivated, but the Chinese variety is by far the most common. The fruit is available fresh, tinned or dried. The tree has been introduced into India, New Zealand, South Africa and Florida.

History

The tree is native to China and has been used extensively by the Chinese as a source of food for over two thousand years.

The small fruit was introduced to the British public in the latter half of the twentieth century, with the influx of Chinese restaurants and the resulting popularity of Chinese cookery. Throughout Britain today, specialist Chinese supermarkets have opened in the majority of cities, thus making Chinese ingredients such as the lychee easily available.

M

✏ MACAROONS – MACARONS ✏

Macaroons are small almond cakes which are made with a mixture of sugar, ground almonds and egg whites. Sometimes honey, apricot jam or inverted sugar are added to the mixture. They can be made in a variety of flavours, for example, vanilla, coffee or chocolate. The Macaroon mixture is piped into small round shapes which are then baked in a moderate oven. The Macaroons can be sandwiched together with a variety of fillings such as butter cream, ganache, jam or praline. There are numerous recipes for these small cakes.

History

The recipe for Macaroons originated in Venice in the thirteenth century. The Venetians christened the small almond cakes Macerone, which was the Venetian spelling of the Italian word *maccherone*, meaning a fine paste. The English word Macaroon is a derivative of the French word *Macaron*. The Italian word *macaroni* refers to a type of pasta. However, many countries in the East use the word macaroni to describe the small almond cakes.

In the Middle Ages, fleets of ships from Asia arrived in the port of Venice laden with cargoes of exotic goods. Hundreds of tons of almonds were imported to Venice to meet the demands of the Europeans, who adored the small delicately flavoured nut. During this period, the almond was at the height of its popularity in Europe. Many European dishes were created using the nut as a main ingredient, the recipe for Macaroons being just one of many.

In the sixteenth century, Catherine de' Medici, an Italian noblewoman, married King Henry II of France in 1533. Catherine was responsible for introducing into France many Italian customs and recipes. She brought with her to her new homeland an entourage of chefs, servants and courtiers. She adored Macaroons, and it was not long before they became fashionable within the French court. The popularity of the small almond cake quickly spread throughout France, and eventually many cities in France produced their own special recipe for Macaroons.

The Macarons de Saint-Jean-de-Luz were named after the town where they were first created. They were the creation of a young French patissier called Adam, who worked in a patisserie in the town. He made them to commemorate the marriage of Louis XIV (1638–1715), who was King of France from 1643, to the Infanta, Maria Theresa of Spain. The Macarons de

Saint-Jean-de-Luz remain popular today, and are still regarded as a regional speciality.

In the eighteenth century, the Macarons de Nancy were created. The recipe originated in the city of Nancy, in a convent of the Carmelite nuns, a religious order which had spread into Europe from the East in the thirteenth century. The nuns were forbidden to eat meat during Lent. It was widely known, even at that early date, that almonds were extremely nutritious, and almond-based dishes were often eaten as a substitute for meat during Lent. St. Thérèse d'Avila was quoted as saying, 'Almonds are good for the sisters who cannot eat meat'. It was the time of the French Revolution and France was in turmoil; religious persecution by the new order was widespread throughout the land. The Carmelite nuns of Nancy were forced to flee from their convent. Two sisters, Sister Gaillot and Sister Merlot, sought refuge in the home of a local doctor, where they remained hidden. The nuns repaid the doctor's hospitality by cooking and cleaning for him. As a special treat they baked him the little Macaroons which were a speciality of the convent and the recipe for which, until then, had been a closely guarded secret. The Macarons de Nancy became one of the most popular recipes for the almond cakes, and today they are renowned worldwide.

A creation of the twentieth century are the renowned Macarons Ladurée, which were created by a young French patissier called Paul Desfontaines. Whilst working in Switzerland, in a small patisserie in Lausanne, he was greatly impressed by the speciality of the establishment, which was a biscuit-based gâteau with a ganache filling. On his return to France he started working for his uncle, Jean Ladurée, who owned a small patisserie. He decided to adapt the recipe for the biscuit-based gâteau and, instead of the biscuit base, he used individual Macaroons which he sandwiched together with a variety of different flavoured ganaches such as lemon, pistachio, chocolate and coffee. He christened his new creation Macarons Ladurée in honour of his uncle. They were an instant success!

∾ McCALLUM ∾

Is vanilla ice cream served with a raspberry syrup.

History

The sweet originated in Glasgow in the twentieth century. A Scotsman called McCallum, who was an avid supporter of the Clyde football team, which is a famous Glasgow football club, ordered an ice cream in a Glasgow café and asked for his vanilla ice cream to be served with raspberry syrup, which represented the colours of his football team, red and white. The sweet was extremely popular in Glasgow, especially with Clyde football supporters in the early twentieth century.

❧ MADEIRA CAKE ❧

Is a rich sponge cake made with butter, sugar, eggs and flour. The sponge is flavoured with lemon peel, which gives the cake its own distinctive flavour. It is usually oblong in shape and is cut into thin slices and served with afternoon tea.

History

The cake dates back to the middle of the nineteenth century and is an English creation. The English found the rich sponge cake a perfect accompaniment to a glass of Madeira wine, a fortified wine which was imported from Portugal. The port wine trade had been established with Portugal since the fourteenth century. In the eighteenth century, the Methuen Treaty (1703) was signed between the two countries, which meant that tax duties on Portuguese wines were much lower than taxes imposed on French or Spanish wines. Fortified Portuguese wines became the favourite tipple of the English gentry, especially Madeira wine, and it was not uncommon for the English to drink a glass of Madeira mid-morning with a slice of the sponge cake which they christened Madeira Cake after their favourite drink.

❧ MADELEINES ❧

Madeleines are small sponge cakes made from butter, sugar, flour, eggs and baking powder. The mixture is put into shell-shaped moulds and baked.

History

These small shell-shaped cakes were created in the seventeenth century in France. They were created by a French cook called Madeleine Simonin, who was the personal cook of Jean Paul de Gondi, Cardinal de Retz, an ecclesiastic of Paris during the reign of young Louis XIV of France (1638–1715), who was King from 1643. Madeleine created the recipe in 1661 in the kitchens of the Cardinal's residence in the city of Commercy, in the district of Lorraine, which is in the north-east of France. He was so delighted with the little cakes that he christened them Madeleines after his cook.

MAIDS OF HONOUR ❧

These are small tartlets which are made with shortcrust pastry or puff pastry trimmings, with a filling of ground almonds, caster sugar, eggs, flour, double cream and are flavoured with orange flowers. They are baked in a hot oven until golden brown.

History

They were created in the sixteenth century in Richmond upon Thames, a small town in Surrey, and were regarded as a speciality of the town. Henry VIII (1491–1547), King of England from 1509, often held court at Richmond during the summer months. The name Maids of Honour was given to the tartlets by the King himself. When presented with the tray of pretty little cakes, he commented that they reminded him of the Maids of Honour who were in attendance at the court in Richmond, and so the cakes were named after them. Among the Maids of Honour was a young lady called Anne Boleyn, an English noblewoman who later was to become the second wife of Henry VIII in 1533. They were married shortly after his divorce from his first wife, Catherine of Aragon. Queen Anne was beheaded in 1536 only three years after her coronation. She bore Henry VIII a daughter called Elizabeth, who later became Queen of England in 1558. Elizabeth I reigned for forty-five years; she never married and died childless. The recipe for the small tartlets remained a closely guarded secret for a great many years.

∾ MANDARIN – MANDARINE ∾

Mandarin, *Citrus Reticula*, originated in China. Common mandarins, of which there are many varieties, are grown mostly in China and the United States. However, mandarins are also grown on the Mediterranean coast, in Spain, Italy and Malta. The British usually refer to these mandarins as tangerines. The fruit is smaller than an orange and they are less acidic than oranges. They are a good source of vitamin C.

The patissier uses the small segments for their colour and attractive appearance for decorating pastry goods, iced desserts, small open tartlets and flans. But the fresh and tinned varieties are used. Mandarins are sweet and delicious to eat as a fruit.

History

The Spanish gave the fruit the name Naranja Mandarin because the colour of the fruit closely resembled the colour of the garments worn by the Chinese Imperial officials, who were called Mandarins. The fruit was not introduced into Europe and the United States until the nineteenth century. It first came to Britain at the very beginning of the nineteenth century.

∾ MANGO – MANGUE ∾

The mango tree, *Mangiferu Indica*, produces a large fruit which may have a skin which is yellow and orange with hints of red, or the skin can range from green through to a rich golden yellow colour. There are literally hundreds of varieties. The fruit is not uniform in size or shape. The flesh has a very distinct aroma and is highly flavoured and very juicy. The fruit is rich in vitamins A and C and is a good source of minerals.

The patissier uses the mango in the production of fresh fruit salads, mousses and sorbets. It is delicious to eat as a fruit, but is not very practical because of its size, shape and the large stone which the fruit contains. It is not used a great deal by the patissier because it remains an expensive fruit and is not always available. In cookery, mangoes are used in the making of sauces and chutneys and can also be made into a spice. Mangoes can be tinned, candied or frozen in a puréed state.

History

The mango is native to India and has been cultivated there for thousands of years. It took centuries to spread eastwards and westwards. In the sixteenth century, the tree was introduced into Africa by Portuguese sailors. By the eighteenth century, the mango had reached South America and the West Indies. However, it was not until the nineteenth century that the fruit reached the island of Hawaii and the southern state of Florida in the United States. Today, the fruit is cultivated in the West Indies, Israel, Hawaii, Florida and parts of Australia.

～ MARGARINE ～

Is a butter substitute which is made from animal fats and vegetable oils. Today, margarine is made with vegetable oils, creating a product which is low in saturated fats.

History

The French Emperor, Louis-Napoleon III (1808–1873), Emperor from 1852 to 1870, commissioned French chemists to produce a fat which would keep for long periods and would not go rancid like butter. His soldiers required such a fat for their long journeys, especially his navy, which was engaged in long sea voyages. It was invented by a French chemist called Hippolyte Mège-Mouriés. He obtained authorization to produce his new invention, called margarine, in July 1869, just months before the defeat of Napoleon against the Prussians. Napoleon surrendered in the city of Sedan, in the north-east of France, in 1870.

～ MARMALADE ～

This is a preserve which is a mixture of the juice of Seville oranges and lemons, slices of lemon and orange peel, water and sugar crystals. The process of making marmalade is very similar to the process of making jam. The mixture is boiled until it is greatly reduced, approximately by half. The high pectin content of the fruits which are used in the mixture enable it to set.

History

Originally the main fruit used to make this preserve was the quince. The word 'marmalade' is a derivative of the Portuguese word *marmelada*, which means quince jam, coming from *marmelo*, which is the word for the actual quince fruit. In the sixteenth and seventeenth centuries, the preserve was made with a variety of fruits, including dates, plums, cherries and apples, as well as quinces. The preserve made at that time was also attributed with medicinal properties. It was said to aid the digestion after a very rich meal and was, therefore, often eaten after a meal. During this period, the preserve was quite rare; for example, Henry VIII (1491–1547), who was King of England from 1509, received a gift of the preserve from his friend, the Earl of Exeter, in 1524, illustrating the high value which the English placed upon the preserve. It was a gift fit for a King!

It was not until the seventeenth century, in Britain, that citrus fruits were used in the production of marmalade. The Portuguese introduced Seville oranges into Britain during this period. The oranges were very bitter, but proved to be excellent for making the preserve. With the addition of oranges to the preserve, it was acclaimed as a remedy for the common cold and indigestion. This was two hundred years before the discovery of vitamins in the twentieth century.

At the beginning of the eighteenth century, in the Scottish town of Dundee, on the east coast of Scotland, a very special marmalade was created by a grocer called James Keiller. The preserve was made with Seville oranges which had been imported from Spain. The new preserve was an instant success in the small Scottish town, and its popularity soon spread to other parts of Scotland. However, it was not until nearly a hundred years later that the world's first marmalade factory was built in Dundee to produce the preserve on a commercial scale.

In France, the term 'marmalade' refers to a mixture of apples and sugar cooked into a fruit purée. Other fruits may also be used. The purée is used by patissiers in France as a filling for a variety of pastry goods.

∾ MARRONS GLACÉS ∾

Are sweet chestnuts which are peeled and poached in a syrup solution flavoured with vanilla essence. The chestnuts are poached until they are tender and are then removed from the sugar solution. The next stage in the process is long and complicated. It involves the cooked chestnuts being placed in special containers and submerged in a series of sugar solutions of increasing sugar density until the chestnuts are completely saturated. The chestnuts are then allowed to dry. The whole process can take several days. Marrons Glacés are extremely expensive because of the long process involved in their production.

History

Marrons Glacés were created in France in 1835. Marrons Glacés translated into English means iced chestnuts. *Marron* is a derivative of the Italian word for chestnut, *marrone*. The French word *marron*, translated into English, means brown, which describes the colour of the nut's shell and is a general term used to describe all types of chestnuts. The chestnut which is used in the recipe is the sweet chestnut, *Castanea Sativa*, commonly known in France as the Châteigne, which is the edible variety. Glacé translated into English means ice. Of course, the chestnuts are not in fact iced, but are candied. However, the candying process gives the chestnuts a coating of fine white sugar which in fact does resemble ice, and probably that is why the chestnuts were christened Marrons Glacés. The Châteigne, or sweet chestnut, is cultivated in France; however, it also grows extensively in the wild. The sweet chestnuts used in the production of Marrons Glacés are imported from Turin in the north-west of Italy or come from the Ardêche district in the south-east of France. These two areas reputedly produce top quality chestnuts.

The recipe first appeared in the French pastry book *Le Mémorial Historique et Géographique de la Pâtisserie* (fourth edition), which was written by the French patissier, Pierre Lacam, and was published in 1898. The original recipe remained unchanged for almost a hundred years. A French pastry book called *Traité de la Pâtisserie*, which was published in 1957, contains a recipe for Marrons Glacés which was identical to the original recipe. Today, the process of making Marrons Glacés has improved, as the production is now on a commercial scale. Marrons Glacés are exported from France throughout the world.

∾ MARZIPAN – PÂTE D'AMANDE ∾

There are many different recipes for marzipan. Basically, it consists of ground almonds, glucose syrup and sugar. The addition of glucose makes the marzipan more malleable and retards the drying process of the paste. High quality marzipan will have a high proportion of almonds to sugar, approximately 65 per cent of almonds to 35 per cent of sugar. The proportion of almonds to sugar varies from manufacturer to manufacturer and this determines the quality of the paste. Belgium produces one of the best quality marzipans on the market today.

History

The word 'marzipan' did not enter the English language until the late nineteenth century. Before this date, the English called the paste Marchpane. It was created by the Italians in the fourteenth century. The Italian word for the paste was *Marzepane*, and Marchpane was a corruption of this. The French call the paste Pâte d'Amande, which translated into English means almond paste. The English also refer to the paste as almond paste as well as marzipan.

A type of almond paste dates back as far as ancient Greece; however, it was made with pounded almonds and honey. When the Greek states were conquered by the Roman legions, the recipe for the paste was introduced to the Romans. The Phoenicians, a great sea-faring people, carried the delicacy on their sea voyages and introduced the paste to ports of call on the Mediterranean coast.

However, it was not until the fourteenth century that the recipe similar to the one we know today was created in Italy. The popularity of the new Marzepane spread throughout Europe, and in medieval times it was made in countries such as Greece, Turkey, Italy, Spain, Germany and France. The paste was mentioned during this period in European cookery books. It was a very expensive commodity and was made only in the wealthiest of households.

Marzepane was not introduced into Britain until the fifteenth century. The English found the pronunciation of the Italian word very difficult, and so it became Marchpane. Marchpane not only referred to the paste, but was a word used to describe elaborate display pieces made out of the paste which were presented at the end of medieval banquets. During this period, it was highly valued by the English; for example, when Elizabeth I (1533–1603), who was Queen of England from 1558, visited the city of Cambridge, she was presented with a selection of precious gifts from the people of the city, among which was a piece of marzipan in a presentation box.

Across the Channel in France, marzipan was equally as expensive and was also highly valued at that time. Henry IV (1553–1610), who was King of France from 1589, presented to his new bride, Maria de' Medici, as a token of his love, three hundred small baskets which were filled with a variety of small fruits made out of marzipan. This precious consignment was carried by welcoming courtiers and accompanying guards who were sent to meet her on her journey through Avignon for her forthcoming marriage.

Better quality marzipan products did not appear until the beginning of the nineteenth century. The cost of marzipan also was greatly reduced when it was produced on a commercial scale in factories around the middle of the nineteenth century.

❦ MAZARIN GÂTEAU ❦

Is a round Genoese sponge shell with a filling of candied fruit which is glazed with fondant and decorated with candied fruit. The Genoese shell is achieved by simply scooping out the centre of a baked Genoese sponge.

History

The Mazarin Gâteau was created in the seventeenth century and named after the French politician, Jules Mazarin (1602–1661), who was the Chief

Minister of France during the reign of Louis XIII (1601–1643), King of France from 1610.

❧ MELON – MELON ❧

The melon, *Cucumis Melo*, belongs to the family of *Cucurbitaceae*. The fruit is rich in vitamin C. One of the most popular types of melon is the Cantaloupe, which is small and round in shape. It has a rough-textured skin and the flesh is highly flavoured. The Ogen melon, which was first cultivated in Israel in the middle of the twentieth century, is very small and has a yellow and green striped skin and green flesh. The Charentais, the renowned French variety, is quite distinctive, with its bright yellow skin and succulent orange flesh. Another type of melon is the Water melon, which ripens very slowly. The Honeydew melon comes into this category, and is perhaps one of the most popular melons today. It is much larger in size than the other melons mentioned and has a yellow skin and a delicious pale green flesh.

The patissier uses the fruit in fruit salads, mousses, jelly, jams and ice sorbets. It is delicious when eaten raw and is often served at the beginning of a meal as a starter, or as a dessert. The fruit can also be candied.

History

According to botanists, the melon probably originated in India or Africa. Melons grow wild in Africa. The fruit was highly prized by the Greeks. During Roman times, melons were extremely small, about the size of a medium-sized orange. The Roman Emperor, Nero (AD 37–AD 68), Emperor from AD 54, was reputed to have eaten a dozen melons every lunchtime. After the demise of the Roman Empire, the fruit was cultivated by the Arabs.

The melon was introduced into France from Italy by Charles VIII (1470–1498), who was King of France from 1483, on his return from Italy where he tried to claim the Neapolitan crown in Naples in 1495. He was unsuccessful, and was forced to return to France. By 1550 it was recorded by a French doctor called Jacques Pont that half a dozen different types of melon were grown in France.

The Italian explorer, Christopher Columbus (1451–1506), carried melon seeds on one of his voyages to the New World. One of his ports of call was the island of Haiti, where the seeds were sown by the islanders and so the melon was cultivated in the New World. The plant spread rapidly to the Americas, where it was cultivated by the natives.

In sixteenth-century England, melons were grown during the reign of James I (1566–1625), King of England from 1603. The climate was unsuitable for their cultivation, so glasshouses were erected in order to grow the new fruit. Previously the melons had been imported from France and Italy. By the nineteenth century, the fruit was grown extensively in hothouses throughout England. Melons were grown by the landed gentry as far north as Northumberland, together with such exotic fruits as guavas and passion fruit. However, these fruits were eaten only by the very wealthy and were not affordable by the general public until a much later date.

∽ Meringue ∽

Is a mixture of whisked egg whites and sugar. The mixture can be put into a piping bag and piped into different shapes and sizes. The meringue shapes are baked in a very slow oven until crisp and dry. These meringues can be used to produce a variety of meringue-based desserts. The uncooked meringue mixture can also be used as a topping for a variety of desserts; when used in this way it is cooked for a short period of time in the oven until the meringue turns golden brown in colour. The outside of the topping should be crisp, but the inside should remain soft. The three main types of meringue are as follows.

French Meringue

Is made with egg whites which are whisked until stiff, and then sugar is folded into the egg whites. French meringue is used to produce a variety of meringue based desserts such as Meringues Chantilly, the traditional meringue shells which are sandwiched together with fresh cream. It is also used in the production of Meringue Glacées and as a topping for Lemon Meringue Pie.

Italian Meringue

Is made with egg whites which are whisked until stiff. A boiling sugar solution is added to the whisked egg whites and the mixture is whisked again until cold. Italian meringue is used in the production of Petits Fours and Bombes Glacées. It is also used to mask and decorate the classic ice dessert, Baked Alaska, which is covered with meringue and placed in the oven until the meringue becomes golden brown.

Swiss Meringue

Is made with egg whites and sugar, usually icing sugar, which are whisked together over hot water in a bain-marie. This type of meringue is used in the production of Petits Fours Secs, Vacherin and Meringues Chantilly.

History

The first type of meringue was created in the early eighteenth century by a Swiss patissier called Casparini in his patisserie in a small Saxon town called Mehrinyghen, which at that time was in the Duchy of Saxe-Coburg-Gotha. The creation was named after the town, and eventually the name was shortened to Meringue. At that time, the meringue mixture was spooned into individual shapes onto a baking tray and then baked. It was not until a later date that the piping bag was invented and could be used to pipe the meringue shapes. This first method was called the French method. This method was used in the late eighteenth century by Marie Antoinette (1755–1793), who was Queen of France from 1774. She was said to have made the meringues herself at the Château of Versailles in 1790. The Italian meringue was not created until the early nineteenth century. It was originally called an Italian cream and was used mainly as a filling or a coating for a variety of gâteaux and tortens. It was shortly afterwards that the Swiss meringue was created, in the middle of the nineteenth century.

∾ MILLE-FEUILLES GÂTEAU ∾

The gâteau is made with puff pastry and is oblong in shape. The pastry is rolled into oblong slices which are then baked in the oven. The baked puff pastry shapes are then sandwiched together with pastry cream which has been flavoured with rum or Kirsch. The surface of the gâteau is brushed with boiling apricot jam and then glazed with white fondant. Melted chocolate is piped in horizontal lines across the gâteau using the point of a knife, and a marbling effect is achieved by stroking across the piped horizontal lines in the opposite direction. The sides of the gâteau are masked with roasted nibbed almonds.

History

Mille-Feuilles is a French name and translated into English means a thousand layers or leaves. The name is a perfect description of the gâteau, as it literally consists of layers and layers of puff pastry. *Mille*, translated into English, means a thousand. *Feuille* is a derivative of the Latin word *folia*, which means leaf; the word dates back to the twelfth century.

The gâteau was created by a French patissier called Rouget. The date of its creation is uncertain. However, the first recipe to be published for the Mille-Feuille was in 1807. By 1867, the gâteau was established as a firm favourite of the French. For example, in one patisserie in Paris called Chez Sergent, which was located in the Rue du Bac, Mille-Feuilles Gâteaux were made daily by the hundreds, to meet the demands of its customers.

∾ MINCE PIES, SWEET ∾

These are small pies made with either shortcrust, puff or sugar pastry. The pies can be made as open tartlets or with a pastry topping. The traditional filling for sweet Mince Pies contains currants, sultanas, raisins, diced cooking apples, almonds, dark sugar, shredded suet, the zest and juice of a lemon and spices. The pies are baked and then dredged with icing sugar.

History

Originally the pies were made with a filling which combined sweet and savoury ingredients. The filling included beef offal, beef marrow, sirloin and topside of beef, which were diced together with beef suet. The diced meat and suet was then boiled and, when cold, would be mixed with dried fruits, nuts, sultanas, currants, raisins, candied peel, unrefined sugar and finally spices and liqueurs were added to flavour the filling. The pastry was shaped into a cradle and was free-standing. The filling was then placed into the pastry cradle, covered with a top crust and baked. The cradle shape of the pastry had religious significance, representing the cradle of the baby Jesus. Often a small figure representing Jesus would also be placed on top of the pie. This was a common practice throughout Christian Europe during the medieval period, and religious symbols and tokens were used in many recipes for cakes and pastries baked especially for Christmas festivities.

In the sixteenth century, a religious revolution started in Western Europe. It began in Germany with a new doctrine called Protestantism, led by Martin Luther, and in Geneva by John Calvin. Calvinism was spread to Scotland by John Knox, and Catholicism came under attack. Also during this period, which was known as the Reformation, Henry VIII formed the new Church of England and broke away from Papal control. Christian Europe was in turmoil, and the new religions forbade celebrations such as Christmas and Easter and condemned the use of religious symbols and tokens in pastries and cakes. This period in British history had a lasting effect on many of our religious customs and traditions. The pastry cradle shape did not reappear, but the tradition of eating mincemeat pies at Christmas has survived.

∾ MOKA GÂTEAU – MOCHA GATEAU ∾

Is a gâteau made from coffee-flavoured Genoese sponges, which have been moistened with syrup flavoured with rum. The sponges are sandwiched together with a mixture of coffee-flavoured butter cream and chopped walnuts. The surface of the gâteau is decorated with piped coffee butter cream and walnut halves. The sides of the gâteau are masked with roasted nibbed almonds.

History

The word *Mocha*, which is English, and *Moka*, which is the French spelling, refers to the coffee flavouring of the cake, hence the name Moka Gâteau. Mocha is a type of Arabian coffee which comes from the seaport of Mocha, on the Red Sea. The coffee was first exported to Britain in the eighteenth century. The gâteau was created in 1857 by a Parisian patissier in the district of L'Odéon in Paris. The original filling used for the gâteau was called

Crème à Quillet. On a Sunday at that time, as many as two hundred egg yolks and at least ten kilograms of butter were used in the production of Moka Gâteaux in the patisserie.

∾ MONTPENSIER GÂTEAU ∾

Is an enriched Genoese sponge which contains raisins, almonds, candied fruit, glacé cherries, pears and angelica. The sponges are sandwiched together with butter cream.

History

The Montpensier Gâteau dates back to the eighteenth century. It was named after the youngest son of Louis Philippe of France (1773–1850), who was King of France from 1830 to 1848.

∾ MOUSSE GLACÉE ∾

There are basically two types of Mousse Glacée. One is made with a syrup solution, fruit juice or fruit purée and whipped cream. The second consists of an Egg Custard or Crème Anglaise to which gelatine, liqueur and whipped cream are added. The mixtures are then allowed to freeze. Both mousses are very light in texture. They are served as an iced dessert, or may be used as a filling for a Bombe Glacée.

History

The word 'mousse', which dates back to the early eighteenth century, is a derivative of the old French word *mosse*, which dates back to 1226. Translated into English mousse means the froth which appears on the surface of water when it is agitated. The word was later used to describe a dessert which is light and frothy in texture. Glacée translated into English means ice, and is a derivative of the Latin word *glacia*, which dates back to 1160 (Ref.: *Le Petit Robert 1*, 1972).

There is some controversy as to who created the Mousse Glacée. Some attribute its creation to an Italian patissier called Francesco Procopio dei Coltelli in 1720. He was reputed to have devised the dessert for a fair which was given by the Duke of Chantilly. The mousse he created was made with whipped cream. Others attribute the dessert to the renowned French chef, Antoine Carême, who created a Caramelized Mousse Glacé in 1814, in the city of Vienna.

∾ MULBERRY – MÛRIER ∾

Mulberry is a tree of the genus *morus*, which belongs to the family *Moraceae*. There are two types of mulberry; the black mulberry, *Morus Nigra*, and the white mulberry, *Morus Alba*. The mulberry fruit is rich in Vitamin C. The patissier uses the black mulberry in the production of puddings and compotes, often combined with other fruits. The black variety are delicious when eaten raw, and as a dessert they are wonderful served with fresh cream.

History

The white mulberry has been grown in China for thousands of years. The fruit was not cultivated for human consumption, but specifically for the consumption of silkworms. After hatching from their eggs, the silkworms mature on the leaves and fruit of the white mulberry trees. Sericulture, which is the science of raising silkworms, began in China over 2000 years ago. It was introduced into France during the reign of Charles VIII (1470–1498), who was King of France from 1483. At a later date, Henry IV, King of France from 1589, had special greenhouses erected in the gardens of the Tuileries, a famous palace in the centre of Paris. James I (1566–1625), King of England from 1603, also saw the potential of sericulture and thought it would aid the English economy. He was responsible for introducing the tree into Britain, and eventually mulberry plantations spread throughout the south of England.

The black mulberry originated in the mountains of Nepal. The fruit was introduced into Europe thousands of years ago. The black variety of the fruit has been eaten since Roman times. It was the Romans who introduced the fruit into Britain, France and Spain.

N

∽ Neapolitan Slice – Cassata Napolitaine ∽

Is an ice dessert which is made in a rectangular-shaped mould. It consists of layers of ice cream and sorbets of different flavours and colours. The dessert is usually made with vanilla, strawberry and chocolate – this is the most popular combination associated with the dessert. When the dessert is turned out of the mould, the result is a rectangular-shaped ice cream divided into three different coloured slices. The Neapolitan Slice is decorated with fruit and whipped cream. It is often served with an egg custard or fruit coulis. It can also be used as a filling for Bombe Glacée.

History

It was created by an Italian confectioner called Tortoni at the beginning of the nineteenth century. He named the ice dessert after the city of Naples in Italy where he worked.

∽ Nectarine – Brugnon ∽

The nectarine, or *Prunus Persicavar Nectarina*, belongs to the family of the *Rosaceae*. The fruit, which is a type of peach, is a rich source of vitamin C. The skin is like a plum and the peach-like flesh may be white or yellow. Nectarines are delicious eaten raw, and the patissier uses them in the making of fruit salads, tarts and to decorate finished goods.

History

The name 'nectarine' comes from the Greek word *nectar*, which in Greek mythology meant the drink of the gods. The origin of the fruit is not known. It appeared in Britain in the seventeenth century, when several varieties were known.

∽ Nesselrode ∽

Is a cold pudding which consists of custard, purée of chestnuts and mixed candied fruits.

History

The dessert is named after the Russian diplomat, Count Karl Nesselrode (1780–1862), who successfully negotiated the Treaty of Paris in 1856 during the Crimean War in which Russia and Britain were in conflict. His personal chef created the pudding especially for his employer.

∾ NIEULLE ∾

Is a small cake which is made with plain flour, butter, caster sugar, milk and eggs. The mixture is placed in a type of waffle mould and baked.

History

The cake, which resembles a waffle, dates back to the Middle Ages in France. It was created in a French district near the Spanish border. The French word *nieulle* comes from the old Spanish word *niole*, which translated into English means crumbs. Nieulles were made in different districts in France and each district had its own name for the speciality cake. Traditionally, the cakes were made to celebrate special festivities throughout the year. Thousands of the cakes were made all over France at Easter and Christmas and were thrown from the windows of the local Hôtel de Ville to the children of the towns and villages. The Hôtel de Ville is the French equivalent of the English Civic Centre. The cake is no longer made in France.

∾ NIFLETTE ∾

Is a cake made with puff pastry and frangipane. It is very similar to the Gâteau Pithivier.

History

This particular cake originates from the Brie district of France, north of Paris.

∾ NOUGAT DE MONTÉLIMAR ∾

Nougat de Montélimar is a preparation made with a solution of honey, sugar crystals, water, glucose, vanilla pod, whisked egg whites, whole almonds, walnuts, pistachio nuts and glacé cherries. The confectionery is made in five stages and is a very involved process. First of all, the honey is melted and poured slowly into the whisked egg whites; the mixture is then beaten over a bain-marie. A cooked sugar solution consisting of the sugar crystals, water and glucose, which has been flavoured with a vanilla pod, is then poured slowly into the meringue mixture and cooked until it reaches the correct consistency. The nuts and fruit are then added to the mixture.

The mass is moulded into squares and, when cool, is cut into various sizes and shapes. The consistency of the confectionery resembles that of a soft chewy toffee. This speciality nougat is always made in the three main colours of white, pink and green. It can also be made in two-colour combinations of pink and white, or white and green. It is also used in the production of a variety of chocolates and sweets.

History

Nougat is a French word dating back to 1750. It is a derivative of the Provençale name for the confection, *nogat*. *Nogat* comes from the Latin word *nux*, meaning nut (Ref.: *Le Petit Robert 1*, 1972). Nougo was a speciality of the district of Pays d'Oc in the south of France, and was made with walnuts preserved in honey.

Nougat originated in the Orient. It was brought back to France by the Crusaders returning from the Holy Wars against the Infidels in the eleventh and twelfth centuries. The original recipe from the East contained walnuts; however, the French decided to add to the recipe pistachio nuts, almonds and cherries. The new Eastern delicacy was first made in the city of Montélimar in the south of France from where the nougat takes its name. However, towards the end of the fifteenth century the French city of Marseille had the monopoly in the production of the nougat.

By the sixteenth century, Nougat de Montélimar was known throughout France and was in great demand. The city of Montélimar was determined once again to become the largest producer of the now famous nougat, which they regarded as a speciality of the city. This became possible because of the introduction of the almond tree to France. At that time, the almond tree was regarded as an Asiatic novelty. Cultivation of the almond tree in the region was started by a Frenchman called Oliver de Serre. He was aided by his good friend the Duke of Sully, who was Superintendent of Finances under Henry IV (1553–1610), King of France from 1589. Hundreds of almond trees were planted in order to produce sufficient almonds for the production of the delicacy in the Montélimar district.

Over the centuries, the Nougat de Montélimar gained in popularity and value. For example, the Dukes of Burgundy and Berry, who accompanied their brother Louis XV (1710–1774), King of France from 1715, on a journey to Spain, were presented, as a token of his gratitude, not with gold or jewels, but with forty-two kilograms of Nougat de Montélimar, highlighting the value of the confectionery at that time.

The renowned French gastronome and promoter of French cuisine, Jules Gouffé (1807–1877), opened a patisserie in 1860, in the Saint Honoré district of Paris. The speciality of the patisserie was the elaborate display pieces made by Gouffé. The showpieces were made entirely with Nougat de Montélimar and nougatine.

Towards the end of the First World War (1914–1918), the nougat started to be produced commercially in large factories in France. Today, the Nougat de

Montélimar is sold worldwide. It is estimated that the city of Montélimar remains the largest producer of the confectionery. Each year the city produces two thousand tons of nougat!

∾ NOUGATINE – CROQUANT ∾

This is a preparation made with a caramelized sugar solution to which nibbed almonds are added. Nougatine is brittle when it is cold, and in order to mould or shape it, it must be heated until it is soft and malleable. Nougatine is mainly used by patissiers in the production of dipped chocolates, moulded chocolates, gâteaux and for display purposes. For example, a Croquembouche is mounted on a nougatine base and decorated with nougatine.

History

Nougatine was created by a French patissier called Louis Jules Bourumeau in 1850, in the city of Nevers in central France. In 1862, Eugénie (1826–1920), Empress of France and wife of Napoleon III, visited the city of Nevers. The Empress was presented with a box of nougatine, which by that time had become a speciality of the city. She adored the sweet and introduced the new confection to the French court. Nougatine was established! Eight years later, her husband, Napoleon III (1808–1873), who was fighting against the Prussians, was forced to surrender at Sedan in the north-east of France. The empire collapsed, and he was forced into exile in England. Eugénie accompanied him to England, and she was responsible for introducing nougatine to the English. Napoleon III never returned to France, and died in England. Nougatine has not only remained popular in Britain and France; its popularity has spread throughout the world.

∾ NOZZLES – DOUILLES ∾

A nozzle is a small metal or plastic funnel used in conjunction with a piping bag to garnish or decorate sweet or savoury dishes. Nozzles are made in a variety of designs to pipe different patterns.

History

The nozzle was invented in the middle of the nineteenth century by a French patissier called Trottier.

∾ NULLE ∾

This consists of egg yolks and cream which are mixed together and poured into a mould. It is then baked in the oven. The dessert is sprinkled generously with spiced sugar before serving.

History

It is an old French dessert which was created by an Italian chef called Nullio, hence the name Nulle. It dates back to the seventeenth century during the reign of Louis XIV (1638–1715), who was King of France from 1643. The Nulle is a simpler version of the classic French dessert, Crème Brûlée, which was created some years later.

∾ NUTMEG – NOIX DE MUSCADE ∾

The nutmeg is the kernel of the seed of an evergreen tropical tree *Myristia Fragrans*, which belongs to the *Myristiceae* family. The nutmeg is extracted from a hard outer shell which produces another spice, called mace. The tree grows to about ten metres in height.

History

The tree is native to the Moluccas Islands and Indonesia. *Noix* is a French word which is a derivative of the Latin word *nux*, which translated into English means nut. *Muscade* is an old French word dating back to the twelfth century. In the Provençal language it was spelt *muscada*, a derivative of the Latin word *muscus* (Ref.: *Le Petit Robert 1*, 1972), meaning musk in English. The French name Noix de Muscade translated into English therefore means musky nut, referring to the perfumed smell of the nut which bore a resemblance to musk. Noix de Muscade in old French was Noiz Miguede, and it is possible that the English word 'nutmeg' is a corruption of the old French name for the spice.

The spice is an ancient one and was known to the Romans. The Roman historian, Pliny the Elder (AD 23–AD 79), informs us in his writings that nutmeg was grated and used to flavour Roman dishes. The spice was brought into Spain by the invading Moors in the early eighth century. By the Middle Ages, nutmeg, along with other exotic spices, was imported into England. They were extremely expensive, as they were not shipped directly to English shores but had to be purchased on the continent, then brought back to England.

Portugal dominated the world in the spice trade during that time. The Portuguese navigator, Vasco da Gama (1469–1525), discovered the route to India in 1497 and brought back cargoes of spices which included pepper, cinnamon, cloves and nutmeg.

Between 1509 and 1512, he visited the Moluccas Islands, where nutmeg and cloves grew in the wild; thus the spice route was opened. The spice ships sailed directly with their cargoes to ports in the south of England. In the centuries that followed, nutmeg was to remain an essential spice in the British kitchen and was used as a flavouring in a variety of baked goods and puddings. Small graters were even invented in Britain specifically for the small spiced nut. Such was the popularity of the spice that it was mentioned in a popular children's song of the day:

> 'I had a little nut tree, nothing would it bear
> But a silver nutmeg and a golden pear'!

O

❧ OATCAKE ❧

Is a type of unleavened bread which is made from a mixture of oatmeal, fat, salt and hot water. Initially, bacon fat or lard was used to bind the mixture. Today, butter has replaced these fats. The mixture is rolled and cut into a variety of shapes, usually small rounds. The biscuits are cooked on one side on top of a hot girdle. They are then removed from the girdle, and the uncooked side is allowed to toast under a grill for a few minutes.

History

During the Roman invasion of Britain, the savage natives, known as the Gaels, would light a peat fire around which a series of stones would be placed. This provided a hot surface on which the biscuits were cooked. Originally they were called hearth cakes because they were cooked on the hearth. In fact, this was probably the first type of girdle! The word 'girdle' is a derivative of the Gaelic word *Greadeal*. Roman soldiers in the far north of England often carried oatcakes on their long marches. They needed to carry food which was not perishable, and their diet was often made up of these tiny biscuits.

As far back as the fourteenth century, the Scottish soldier would carry on his person a small bag of oatmeal and a flat piece of metal – in fact, a type of girdle. When the army set up camp, the fires would be lit and the soldiers would make their own fresh oatcakes. In the home during that time, the oatcakes would be cooked on a metal plate which would be placed on a type of support over an open peat fire.

Oatcakes were made not only in Scotland, but also in Northern Ireland, Yorkshire and Lancashire, where they were referred to as havercake or middlecake. In the northwest of England, in Westmorland, Cumberland and Lancashire, a type of leavened oatcake was made and was called haverbread or oatbread. In the remote Scottish islands of the Hebrides, they were called Ollags.

Today, oatcakes remain extremely popular in Scotland and are often regarded as a Scottish creation. However, history illustrates that they were made in different regions in Britain in the past, although the method of making them varied from region to region.

❦ OMELETTE ❦

An omelette is made with eggs. There are two main types of omelette. The first is called a plain omelette, which can be either sweet or savoury, and is shallow fried in butter in a specially designed omelette pan. The second type is a soufflé omelette, and is always served as a sweet at the end of a meal.

Plain Omelette: Sweet or Savoury

When making a plain omelette, the whole eggs are whisked together in a bowl and seasoned. The mixture is then poured into a heated omelette pan which has been well greased with butter. The omelette pan has a thick bottom which retains sufficient heat to cook the egg mixture as quickly as possible. The mixture should only cook for two to three minutes; this is the secret of a successful omelette. If cooked too long, the omelette will become tough. The eggs are stirred gently over a moderate heat until they are set. The omelette should be golden underneath, but remain creamy on top. A fork should be used to fold one-third of the omelette to the centre, then the other third of the omelette should be folded before it is turned out onto the serving plate. A savoury or sweet filling should be added before the omelette is folded. The sweet filling is usually hot jam. The list of savoury fillings is endless, and includes tomatoes, cheese, mushrooms and bacon. The sweet omelette is usually dredged with icing sugar and the sugar is caramelized with a hot metal poker before serving. The plain omelette can also be finished off under a grill until golden brown before the filling is added and finally folded and served.

Soufflé Omelette

The main difference between the plain omelette and the soufflé omelette is that the eggs are separated. The yolks are whisked with caster sugar and flavoured with vanilla and liqueur or chocolate, coffee or praline, and the whites are whisked separately. Both mixtures are then gently folded together. The mixture is then baked in a hot oven, in a well greased earthenware dish. When cooked, it is dredged with icing sugar. It must be served immediately so as to avoid the dessert collapsing. Some professionals add a little flour in the yolk mixture to prevent this.

History

Omelette is a French word which dates back to 1548. The word is a derivative of the old French word *amelette* (Ref.: *Le Petit Robert 1*, 1972). Subsequently the plain omelette was probably created in the sixteenth century. The omelette as we know it today was probably a French creation, although a type of omelette was made by the ancient Romans. However, the form and method of making the egg dish during that period would differ greatly from the omelette with which we are familiar today. The dish would have been cooked with crude utensils over an open fire and would probably have been seasoned with salt or sweetened with honey.

The Soufflé Omelette was created in the nineteenth century. Antoine Carême created the soufflé during this period; therefore the Soufflé Omelette could not have been created before this date.

∾ OPÉRA GÂTEAU ∾

Is a gâteau which has a base made with a paste consisting of plain flour, icing sugar, butter and milk. The paste is put into a piping bag and piped into a circular shape in a series of whirls to form a base. It is then baked in the oven at a low temperature. The base is allowed to cool. The surface of the base is then decorated with piped butter cream which has been flavoured with praline paste and Curaçao liqueur. The gâteau is then put into the refrigerator until the butter cream hardens and is then dredged with chopped nougatine.

History

The gâteau was created at the beginning of the twentieth century by a French patissier called Louis Clichy. He was later to become the personal chef of the Marshal of France, Ferdinand Foch (1851–1929), during the First World War (1914–1918). Today the gâteau is a speciality of an exclusive patisserie in Paris called Bugat which is located at 5, Boulevard Beaumarchais.

∾ ORANGE – ORANGE ∾

The orange, *Citrus Sinensis*, belongs to the family *Rutaceae*. The small tree grows in the sub-tropical regions of the world. The best season for oranges is from December until the end of April. The main orange-growing countries are the USA, Brazil, Mexico, Spain, Italy and Israel.

The orange is the most popular of all the citrus fruits. There are two types of oranges, bitter and sweet. The main varieties of sweet oranges are Washington, Hamlin, Jaffa and Valencia. Bigarade and Seville are the two main varieties of the bitter orange. The fruit is very rich in vitamin C. It also contains vitamin B and is a good source of the sugars, fructose, glucose and saccharose. Oranges are also rich in the minerals calcium and potassium.

It is an extremely versatile fruit and is widely used by both the chef and the patissier. It is used by the patissier in the production of flans, mousses, ice creams, bavarois and sorbets. The zest and juice are used by the chef to flavour sauces and dishes in cookery. The fruit is used in such classical dishes as Canard à l'Orange and Crêpe Suzette. The bitter variety of orange is used to produce marmalade, the famous British conserve! As a decoration or garnish, its wonderful bright orange colour enhances gâteaux, fruit salad and a variety of cookery dishes. The juice of the orange is the most popular fruit juice available on the market today. The fruit is also used to flavour world-famous liqueurs such as Grand-Marnier, Curaçao and Cointreau.

Today, oranges are plentiful, cheap and available all the year round. For export purposes and to extend their keeping quality, orange trees are treated with Diphenyl. It is therefore advisable, when using the zest of the orange for cooking purposes, that the oranges should be thoroughly washed.

History

The orange seems to have originated from the tropical regions of India and China. It was then introduced to the Middle East and was later brought back to England by the Crusaders in the late thirteenth century. Richard the Lionheart enjoyed the fruit whilst fighting in the Holy Wars in the late twelfth century. However, this was not the sweet variety of orange that we know today, but a bitter variety. The sweet orange was not introduced into Europe until the beginning of the fifteenth century. The Portuguese navigator, Vasco Da Gama (1469–1525), was responsible for bringing the fruit back to Spain from one of his long sea voyages of discovery.

The French began growing the orange tree not for the fruit, but as an ornamental tree, to enhance the gardens of the châteaux belonging to the French aristocracy. According to one story, the pip from a sweet orange was planted in a pot in Spain by a member of the Spanish court. The young tree was then offered as a gift to a member of the French aristocratic Bourbon family. The tree was nurtured at the Château of Chantilly, then moved to the Château Fontainebleau, and finally it was housed in the great conservatory at Versailles in 1684. The tree survived until 1850. Louis XIV (1638–1715), King of France from 1643 and also known as the Sun King, was responsible for making the orange tree fashionable, and an essential ornament in the garden. He grew orange trees in the magnificent gardens at his château in Versailles. Huge ornate conservatories were constructed to house the trees, as they could not survive the harsh Western winters.

In the middle of the eighteenth century, oranges were introduced to France as a commercial crop, but were only grown in a small region in the South of France. Today, oranges are available throughout the year in our markets worldwide. They are highly valued for their nutritional content, versatility and taste.

❧ OVENS, PASTRY ❧

In the early fifteenth century, the bakers and patissiers in France used ovens which were partly built outside the bakehouse. During that period, the ovens were fuelled with wood which was stoked outside and left to burn until the interior was hot enough. Long-handled rakes were used to remove the ashes, whilst long, flat, wooden shovels were used to lift the baked goods in and out of the ovens.

Pierre Lacam, in his book *Mémorial de la Pâtisserie* (fourth edition), which was published in 1898, tells us that the first oven to be heated by coal was installed in a bakery in the Boulevard Sébastopol in Paris in 1858. By the year 1860 in France, coal had replaced charcoal and wood as a fuel for heating pastry ovens.

P

∽ PAIN AU CHOCOLAT – CHOCOLATE BUN ∽

Is a small bun which is made with either croissant or brioche dough. The buns are oblong in shape and have a filling of dark chocolate.

History

The small buns were created in the late seventeenth century.

∽ PAIN AU LAIT ∽

Is made like a brioche dough; however, it is not quite as rich. Most of the eggs have been replaced with milk, thus its name, which translated into English simply means Milk Bread. Also, less butter is used than in the recipe for brioche; therefore Pain au Lait is much cheaper to make.

History

The recipe for this bread originated in France between the sixteenth and seventeenth centuries.

∽ PAIN PERDU – FRENCH TOAST ∽

Is made with stale bread which is sliced and then allowed to soak in a mixture of milk and eggs. The bread is then shallow fried in butter or oil and drained. It is sprinkled with caster sugar and served hot. It is interesting to note that in France the dish is served sweet, whereas in Britain it is usually seasoned with salt and pepper and served as a savoury dish. In America, a savoury dish is made with the addition of spring onions, parsley, bacon and seasoning.

History

The French name Pain Perdu is a derivative of the old French name Pain Perdy, which translated into English means Lost Bread. Obviously the name is extremely apt because the stale bread used in the recipe would otherwise have been wasted or lost. A similar recipe was known to the ancient Romans. Crusts from old bread were removed and soaked in milk. The bread was then fried in oil and coated with honey.

In the eleventh century, the Anglo-Normans were very fond of Pain

Perdu. The bread was soaked in a mixture of milk and eggs and then fried in oil and coated in honey and spices. It is quite possible that the French introduced the recipe to the British, as we refer to the dish as French Toast. Throughout the centuries the dish retained its popularity and survived probably because it was economical, nutritious and quite substantial, especially for poor people who could not afford to throw away stale bread. At a later date, such classic puddings as Bread and Butter Pudding and Cabinet Pudding were made with stale bread.

Today, the popularity of Pain Perdu has diminished, primarily because of our more affluent society and also the availability of mass-produced puddings and pastries.

∾ PALMIER – PIG'S EARS ∾

Is a small pastry which is made with puff pastry. The pastry is rolled into a square and dredged generously with caster sugar. It is folded several times and then cut into slices in order to achieve the distinctive shape of the pastry, which when baked resembles the leaves of a palm tree. The pastry shapes are then baked in a hot oven until the underside of the pastry starts to caramelize slightly. They are then turned over and baked until crisp and golden. Palmiers can be made very small in size and used in the production of Petits Fours Secs, or they can be made larger and served for afternoon tea. Sometimes they are sandwiched together with jam and whipped cream.

History

The word *Palmier* is a French word which dates back to 1119 (Ref.: *Le Petit Robert 1*, 1972). Translated into English it means palm tree. The small pastry was called Palmier because it resembles the leafy part of the palm tree. In Britain, it has been christened Pig's Ears because the shape of the pastry resembles the shape of a pig's ear. Palmiers are a French creation, but were not created until the early twentieth century. It is probable that they were created in Paris, where they are regarded as a speciality of the French capital.

∾ PAPER PIPING BAG – CORNET PAPIER ∾

Is a small, conical-shaped paper bag which is made from greaseproof paper. The point of the bag is cut off. It is used by the patissier to decorate pastries and gâteaux with royal icing, chocolate and butter cream. It is ideal for intricate decoration and fine work.

History

The bag was invented in the nineteenth century by a French patissier called Lorsa de Bordeaux. While working in the kitchen, he observed a young apprentice patissier piping his name in royal icing, using an empty paper cornet in which sugar almonds had been boxed. He had simply cut the point off the cornet and put the royal icing into the bag. Lorsa copied the idea using greaseproof paper to make a conical-shaped piping bag. This simple invention has proved to be of immeasurable value to the patissier.

∾ PARIS-BREST GÂTEAU ∾

Is a large circular gâteau which is made with choux pastry. The pastry is placed into a piping bag and, using a star-shaped nozzle, is piped into a circle. It is then dredged generously with flaked almonds and baked in the oven. When cooked, it is allowed to cool before being split through the middle. The top and bottom of the gâteau are then sandwiched together using a Crème Mousseline which has been flavoured with praline and rum. It is then dredged liberally with icing sugar. Small individual Paris-Brest gâteaux are also very popular.

History

The origin of the gâteau is a subject of controversy. Some claim that it was created in 1912, by a French patissier, to commemorate the opening of the British railway line called Agence Cook. The line ran between the French cities of Paris and Brest. Others claim that this classic gâteau was created by a French patissier in 1891, to commemorate the famous bicycle race from Paris to Brest, which took place in the same year. They insist that the gâteau was made to resemble the shape of a bicycle wheel.

∾ PARMEZANE ∾

Parmezane is a savoury pastry. It is made with puff pastry which is rolled and cut into small individual rounds. The round pastry shapes are dredged with Parmesan or Gruyère cheese and then baked. When cooked, the shapes are split in half and the base is covered with a rich Mornay sauce, which is generously dredged with Parmesan or Gruyère cheese. Finally a few knobs of butter are placed on top of the filling. The filling is then covered with the pastry top and served piping hot. Parmezanes are usually served as a snack at lunchtime. They can also be made much smaller in size and served at buffets.

History

The savoury was created in France in the early twentieth century.

∾ PASSION FRUIT – GRENADILLE ∾

The passion fruit belongs to the family *Passifloraceae*. The edible fruit is produced from a climbing shrub. The fruit is the size of a plum and has a dark purple, brittle skin. The pulp of the fruit is orange in colour and contains hundreds of tiny seeds which are edible. The flesh has a highly distinctive pungent flavour which is delicious. There is also another type of passion fruit which is yellow in colour. Passion fruit contains vitamin C and minerals.

The patissier uses the fruit mainly in the making of sorbets, fools, mousses, coupes glacées, bavarois and sweet sauces. It is used more as a flavouring rather than as a fruit because of the intense perfume of the flesh. The fruit remains an expensive ingredient in the production of desserts.

History

The passion fruit is native to Brazil. Since the nineteenth century, the purple fruit has flourished in Australia, New Zealand, South Africa, Hawaii and Israel. The yellow fruit is grown only in Hawaii and Fiji.

∾ PASTEURIZATION ∾

Is a process which involves the treatment of food in order to reduce the number of micro-organisms the food contains. For example, the pasteurization of milk involves partially sterilizing the milk by heat treatment. The milk is heated to 72°C for fifteen seconds, then cooled to 10°C. This process kills salmonella bacteria, prolonging the life expectancy of milk to five days.

History

This process was discovered by the French chemist, Louis Pasteur (1822–1895), while he was experimenting on wine.

∾ PASTILLAGE – GUM PASTE ∾

Pastillage is made with icing sugar, water and gelatine, to which a few drops of lemon juice or vinegar are added. The gelatine is softened in cold water in a bowl and then heated over a bain-marie until the gelatine melts. A few drops of lemon juice are added, and finally the sifted icing sugar is mixed in. The mixture can be worked by hand or in an electric mixter, until thoroughly mixed. Pastillage can be stored in a plastic bag in a refrigerator for a few days. The patissier uses it mainly to make elaborate showpieces called Pièces Montées.

History

The original recipe for Pastillage was the creation of an Italian patissier named John Pastilla. He was the personal patissier of Catherine de' Medici, and was employed in the royal household of her husband, Henry II, who was King of France from 1547 until 1559. Pastilla had brought with him to France a recipe for sweets which he had created several years earlier in his native Italy. These small sweets were flavourings and were known in Italy as Pastils. They were extremely fashionable in Italy and the Italian nobles carried them in their garments to eat at their leisure throughout the day. It was Catherine de' Medici who introduced them to the French court.

It was from this simple recipe that Pastillage was created. At a later date, the recipe was modified, and with the discovery of gelatine, the Pastillage as we know it today was created. Pastillage has been used for hundreds of years in France to create Pièces Montées.

∾ PASTIS ∾

There are several different types of Pastis, the method of making which varies from region to region. The two most popular types are, Pastis Bourrit, which originated in the Basque region of France and is a type of brioche which is sweetened and flavoured with lemon zest and rum. It is usually served hot and is dredged with icing sugar. Pastis from Béarn is made with thin rounds of pastry which are brushed with oil and honey, then placed on top of each other and baked in the oven. When cooked, the Pastis is brushed with warm honey and served hot.

History

The word 'Pastis' is derived from the Latin word *pasticius* (Ref.: *Le Petit Robert 1*, 1972). The Pastis was originally introduced to the Spanish by the Moors, who invaded the Spanish mainland in 711. As the Moor invasion crossed the Pyrenees, because of the mountainous terrain their progress was painstakingly slow. During their march over the mountains, they introduced to the Basque people many of their recipes, Pastis being one of them. The Moors pushed their advance into the French interior, and at Poitier, in 732, they were beaten in battle by the French, under the command of the Frankish ruler, Charles Martel, who was nicknamed 'The Hammer', thus ending the Moors' invasion of France. The Moors left behind culinary knowledge which was to have a considerable influence on French cooking in the years to come.

∾ PASTRY CUTTER – EMPORTE PIÈCE ∾

This piece of equipment is essential to the patissier. It is made of aluminium or plastic, comes in a variety of shapes and sizes and is used to cut pastry.

History

The pastry cutter was invented in the eighteenth century by an executive chef who was employed in the court of Frederick II (1712–1786), King of Prussia from 1740. He was also known as Frederick the Great. The first pastry cutter that the chef used was made from an old spur taken from his master's boots!

～ Pâte à Bombe ～

Is a mixture of egg yolks and a cooked sugar solution which is whisked together until cold. It is often added to Italian meringue and is used in the production of Baked Alaska, piped over the ice cream. Pâte à Bombe is also used by the patissier in the production of Bombes Glacées. Whipped cream or Italian meringue is added to the mixture and it is used as a filling for the Bombes.

History

It was created in Italy in the eighteenth century.

～ Pâte de Fruits ～

This consists of a fruit purée or fruit juice, pectin, sugar and glucose syrup, to which citric acid or tartaric acid is added in order to harden the solution. It is used extensively in the production of confectionery, for example, Turkish Delight.

History

It was created in the seventeenth century by a French patissier called Gilliers. During that period, however, pectin was not used in the recipe, but was replaced by gelatine, which was extracted from the bones of dead animals. Originally it was a mixture of fruit purée, brown sugar, gelatine and spices. The region of the Auvergne in the south-west of France is renowned for its Pâte de Fruits.

～ Pâté en Croûte ～

Is a meat joint or forcemeat, or a combination of both, which is enclosed in pastry and baked.

History

A type of Pâté en Croûte was made during the early Roman civilization. Originally the filling was either sweet or savoury. The Pâté en Croûte as we know it today was created by a French patissier called Noël in 1759. While he was working in a small patisserie in Paris, Noël had the idea to cover a whole ham joint with a savoury shortcrust pastry and then bake it in the oven. When it was cooked, he carved it into slices; each slice of ham was surrounded by pastry. It was a new idea, and the Parisians loved it. Jambon en Croûte was then followed by the classic Beef Wellington, which was made with the whole fillet of beef. The beef was placed on an oblong of puff pastry, which had been spread with a layer of forcemeat, or pâté. The fillet was then enclosed in the pastry and baked. Several years later, a French patissier was inspired to replace the puff pastry with a brioche dough, and the Filet-en-Croûte Brioché was born! Pâté en Croûte can be made with a variety of different meats and fish.

❧ PAVLOVA GÂTEAU ❧

Is made with French meringue, which is piped into a large round shape. The meringue is baked in a slow oven. When cooked, the base should have a firm outer crust, but the centre of the meringue should be soft and quite chewy. When cool, the surface of the meringue is piped with freshly whipped cream and decorated with a variety of fresh fruits.

History

The Pavlova Gâteau is a creation of the twentieth century. It was named after the famous Russian ballerina, Anna Pavlova (1885–1931). Anna popularized Russian ballet worldwide. It was during a tour in Australia, at the beginning of the twentieth century, that the gâteau was created in her honour after her acclaimed performance in the ballet *Swan Lake*.

❧ PEACH – PÊCHE ❧

The peach, *Prunus Persica*, belongs to the family *Rosaceae*. A distinguishing feature of the fruit is the soft, velvety texture of its skin. The peach has both white and yellow flesh. There are two types of peach, clingstone and freestone. The peach is a rich source of vitamin C and minerals.

Both fresh and tinned peaches are used extensively by the patissier. Peaches which are tinned maintain their flavour better than most fruits. The fruit is used in the production of flans, tartlets, mousses, fruit salads, and such classic desserts as Peach Melba and Peach Bourdaloue. Peaches can be conserved in alcohol, candied, dried, or bottled. The fruit is delicious when eaten raw.

History

The peach originated in China, where it has grown wild for thousands of years. It is a fruit which flourishes in temperate climates, but also requires warmth. For many years it was regarded as having originated from Persia because of its name, *Persica*, but the cultivation of the fruit had spread from China to countries which could provide suitable growing conditions. From Persia the fruit spread to Greece. It was the Roman Emperor Claudius (10 BC–AD 54), Emperor from AD 41, who introduced the tree into Italy. From Italy the fruit was introduced into other countries in Europe. The Crusaders brought the peach to Britain from the Holy Wars. The English climate was not an ideal one in which to cultivate the fruit, but orchards in a sheltered position thrived in Britain.

Today, the main producers of the fruit are Spain, Italy, France, North America and South America. A large percentage of peaches grown are now canned. Wild peach trees still flourish in China today. Britain produces some very good varieties of peaches, for example, the Duke of York and the Peregrine.

❧ PEAR – POIRE ❧

The pear, *Pyrus Communis*, and other species belong to the family *Rosaceae*. The colour of the skin of the fruit varies from yellow to green, some being marked with a russet colour according to the particular variety. The main varieties are Bartlett, Beurre, Comice, Conference and William. The pear, although low in vitamin C, contains other vitamins and minerals and is a rich source of pectin.

The pear is used extensively by the patissier in the production of fruit slices, fruit flans, coupes, compotes, coupes glacées, and to decorate gâteaux. The fruit can be tinned, bottled, dried and can also be preserved in alcohol. Pears are used in the classic desserts; Pear Belle-Hélène, Pear Bourdaloue, Pear Bourguignonne and Pear Condé. They are one of the most popular fruits when eaten raw, and are a close rival to apples.

History

The word 'pear' is an ancient one. The French word for pear is *poire*, which is a derivative of the Latin words *pira* and *pirum*. Pears have been known to man for thousands of years. The pear tree originated in the Caucasus, the mountain range between the Caspian and the Black Sea in the USSR, and gradually the fruit spread into Europe and India. The Ancient Greeks prized the fruit highly.

Pliny the Elder, Gaius Plinius Secondus (AD 23–AD 79), a Roman scientist and historian, stated in his writings that during this period there were thirty-eight different varieties of pears. The pears were eaten in their raw state or sometimes were preserved in honey. It was the Romans, during the invasion of Britain, who introduced the pear to the British. It was to become one of Britain's most extensively grown fruits.

In Europe during the sixteenth and seventeenth centuries, pear growing escalated. In England at that time, over sixty varieties of pears were being grown, whilst in France, cultivation of different varieties was also flourishing. For example, the Bon-Christien pear was introduced into France in the middle of the fifteenth century by Saint François de Paul, who was known as Le Bon Christien, which translated into English means the good Christian. Another variety called Le Doyenné was cultivated in 1640 and named after an elderly priest who was living in a house adjacent to a church, which was surrounded by orchards of pears. The pear was introduced to America in the early seventeenth century.

However, it was the Belgians during the eighteenth century who gained the reputation for cultivating the best quality pears, with such varieties as the memorable Beurre. Today, there are over a thousand different varieties of the fruit grown worldwide.

∾ PECTIN – PECTINE ∾

Is found naturally in fruits. Pectin content is especially high in bitter or acidic fruits such as gooseberries, quinces, cooking apples, red and black-currants, lemons and oranges. Pectin allows jams and jellies to set.

History

The word 'pectin' is derived from the Greek word *pektos*, which translated into English simply means coagulation.

∾ PEPPER – POIVRE ∾

The pepper, which is produced commercially, belongs to the *Piperaceae* family. It is obtained from the dried berries of the *Pepper Nigrum*, a shrub which grows up to a height of four metres. The shrub grows extensively in India. Pepper is used by the patissier to flavour savouries such as pies, pasties and quiches.

History

During the period of the great Roman Empire, the spice was imported from India. It is well documented in the reign of the Emperor Diocletian, Gaius Aurelius Valerius Diocletianus (AD 245–AD 313), that white pepper and black pepper were sold at that time at seven dinar for five hundred grams. The dinar was the Roman coinage of that period.

∾ PETITS BEURRES ∾

Are biscuits made with a dough consisting of flour, butter, sugar and salt. The biscuits are oblong in shape and have scalloped edges. In France, they are served with champagne, or as an accompaniment to desserts such as mousses. In Britain, they are served with tea.

History

Petits Beurres translated into English simply means little butter, referring to the butter content of the biscuits. The biscuits originated in the city of Nantes, which is situated on the River Loire, in the north-west of France. The little butter biscuits were to become a speciality of the city. In 1862, the first factory to produce the biscuits on a commercial scale was opened in the city. It was not until the beginning of the twentieth century that the British became acquainted with the little biscuits, which were to keep their French name, Petits Beurres.

∾ PETITS FOURS ∾

Petits Fours can be either sweet or savoury. However, they are usually cakes or biscuits which are made so tiny that they can be popped into the mouth and eaten. Sweet Petits Fours, which are elaborately decorated and made in an array of beautiful colours, are served at the end of a meal with coffee. There are six main types of Petits Fours.

Petits Fours Secs

The following Petits Fours come under this heading: Tuiles aux Amandes, Rochers aux Amandes, Cigarettes, Palets de Dames and Biarritz. There are many types of Petits Fours Sec. *Sec*, translated into English, simply means dry.

Petits Fours Amandes

The main ingredient used to flavour this type of Petits Fours is almonds, and that is why they are called Petits Four Amandes. Macaroons come under this classification.

Petits Fours Frais

These are tiny replicas of larger cakes. For example, tiny Eclairs are called Carolines, small fruit barquettes or tartlets are called Mignonnettes and small Rum Babas are called Pomponnettes. These are just a few examples of Petits Fours Frais.

Petits Fours Glacés

These are tiny cakes which are glazed with fondant. They are usually made with a sponge or biscuit mixture. They are sandwiched together with ganache or butter cream, glazed with fondant icing and then decorated.

Petits Fours Déguisés

These Petits Fours are made with fresh fruit such as grapes, cherries or orange segments which are dipped in a sugar solution. Dried fruits such as prunes, dates or apricots are also used. The stones of the dried fruits are removed and the centre is then filled with almond paste. They are then rolled in sugar, or dipped in a sugar solution. Tiny replicas of fruit which are shaped with coloured marzipan also come under this description. Fruit which has been preserved in alcohol, such as cherries, can also be dipped in chocolate or fondant and served as Petits Fours Déguisés; these are called Griottines.

Petits Fours Salés

These savoury Petits Fours are also referred to as Amuse-Gueules. They can be made with puff pastry, savoury shortcrust pastry or choux pastry. Tiny Gougères, Vol-au-vents or Bouchées are filled with a savoury mixture. One of the most popular Petits Fours which come under this heading are Cheese Straws. Salted almonds are also classified as Petits Fours Salés.

History

Petits Fours originated in France. The name Petits Fours is French, and translated into English simply means small ovens. The exact date as to when the original Petits Fours were first created is unknown. However, Petits Fours Frais and Petits Fours Déguisés were created by the renowned French chef and gastronome, Antoine Carême, in 1815. Seventeen years later, he created the Petits Fours Secs.

∾ PETS-DE-NONE ∾

Are small buns which are made with choux pastry. The buns are deep fried in hot oil. When placed into the hot oil, the choux pastry balls puff up and produce light, airy buns which could be described as having a soufflé appearance.

History

Pets-de-None are a French creation. The name, when translated into English, means Nun's Farts. It is perfectly understandable why the English translation of the name is not used! There is a great deal of controversy as to who created the recipe for these small choux buns. Some professionals claim that they were created by the Nonnes de Baume aux Dames, who lived in an abbey in the French district of Doubs, in the Jura mountains, near the Swiss border. This would certainly explain the second half of the strange name. Others claim that in 1770 a French chef called Tiroluy created a new recipe for fritters using choux pastry and called them Pets-de-None.

∾ PIE ∾

A pie is made with pastry which encloses a sweet or savoury filling. Pies are usually round in shape and can be in a variety of sizes. Different types of pastry can be used to make a pie, the main ones being shortcrust, flaky, rough puff, sweet shortcrust and hot water pastry. There are different types of pies. For example, one of the most popular pies made today is the closed pie, which has a top and bottom layer of pastry and encloses a sweet or savoury filling in the middle. Another type of pie is when the filling is placed on a plate or in a deep dish and is then covered with a layer of pastry on top. This type of pie is known as a single crust pie. The third type of pie is simply a pastry shell or case which has a savoury or sweet filling. This type of pie is commonly known as a tart or flan. Often tarts and flans have a topping added, for example, when meringue is added to a sweet lemon flan it is called Lemon Meringue Pie.

History

It is thought that the pie originated in ancient Greece. The Romans were undoubtedly responsible for introducing the pie to Britain during the

Roman invasion. The pastry at that time was made with oil, flour and water, which was moulded by hand, and the pastry enclosed meat.

As far back as the twelfth century in England, pie-makers were established in large towns. By the fourteenth century, health and hygiene regulations were laid down regarding the production of pies. The closed pies which were made during this period were made only with savoury fillings. They were huge and the pastry was free-standing. Open pies and tarts were simply pastry cases which were baked blind and filled with eggs, fruits and cheese. It was at a later date that pies, tarts and flans were supported by moulds such as plates, flan rings and deep dishes.

Sweet fruit pies did not become popular until the sixteenth century. In Elizabethan England, the fruit pie was immensely popular. It is documented that Elizabeth I (1533–1603), Queen of England from 1558, was extremely partial to sweet cherry pies. The sweet and savoury pies made during this period were extremely elaborate and were made in a variety of different shapes. The tops of the pies were decorated with an array of flowers and leaves.

It was during this period that trick pies became popular. The trick pie was not edible, but was simply a free-standing container made of pastry. It had no filling as such, but small birds or animals were placed inside the pastry container and then concealed with a pastry lid. The trick pie was merely a form of amusement for Elizabethan nobility at their banquets. This type of trick pie was immortalized in the following lines of the old children's nursery rhyme:

> 'Sing a song of sixpence, a pocket full of rye,
> Four and twenty blackbirds baked in a pie,
> When the pie was opened,
> The birds began to sing,
> Wasn't that a pretty dish to set before the King'.

Mincemeat pies were also very popular at that time and were eaten during Christmas festivities, a custom which has survived until the present day. The original recipe for mincemeat pies included meat.

Pie is a term which is used uniquely by western Europeans and Americans. The word 'pie' was spread across the Atlantic to the New World by the early settlers. Countries in the East do not use the word, and there is no equivalent for it in many Eastern languages.

∾ PIÈCE MONTÉE – DISPLAY PIECE ∾

This is a term used in France to describe a variety of elaborately decorated displays, which can be made with pastillage, Genoese sponge, choux buns, candied fruit, croquant and poured sugar. (Poured sugar is a solution of sugar, water and glucose which is heated to a temperature of 155–158 °C and then poured into moulds.) These sugar replicas are then used for display purposes. Some of these displays are edible; however, many Pièces Montées are made purely for display purposes.

Pièce Montée made with Genoese Sponge

This is a celebration cake and is usually made for weddings and christenings. Although it is classified as a display piece, it can also be edible and is usually eaten at the end of the wedding reception. It is the equivalent of the British wedding cake.

One of the most popular genoese based Pièces Montées in France is known as Gâteau Breton. The Genoese sponges are baked in special moulds, and some Pièces Montées have as many as six tiers. They are made in different sizes. The largest sponge is used as a base and the other sponges are placed on top of each other according to their size, the smallest sponge being placed on the top to achieve the desired tower effect. The gâteau is then glazed with fondant and decorated with piped chocolate, glacé cherries, angelica and crystallized violets.

Pastillage Pièce Montée

The Pièce Montée which is made with pastillage is made exclusively for display purposes. These displays can be made up to a height of three or four feet and can have as many as five or six tiers, which are supported by pillars. They can be decorated with chocolate, royal icing, pulled sugar in the form of flowers and ribbons or soufflé sugar in the shape of fruits, birds or animals. These display pieces are truly memorable and are considered as a work of art today. This type of display can also be made in croquant or poured sugar. Some Pièces Montées are decorated with petits fours.

Croquembouche

This is made with choux buns and is also edible. It is also considered as a celebration cake and is made for weddings and christenings. *See* Croquembouche.

Regional Speciality Pièce Montée

Throughout France, edible Pièces Montées are made in different regions. For example, in Niort, in the south-west of France, a Pièce Montée is made entirely with candied fruit. This is just one example of the regional variations.

History

The first type of Pièce Montée which was made in France consisted purely of candied fruits. The fruits were simply placed on top of each other in the shape of a pyramid. The Pièces Montées with which we are familiar today came at a later date. They were said to be modelled on the Hanging Gardens of Babylon, which was an ancient staged temple, seven storeys high and approximately a hundred metres in height.

The Pièce Montée which is used mainly as a celebration cake and made with Genoese sponge was not created until the end of the eighteenth century. The Gâteau Breton, for example, was very popular up until the nineteenth century, but its popularity diminished and the Croquembouche has become the traditional celebration cake for weddings and christenings.

The use of pastillage as a medium to produce huge, elaborately decorated pieces which were for display purposes only started after the creation of pastillage in the late sixteenth century in France. The first display piece made out of pastillage was created by the head chef of the Duc D'Orléans, who was known professionally by his Christian name, Noël. He carved shapes of animals, flowers and birds from pear wood using a chisel and he used these wooden moulds for his elaborate pastillage displays. The displays were constructions of five or six storeys, supported by pillars, and were lavishly decorated with the sugar shapes from the wooden moulds. However, these displays were quite crude in comparison to the pastillage Pièces Montées created at a later date, when the recipe for pastillage was modified and included gelatine, which produced a superior pastillage.

In fifteenth-century England, the equivalent of the Pièce Montée was the Marchpane, which was made from marzipan. Marzipan was made from ground almonds and sugar. It was created in Italy in the fourteenth century and later became popular in Europe. The Marchpane consisted of a large round base which was made with marzipan. Models of animals, birds and flowers, which were made with sugar syrup or almond paste, were moulded in wooden shapes and mounted on the marzipan base in a way similar to the method used by Noël in France. The English displays were often gilded with gold leaf.

At the end of the eighteenth century in France, Pièces Montées made from pastillage were to reach the height of their popularity. Most national celebrations would include the display of a large Pièce Montée. For example, in 1796 a French patissier called Frascati was commissioned to create an elaborate Pièce Montée of ten tiers to commemorate the French victory at the Battle of Lodei, a city which is twenty miles south of Milan, in Italy, where Napoleon defeated the Austrian army.

At the end of the nineteenth century, the famous French chef, Antoine Carême, created the Croquembouche which we know today (*see* Croquembouche). He was also responsible for making the pastillage Pièce Montée a true work of art, creating enormous and elaborately decorated displays of churches, castles and monuments.

❧ PINEAPPLE – ANANAS ❧

The pineapple, *Ananas Comasus*, belongs to the family *Bromeliaceae*. The edible fruit is produced from a low-growing plant which has long green leaves. Today, an average pineapple weighs around one kilogram and consists of over a hundred small fruits. The pineapple is a good source of vitamin C and is rich in minerals such as magnesium and potassium.

The fruit must be one of the most prized exotic fruits used by the patissier. Its attractive appearance and colourful yellow pulp are ideal for decoration purposes. The pineapple contains an enzyme called bromeline, which prevents gelatine from setting. However, when the fruit is cooked the enzyme is destroyed, and such sweets as bavarois and mousses can be made. Its wonderful flavour, perfume and succulence ensure that the fruit is at the top of the list for the production of tarts, tartlets, fruit salads, mousses, bavarois and iced sorbets and for the decoration of gâteaux such as Gâteau Singapore, Croûte aux Fruits and Coupe Jamaïque, which have all become classic desserts. A large percentage of the fruit grown today is canned. The pineapple is excellent when eaten in its raw state and is one of the most popular exotic fruits in the world today.

History

The pineapple is native to Brazil, where the Ananas grow wild. The Indians in Brazil called the fruit *Nana*, which translated means perfume, which later became *Ananas* from *Nana-nana*, or *Anana*, which translated means the perfume of perfumes, referring of course to the highly perfumed flesh of the fruit. The word Ananas is used in many different languages such as French, Italian, Portuguese, Greek and Arabic. However, the British thought the fruit resembled the pine cone, and it was given the name 'pineapple'.

On his second voyage of discovery, the Italian explorer, Christopher Columbus (1451–1506), reached the island of Guadeloupe in 1494 and discovered the Ananas growing wild on the island. He introduced the fruit to Spain, and by the early sixteenth century European gardeners were successful in cultivating the fruit. One of the first pineapples grown was presented to the Spanish King Charles V (1500–1558), Holy Roman Emperor from 1519. However, it was Portugal which played a large part in the spread of the cultivation of the Ananas throughout the tropics.

In England, the first pineapple was grown in a hothouse in 1661. The gardener of the Duchess of Cleveland grew pineapples in a greenhouse on the Duchess's estate, and his first success was presented by the Duchess to Charles II (1630–1685), King of England and Scotland from 1660. The French were quick to follow, and in 1670 the first pineapple was grown in France in a heated greenhouse. Pineapples grown in greenhouses in France were presented to the French King, Louis XV, as a gift in 1733.

It was during the reign of Victoria, Queen of Great Britain and Ireland from 1837 to 1901, that gardeners in England developed different varieties and the cultivation of the fruit escalated.

In the late nineteenth century, fruit grown in Hawaii and Singapore were canned for the first time. The familiar pineapple rings were cut from the fruit in order to fit them into the tins. Today, the main producers of pine-apples are Hawaii, Puerto Rico, Brazil and Malaysia.

⤬ PIPING BAG – POCHE ⤬

A piping bag is a conical-shaped pocket which is made out of plastic. At the point of the bag there is a hole into which a nozzle can be inserted. The bag is used to decorate or garnish a variety of sweet and savoury goods and is filled with either sweet or savoury mixtures. A variety of different shaped nozzles can be inserted into the bag for decorating purposes.

History

The piping bag was invented in 1847 by a Frenchman called Aubriot. Originally the piping bag was made out of a cloth material. However, today it is made out of plastic, which is more hygienic and can be disposed of immediately after use.

⤬ PITHIVIER GÂTEAU ⤬

Is made with puff pastry which is rolled into two large rounds. They are then sandwiched together with almond cream or frangipane. The edges of the gâteau are scalloped, using a sharp knife. The surface of the gâteau is then egg-washed and a design of a sun-ray is made on the surface with the point of a sharp knife. It is then baked in the oven. Just before it has finished cooking, the gâteau is removed from the oven and dredged with icing sugar. It is then returned to the oven for five minutes or so, in order to achieve a glaze on the surface of the gâteau.

History

The gâteau was created in 1506 by a French patissier who worked in the city of Pithivier, which is about seventy kilometres south of Paris. During the reign of Louis XIV (1643–1715), the gâteau reached the height of its popu-larity in France and was exported all over the country from the north. Today, the Pithivier Gâteau is regarded as one of the classic French pastries.

⤬ PLINY THE ELDER ⤬

A Roman historian. His real name was Gaius Plinius Secundus.

History

He was born in AD 23. His historical manuscripts provided a wealth of information on everyday life in Rome during that period. For example, he recorded information on the different types of crops and foods grown at that time. His writings also included numerous recipes and the diet and eating habits of the ancient Romans. He was killed in AD 79, when the volcano of Mount Vesuvius erupted, burying the ancient city of Pompeii.

∾ PLOMBIÈRE GLACÉE ∾

This is an ice bombe, filled with candied fruits which have been macerated in alcohol such as Kirsch or in a liqueur such as Maraschino.

History

The iced dessert originated in France in 1838 and most probably took its name from the city of Plombières in the district of Vosges, where it was created.

∾ PLUM – PRUNE ∾

The plum is the fruit of *Prunus Domestica*, which belongs to the family *Rosaceae*. Greengages and mirabelles are types of plums. The fruit is low in vitamin C, but is a good source of pectin, minerals and other vitamins. There are approximately two thousand species of plums and the trees can be found growing throughout the world. Plums are used in the production of flans, tarts, fruit fools, mousses and are used a great deal in jam and jelly making. They are delicious eaten in their raw state, especially the large purple Victoria plum and the smaller green-coloured greengage.

History

The plum originated in Asia and was known to the ancient Syrian, Greek and Roman civilizations. It was after the Holy Wars that the Crusaders brought the fruit back to Western Europe. They were cultivated as early as the end of the twelfth century.

During medieval times in England, the fruit was used in the making of pies. It was not until much later that the plums were dried and used for puddings and tarts and given the name 'prune' in England. In the sixteenth and seventeenth centuries, the dried fruit was replaced by other dried fruits, for example, raisins, in the making of such sweets as Plum Pudding. In 1840, the large, gloriously purple coloured Victoria plum was introduced.

In France, the fruit was known as early as the twelfth century, and was also used in medieval times in the production of tarts and pies. The French word for plum is *prune*. A small dark-coloured plum was brought back to France in the thirteenth century from Damascus, in Syria, by the Comte d'Anjou and was christened by the French the Prune de Damas. In England, the fruit became known as the damson. The original greengage arrived in France during the sixteenth century. It was brought back from Armenia. The King of France at that time was Francis I (1494–1547), King from 1515. His wife was called Claude and the fruit was named after her, Reine Claude, which translated into English means Queen Claude. The Reine Claude was imported into England from France in the early eighteenth century and was to become known as the greengage.

Another plum which was to become something of a French speciality is the small golden plum called the mirabelle. It was first introduced into France from the East in the middle of the fifteenth century. Today, the small fruit is highly regarded by the French. It is grown in the north-eastern regions of France, where there are two specialities grown, the mirabelle de Nancy and the mirabelle de Metz. The fruit is also used in the production of a white colourless alcohol. It is made by distilling the fermented fruit juice to produce a mirabelle brandy.

∾ POLKA GÂTEAU ∾

This is a flan which is made with shortcrust pastry. The flan is filled with pastry cream, over which a crown of choux pastry is piped. The flan is then baked in the oven. It is removed from the oven ten minutes before it has finished cooking, dredged liberally with icing sugar and returned to the oven for the remaining cooking time. This gives the surface of the gâteau a shiny glaze.

History

The gâteau was created in France in the early nineteenth century. It was named after the Bohemian folk dance called the polka. The dance spread from Bohemia into Germany, and in the early nineteenth century was a popular dance throughout Europe. The Parisians adored the lively new dance, and it became all the rage within fashionable society in the early 1830s. Sadly, the gâteau, like the dance it was named after, has diminished greatly in popularity with the French.

∾ POMEGRANATE – GRENADE ∾

The pomegranate, *Punica Granatum*, is the edible fruit which comes from a small tree belonging to the family *Punicaceae*. The fruit is small and round in shape and has a topknot. The skin of the fruit is orange to red in colour; it is hard and encases hundreds of seeds, which are surrounded by the edible red pulp. The flesh is sweet and delicious to eat. However, eating a pomegranate can be a long and tedious task, and this is the main disadvantage of the fruit. Today, some cultivated varieties are almost free of seeds. Pomegranates contain vitamin C and, if the seeds are eaten, are a good source of fibre.

In the West, the fruit is used mainly in the production of a concentrated syrup called Grenadine, which is a speciality of France. The sweet syrup is often used in small quantities to flavour and liven up other drinks, for example, lemonade. A delicate and quite distinctive jelly is also made with the fruit. The fruit is not used a great deal by the patissier, mainly because of the difficulty of extracting the edible pulp which contains seeds.

However, pomegranates are sometimes used in the production of sorbets. In the East, where the fruit originated, pomegranates are widely used in cookery, as an ingredient in many traditional dishes. A Mexican liqueur, Aguardiente, is made from the fruit.

History

The pomegranate is native to Persia, today known as Iran. It is well documented in biblical times. The fruit is an ancient one, it was known to the Greeks and is mentioned in Greek legends. The Romans called the fruit Carthage's Apple, named after the city from which they were imported into Rome. Carthage was a Phoenician city on the Gulf of Tunis which was founded around 814 BC.

In the eleventh century in Spain, the fruit is well documented. Rodrigo Diaz de Vivar (1043–1099), who was known as El Cid, which translated into English means 'The Lord', ate the fruit during this period. The pomegranate had been brought into Spain by the invading Moors. The Spanish were responsible for introducing the fruit to the New World in their great voyages of exploration to the Americas. However, the fruit was not imported into Britain until the middle of the sixteenth century.

Today, the pomegranate is cultivated throughout the world in Iran, Afghanistan, India, the Mediterranean region, South America, Mexico and California.

～ POMME ANDRÉ ～

Is a flan which is made with sweet shortcrust pastry. The base of the flan is covered with sliced apples and a filling of pastry cream, which has been flavoured with Calvados, is poured over the apples. The flan is baked in a medium oven. When cooked, it is allowed to cool and the surface of the flan is brushed with boiling apricot jam.

History

This recipe was created by the author and was named after his late father, André Juillet, who died on 16 March 1985. His father was born in Normandy, a region in France which is renowned for its apples and the apple brandy which is distilled from cider and is called Calvados. André was a true Norman at heart and he adored the specialities of the region. The recipe embodies two of his favourite ingredients, apples and Calvados. He would have adored Pomme André, especially if served with a glass of cider, his favourite drink. Salut, André.

❧ POMME-DE-TERRE – MARZIPAN POTATO CAKE ❧

These are small cakes which are made with stale Genoese sponge. The sponge is mixed with candied fruit and flavoured with rum. The cakes are shaped into small balls and coated with marzipan, then rolled in cocoa powder and decorated with almonds, to resemble a small new potato.

History

The recipe was created by a patissier in France in 1903. Presented with a large quantity of Genoese sponge which had become stale, he created the recipe to use up the left-over sponge. He had the inspiration to make the small cakes look like potatoes. He shaped them like small potatoes, achieving the colour of potatoes by rolling them in marzipan and coating them in cocoa powder and finally decorating the potato cake with whole almonds to imitate the eyes of the potato. The novelty cakes were an instant success, especially with children. The marzipan potatoes were introduced to the British market in the early twentieth century.

❧ POTATO – POMME-DE-TERRE ❧

The potato, *Solanum Tuberosum*, is a perennial plant which belongs to the family *Solanceae*. It has edible tuberous roots which are rich in starch. The potato is a carbohydrate and is particularly rich in roughage when eaten with its skin on. The patissier uses the vegetable in the production of dishes such as savoury pastries and potato cakes.

History

Potatoes were eaten by the Andean Indians, inhabitants of the Andes mountains, a range of mountains in South America, over two thousand years before the Spanish invaded the continent.

In 1586, the potato was introduced to Great Britain by Sir Walter Raleigh, a British explorer, who brought the vegetable back from South America. Looking for a market further afield for his new discovery, he took the potato across the sea to Ireland and sold the humble vegetable to the Irish for enormous sums of money, claiming that the South American vegetable was an aphrodisiac. The potato was to become the staple diet of the British and Irish lower working classes over a period of years, although it was a very gradual process.

In the eighteenth century, the vegetable was brought to France to be cultivated on a commercial scale by Antoine Augustin Parmentier, financed by Louis XVI (1754–1793), King of France from 1774. The potato had already been introduced into France, but grown only on a small scale. The French King believed that the cheap vegetable would sustain the population in times of famine. Parmentier devised a ploy to trick the French peasants into believing that the potato was a valuable source of food, because the peasants were suspicious of the new vegetable. He placed armed soldiers around the fields where the potatoes were grown. The French peasants believed that the new vegetable must be of value and worth stealing, if it was being kept under such close guard. Parmentier was successful! The potato was stolen in great quantities by the peasants. This devious scheme was how the vegetable became a part of the French peasants' diet.

By the nineteenth century, the potato had become the staple diet for the poor in Britain and Ireland. In 1845, the Irish potato crop was destroyed by a parasitic fungus. This had a devastating effect on the Irish population and resulted in thousands of deaths in the country. The famine led to thousands of Irish people emigrating to America during that period.

In the twentieth century, the potato crop on mainland Britain was largely harvested by Irish peasants, who arrived at British ports in their droves to pick potatoes in the fields around Britain. They were paid a meagre pittance. Today, the potato is the most popular vegetable in the Western world.

✑ PRALINE ✑

This is a solution of sugar and glucose, which is cooked over a fierce heat until the solution caramelizes. Nibbed or whole almonds or hazelnuts are then added to the caramelized sugar solution. It is allowed to cool, and the mixture is then pounded between special steel rollers until the desired praline paste is obtained. There are many different recipes and methods used in the production of this highly flavoured paste. It is widely used by the patissier in the production of cakes, gâteaux, petits fours, confectionery and iced desserts. The classic French pastry, the Gâteau Paris-Brest, is flavoured with praline.

History

Praline was created in 1731 by a French head waiter called Clement Jaluzot. He was employed by the Duc de Choiseul, Comte de Plessis-Pralin (1719–1785). The Duc became a French Marshal during the reign of Louis XV, King of France from 1715 to 1774. The idea for the paste was sparked off by one of Jaluzot's apprentices, who was eating almonds with pieces of caramel. He commented to Jaluzot on the delicious combination of the nuts and confectionery. Jaluzot named the paste Praline, in honour of the Duc.

The new praline paste, in the shape of bonbons or confectionery sweets, was first served with the desserts at a banquet hosted by the Comte de Plessis-Pralin on the outskirts of the city of Bordeaux in France. The city had rebelled against the French King, and the Comte was given command of the French army in order to quash the rebellion. Unable to take the city, he decided to negotiate with the enemy. In order to promote goodwill, he invited the dignitaries of the city to a lavish banquet to talk around the table. The negotiations were successful; whether or not this can be attributed to the delicious new bonbons which were served is open to speculation!

∽ PROFITEROLES ∽

These are small buns which are made with choux pastry. The buns can have either a sweet or savoury filling. Sweet Profiteroles are usually filled with a flavoured Crème Mousseline or a flavoured pastry cream. The flavourings used are usually chocolate, coffee or praline. In Britain, the filling used for the pastry bun is often whipped cream. When cooked, the small buns are arranged on top of each other in the shape of a pyramid, then covered with a flavoured pouring sauce. The flavour of the sauce is determined by the flavour of the filling. For example, Chocolate Profiteroles should be served with a chocolate sauce. The Profiteroles are then decorated with piped whipped cream. Another variation of this recipe are Profiteroles Glacées, which are small choux buns filled with vanilla ice cream and served with hot chocolate sauce. Savoury profiteroles are individual choux buns which are filled with a Mornay sauce and can either be served hot or cold, as an entrée.

History

The word 'profiterole' originated in the sixteenth century. However, the buns were not created until a much later date. The French cookery writer, Pierre Lacam, in his book *Mémorial de la Pâtisserie*, which was published in the nineteenth century, describes how Profiteroles were made during that period. It is interesting to note that the filling used then was whipped cream, and it was not until a later date that pastry cream and Crème Mousseline were used. Profiteroles Glacées were not created until the twentieth century.

The idea for Profiteroles as a sweet dish came from the larger and more elaborately decorated sweet, the Croquembouche. The Croquembouche is made by the patissier, who is employed in a patisserie in France. It takes a great deal of time to make the large cake, and the decoration is laborious and time-consuming. In a patisserie the patissier is allowed the amount of time required to make the Croquembouche. Profiteroles are usually made in hotels and restaurants where the patissier is making a variety of sweets to order. Time is of the essence, and Profiteroles are much quicker and easier to make because they are much smaller.

∽ PUDDING ∽

Puddings can be either sweet or savoury and may be served hot or cold. The term covers a wide variety of sweet and savoury dishes. For example, sweet puddings include suet puddings, sponge puddings or milk puddings which are made with sweetened and flavoured cereal products such as rice or semolina. Savoury puddings include black pudding, white pudding, haggis or puddings made with suet pastry enclosing a savoury filling. Puddings today can be boiled, baked, steamed or microwaved.

History

England is the home of the pudding! They simply adore the dish. The English word 'pudding' is a derivative of the old English word *poding*, which dates back to the thirteenth century. The earliest puddings were boiled in the clean guts of newly slaughtered animals. The French word for pudding is *boudin*, which is a type of sausage. For example, Boudin Blanc translated into English simply means White Pudding; it is an old French recipe for a white sausage which is traditionally eaten at Christmas.

In the seventeenth century, a new method of cooking sweet or savoury puddings was invented. The mixture for the pudding, instead of being enclosed in the clean guts of an animal, was placed in a pudding cloth or bag and boiled. The term 'pudding' may have been used to describe this new method of cooking because it was similar to enclosing the boudin or pudding, which was a type of sausage in a skin. In England, these puddings were referred to as Bag Puddings, but in Scotland they were christened Clootie Dumplings. Clootie is an old Scottish word meaning cloth. The invention of the cloth meant that puddings were more convenient to make, as it was not necessary to wait for an animal to be slaughtered to obtain the guts.

The English national dish, Plum Pudding, was not created until 1675 and was boiled in a cloth bag. Baked puddings, or pudding pies, were baked in the oven during this period. Suet puddings were also made with the cloth bag, and were both sweet and savoury. The bag was lined with suet pastry and filled with savoury fillings such as meat or game or sweet fillings such as fresh and dried fruit with lashings of butter. Haggis was eaten throughout Britain during this period and did not become the national dish of Scotland until the eighteenth century.

At a later date, sweet boiled milk puddings made from cereals were made in abundance and were extremely popular because of the availability and cheapness of sugar. For example, rich rice puddings, sponge puddings and whitepots, which was the ancestor of one of our best loved puddings, Bread and Butter Pudding, were great favourites of the English at that time.

Today in Britain, the term 'pudding' is often used to describe the sweet dish served at the end of a meal.

∾ PUFF ∾

A puff is a term which applies to a pastry made with puff pastry and enclosing a filling. The name of the puff is determined by the filling. For example, a pastry with almond filling would be called an Almond Puff and so on.

History

The term 'puff' dates back to the eighteenth century and was extensively used in England during that period. At that time puffs could have a sweet or savoury filling.

❧ PUFF PASTRY –
PÂTE FEUILLETÉE ❧

Puff pastry is made with flour, cold water and salt, into which fat is incorporated. The flour used in making this particular type of pastry should be strong flour, which is rich in gluten. Strong flour will give the elasticity to the pastry dough which is essential, because of the amount of rolling and handling required to make the pastry. Acid, such as lemon juice, is sometimes added in order to give more elasticity to the gluten. The water used should be ice cold. Two types of fat may be used when making this type of pastry, depending upon the quality of the pastry required. Butter will produce the best quality puff pastry, but pastry fat can also be used; however, the quality is inferior. The quality of the pastry also depends upon the quantity of fat used to the flour.

There are three main methods of making this type of pastry. They are known as the French method, the English method and the Scottish method, which is commonly referred to as rough puff pastry. In the English and French methods, the quantity of fat to flour can be equal if butter is used as the fat. If pastry fat is used in these methods, less fat is required. In the Scottish method, half the quantity of fat to flour is used. The main difference between the methods of making these pastries is how the fat is incorporated into the pastry. Each method involves a succession of rolling and a series of turns. When the pastry is baked in a hot oven, steam is created, causing the pastry layers to rise and puff up, hence the name Puff Pastry. Other methods of making puff pastry are the chocolate method, the inverted method and the Viennese method.

Puff pastry is used extensively by the patissier in the production of sweet and savoury pastry goods. For example, such classic pastries as Gâteau Mille-Feuilles, Gâteau Pithivier, Apple Turnovers, Jalousie and Vol-au-Vents are all made with puff pastry. The list is endless.

History

The origins of puff pastry have been a subject of controversy for a long time. However, it is highly probable that a type of rough puff pastry originated in Persia, perhaps as early as the ninth century. Some professionals claim that the earliest recipes came from Egypt. Spanish cuisine had been greatly influenced by the Moors during the invasion of Spain in the eighth century. Early manuscripts in Arabic, which were written in Spain, lay testament to the fact that recipes for different types of layered pastries existed during that period and were used by the Spanish. However, it was a type of rough puff pastry. In the eleventh century, the first Crusaders brought back to other parts of Europe from the East a very crude method of making rough puff pastry. The pastry was brushed with melted animal fat and rolled and turned to incorporate air between the pastry folds.

In neighbouring France, during the reign of Charles V, known as Charles the Wise (1338–1380), who was King of France from 1364, a type of puff pastry was made in the city of Cahors in the south-west of France, near the Spanish border. Oil was still being used to make the pastry. However, it was not until the seventeenth century that a French patissier called Feuillet created the modern recipe for Pâte Feuilletée, which was made with butter incorporated in a series of turns to produce a pastry with hundreds of layers. La Varenne, who was a renowned French chef and cookery writer during the reign of Louis XIV (1638–1715), who was King of France from 1643, published a recipe for Pâte Feuilletée in one of his cookery books. However, it was not until the early nineteenth century that Pâte Feuilletée was perfected by the famous French chef, Antoine Carême.

∾ Puits d'Amour ∾

Are deep tartlets which are made with sugar pastry. The tartlets are baked blind and are filled with vanilla-flavoured pastry cream. The surface of the tartlet is sprinkled generously with sugar and the surface is then caramelized by using a hot poker.

History

The French name Puits d'Amour, when translated into English, means Well of Love. The origin of the name is very romantic. A young French patissier who created the tartlets was very much in love. In the Rue de la Grande-Truanderie, in Paris, there was a well, into which Parisian lovers would throw coins and then make a wish. The young Frenchman threw a coin into the well, making a wish to be successful in love. He created the tartlets shortly afterwards and named them after the famous well. The original tartlets were vol-au-vent cases and were filled with redcurrant jelly. At a later date, apricot jam replaced the redcurrant jelly. In the middle of the nineteenth century, a new filling of pastry cream flavoured with vanilla was added to the vol-au-vent cases, and the surface of the pastry was sprinkled with sugar and caramelized with a hot poker. Shortly afterwards, sugar pastry tartlets replaced the original vol-au-vent cases.

Q

∼ QUATRE-QUARTS ∼

Is a rich sponge cake which is oblong in shape. The cake is extremely popular in France. The sponge mixture is made with equal quantities of the four main ingredients, which are flour, fat, sugar and eggs.

History

The cake originated in France. It was called Quatre-Quarts because it was made with equal quantities of the four main ingredients weighing one quarter of a kilogram. Quatre-Quarts, translated into English, simply means four of one quarter. The English equivalent of this rich sponge cake is the American/English Pound Cake or Madeira Cake. The Pound Cake was created in Britain in the nineteenth century, and was so called because the recipe consisted of one pound weight of each of the main ingredients.

∼ QUEEN OF PUDDINGS ∼

This consists of a thick egg custard, to which breadcrumbs are added. The mixture is flavoured with vanilla and often lemon zest is added. The custard is poured into an earthenware dish and covered with a layer of jam. A final topping of piped meringue is added to cover the mixture. It is then baked in a very hot oven until the meringue becomes golden brown.

History

This pudding is a traditional British pudding and one of the most popular of the classic English puddings. It was probably created in England in the nineteenth century.

∼ QUICHE LORRAINE ∼

Is a flan which is made with savoury shortcrust pastry and has a filling which is made with eggs, milk and seasoning. An endless variety of savoury ingredients can be added to the mixture, for example, bacon, cheese, asparagus, onions and tomatoes. The flan ring is lined with the shortcrust pastry and baked blind. It is removed from the oven partially baked and the filling is poured into the flan. It is returned to the oven until the egg mixture has cooked and set. The quiche can be eaten either hot or cold and can be made in a variety of sizes. Small individual quiches are served at buffets or as a snack. Large quiches are usually sliced and served in portions as a main course.

History

'Quiche' is a word which dates back to 1845. It is a derivative of the Alsacian word *Küchen* (Ref.: *Le Petit Robert 1*, 1972), which translated into English simply means gâteau. The pastry originated in the district of Alsace-Lorraine, in the extreme east of France, bordering with Germany. The district has changed hands between the Germans and the French on numerous occasions over the centuries.

Originally quiches were made in the district on the first day in May, to commemorate the beginning of spring. The quiches which were made during that period were enormous, much larger than those that are made today. Often they could measure sixty centimetres in diameter! The filling was made up of lard, milk, cream, butter and eggs, to which smoked bacon would be added.

The quiche did not become popular in Britain until the middle of the twentieth century. It is one of the most popular fast food dishes which has been imported to these shores from France. Most menus in this country will include some type of quiche.

∽ QUINCE – COING ∽

The quince tree, *Cydonia Oblonga*, belongs to the family *Rosaceae*. The tree produces a large yellow fruit which has a bumpy and uneven surface. The fruit is pear-shaped and is extremely hard. The inside of the fruit is also hard and has many pips. The flesh is very sour and inedible unless sweetened with sugar. The fruit is extremely rich in pectin and contains some vitamins and minerals. Because of its high pectin content, it is ideal for making jams and jellies. When cooked, the flesh turns pink and has a perfumed flavour which is quite distinctive. Today, the quince is not used a great deal by the patissier.

History

The quince fruit is native to Persia. It is an ancient fruit, and was known in the Middle East as far back as 1000 BC. The Greeks and the Romans used quinces in their cooking. The ancient Greeks grew quince trees in their gardens. They roasted the fruit and then coated it with honey before serving. Often the quince was cooked in honey to allow the fruit to absorb the honey to counteract its sour taste. The Romans made a type of jam with quinces using honey instead of sugar; this has been documented as far back as AD 50.

As centuries passed, the Europeans continued to use the fruit in a variety of recipes. During the Middle Ages, the quince was a popular fruit to use as a filling for pies and to make jams. It remained popular up until the nineteenth century, and the Victorian cookery writer, Isabella Beeton (1836–1865), published recipes which included quinces. Marmalade and jelly made with quinces remained popular until the beginning of the twentieth century. However, by the middle of the twentieth century the hard, sour and unattractive fruit had lost favour with the British public, and today it is seldom seen in this country. However, it remains extremely popular and is used extensively in the cuisine of countries in Eastern Europe, such as Turkey and Romania. Turkey consumes the largest quantity of quinces in the world.

R

RAISINS, DRIED – RAISINS SECS

A raisin is a dried grape. The main types are: the common raisin, the sultana, the seedless raisin and the currant. The process of dehydration results in a loss of vitamin C, but increases the sugar content of fruit. The raisin is therefore high in sugar content. Dehydration reduces the moisture content of the fruit in order to preserve it for long periods of time. Other fruits suitable for drying are apricots, apples, pears, figs, bananas, plums and peaches. Fruit can be dried using three main methods: freeze drying, natural drying in the sun and drying in special ovens through heat. Raisins are used extensively in the bakery and confectionery trade.

History

The English word 'raisin' comes from the old French word *raisin*, which translated into English means grape. The French name for the fruit, *raisin sec*, translated into English means dried grape, *sec* meaning dry. Around 2500 BC, Neolithic man dried raisins in the sun in order to extract the juice. It is well documented that the early Greeks and Romans used dried fruits. The Roman historian Apicius, in his early writings, mentions several different sauces which were made with the juice from raisins. Wine was also made by the Romans from raisins (Ref.: *Hippocrate* Magazine, France, January 1947).

In medieval times, such exotic fruits as prunes, dates and currants were imported into Britain on the great spice ships belonging to Italy, Spain and Portugal. At that time currants were widely used in the production of baked goods, such as the traditional English plum cake. At a later date, raisins were used as a main ingredient in such classic English pastries as Eccles Cakes, Chorley Cakes, Banbury Cakes and Scones.

RAMEQUINS AU FROMAGE – CHEESE RAMEKINS

There are two main types of this savoury cheese dish. The first is a cheese savoury mixture which is poured into special small fireproof china containers known as ramekin dishes and baked in the oven. The small baked savouries are served hot in the ramekin dishes as an entrée. The second consists of small baked pastry tartlets which have a filling of choux pastry quenelles mixed with Mornay sauce. The tartlets are sprinkled with grated Gruyère cheese and are gratinated in a hot oven.

History

Ramequin is a French word which dates back to 1654. It is a derivative of the old Dutch word *rammeken*, which comes from the old Dutch word *rahm*, meaning cream with cheese (Ref.: *Le Petit Robert 1*, 1972). Ramequins au Fromage was created in 1760 by a French patissier called Avice. The original dish consisted of diced Gruyère cheese which was mixed with choux pastry and piped into bun shapes like Gougères and then baked. Over the centuries the original recipe changed, and today different regions of France have their own variation of the cheese savoury. For example, Ramequins Vaudrois is a speciality of the Vaud district and Ramequins Comptois is a speciality of the Franche-Compté in the Jura mountains in the east of France, where Gruyère cheese is the main agricultural resource.

∽ RASPBERRY – FRAMBOISE ∽

The raspberry, *Rubus Indaeus*, grows wild in the northern hemisphere. The fruit is a rich source of vitamin C.

History

The origin of the English name 'raspberry' is not known. The French name for the fruit, *framboise*, comes from the twelfth-century word *brambasia*, then *frambeise* (Ref.: *Le Petit Robert 1*, 1972). The raspberry is an ancient fruit and was known to the early Greeks. The Romans also had knowledge of the fruit, but did not appreciate it and never attempted to cultivate it. It was in the Middle Ages that the French began to be aware of the qualities of the wild fruit and started cultivation of the plant. France introduced the cultivation of raspberries to Britain in the sixteenth century. Over the centuries, raspberries have been used extensively in the creation of a variety of British desserts, such as fruit coulis, ice sorbets, tarts, flans, mousses and the traditional Scottish sweet, Cranachan.

∽ RELIGIEUSE GÂTEAU ∽

The Religieuse Gâteau consists of two choux buns of different sizes, one small and one medium-sized. The buns are either filled with chocolate or coffee pastry cream and are glazed with fondant the same flavour as the filling. The small choux bun is then placed on top of the larger one and the buns are decorated with rosettes of white butter cream. Religieuses can be made as small individual gâteaux or a larger gâteau can be made for several people.

History

Religieuse Gâteau is regarded as a classic French pastry. It was created in 1856 by a Parisian patissier called Frascati. The word *religieuse* is an old French word which dates back to 1165 (Ref.: *Le Petit Robert 1*, 1972). Translated into English, *religieuse* means nun.

The original gâteau had a completely different form. It consisted of a sugar paste flan which had a filling of choux pastry buns containing flavoured whipped cream and glazed with white fondant. In 1890, in a patisserie in the centre of Paris, a patissier called Sthorer totally transformed the shape of the Religieuse. He had the brilliant idea to make the gâteau resemble *une religieuse* or a nun dressed in her black and white habit. He took a medium-sized choux bun and filled it with chocolate pastry cream, then glazed it with chocolate fondant to represent the nun's body. Chocolate fondant was the nearest colour to black, the colour of the nun's habit. He repeated the process for the head and placed the small choux bun on top of the medium choux bun. He then piped white butter cream rosettes between the choux buns representing the nun's white, starched collar. To complete the illusion, he piped a small white butter cream rosette on top of the small choux bun to represent the nun's white hat. The shape of the Religieuse has survived until the present day, and it is an extremely popular pastry in France and throughout the world.

❧ RHUBARB – RHUBARBE ❧

Rhubarb, *Rheum Raphonitacum*, belongs to the *Polygonaceae* family and is one of the oldest species of the plant. The fruit contains vitamin C and is a good source of potassium and manganese. The leaves of the plant contain a poison; it is the stalks of the plant which are edible. There are different species of rhubarb, some of which are inedible or are used only because of their medicinal properties.

History

The French word *rhubarbe* comes from the old thirteenth-century French word *reubarbe* (Ref.: *Le Petit Robert 1*, 1972). The plant originated from the cold countries of Mongolia and Siberia. Rhubarb was used in Persia in 2000 BC as a source of food. However, it was for its medicinal properties that the plant was highly valued by ancient civilizations. It was introduced into North Africa by the Arabs, and from North Africa was introduced into mainland Europe and France in the late twelfth century. However, rhubarb was not at that time cultivated in France.

The plant was introduced into Britain over three hundred years later by the French, and it was called rhubarb (the English dropped the 'e' ending of the French name for the plant). It was appreciated by the British solely for its medicinal properties for the next three hundred years and was not used as a source of food.

British attitudes towards the plant changed in the nineteenth century. The plant was used in recipes for pies, mousses and fools, but the great British favourite of that period was stewed rhubarb served with lashings of hot custard! Not to forget a wonderful home-made wine made from the fruit. It was grown widely in gardens throughout Britain and used extensively by the British housewife, in Victorian England right up until the middle of the twentieth century, to make rhubarb-based desserts and wonderful jams such as the delicious rhubarb and ginger jam. What an exquisite taste!

∽ RICE – RIZ ∽

Rice is a cereal obtained from the grass *Oryza Sativa*. It grows in warm, wet conditions and takes up to five months to mature. Water is essential to its growth. The cereal is nutritious and contains protein and carbohydrates. White rice, which is processed, is the most popular rice on the market today. However, during the husking and polishing process, valuable vitamins are lost. Brown rice, or unhusked rice, although proven to contain vitamins and to be more nutritious, is less popular. There are over seven thousand varieties of rice, and it is the staple diet of over one-third of the world's population, especially in countries in the East. It is used extensively as a main ingredient in Eastern and Western cookery dishes throughout the world in classic dishes such as Risotto and curries.

Today, the cereal is grown all over the world, in parts of Italy, the United States of America, South and Central America, South-East Asia, China, the Middle East and Japan. It is also grown in the wet, marshy area in the south of France known as the Camargue. This area alone produces enough rice for the population of France!

History

The French word for rice is *riz*, a derivative of the old French word *ris*, which dates back to the thirteenth century and comes from the Latin word *oryza* (Ref.: *Le Petit Robert 1*, 1972). The English word 'rice' is a derivative of the thirteenth-century French word. Rice is native to India and South-East Asia, and it was cultivated in China and India as long ago as 5000 BC. A Chinese Emperor in 2800 BC started an ancient custom in China which involved throwing handfuls of rice at newly married couples to ensure fertility. This custom spread to the West, and has survived for thousands of years – this ancient fertility ritual is still carried out at weddings today! The ancient Japanese people worshipped the god of Rice called Inari and built shrines in his honour. It is a custom to pray to the god of Rice for good crops.

In AD 711 the Moors invaded Spain, and it was during the invasion that rice was introduced into Europe. Centuries later, the cereal was used mainly in European countries such as France and England in the production of desserts. Rich rice milk puddings which were baked in the oven were extremely popular in the eighteenth century in England. In France, such classic rice desserts as Gâteau de Riz and Riz Condé were created during that period. It was not until the middle of the twentieth century, when travel to distant countries became affordable, that foreign rice-based dishes became popular in Britain and rice became one of the most popular cereals on the market. Today, it is used in the production of sweet and savoury dishes.

∾ RICE GÂTEAU – GÂTEAU DE RIZ ∾

Rice Gâteau is a sweet shortcrust pastry flan which is served cold, cut into wedges. The sweet filling is a cooked rice mixture which is made with rice, milk, sugar, whole eggs and cream and is flavoured with vanilla and nutmeg.

History

It was created in France in the eighteenth century and was extremely popular during that period. In the twentieth century the Gâteau de Riz, although still made in France, has lost its popularity as a dessert.

∾ RIZ CONDÉ – RICE CONDÉ ∾

This is a sweet milk pudding made with rice. It is served cold and is glazed with jam and decorated with fruits. Riz Condé is usually accompanied by whipped cream.

History

This cold rice pudding is thought to be a creation of the famous French chef, Antoine Carême (1784–1833). Riz Condé was named after the French aristocratic family of the same name. The House of Condé was founded by Louis de Bourbon Condé (1530–1569), who was the uncle of Henry IV (1553–1610), King of France from 1589.

∾ ROLY-POLY PUDDING ∾

Roly-poly pudding is made with suet pastry which is rolled into an oblong shape. The surface of the pastry is spread liberally with jam. It is then rolled, covered in greaseproof paper and tin foil and steamed. It is delicious served with thick hot custard!

History

Another great British pudding! Steamed sweet suet puddings were brought to England by George I (1660–1727), King of Great Britain and Ireland from 1714, from his native country, the Electorate of Hanover. However, it was not until the nineteenth century that the suet pudding Roly-Poly was created, during the reign of Victoria (1819–1901), Queen of Great Britain and Ireland from 1837. Victoria married the German Prince Albert in 1840. He reintroduced and revived the popularity of the German sweet steamed suet puddings of the previous century. A recipe for this sweet suet pudding appeared in Isabella Beeton's book, *Household Management*, which was published in 1860. This classic English pudding was to remain a great favourite of the British people until the middle of the twentieth century.

∽ ROYAL ICING – GLACE ROYAL ∽

This is a mixture of sifted icing sugar and raw egg whites which are beaten together until the correct consistency is obtained. It should be very smooth, glossy and white in colour. Glycerine is often added to the icing to prevent it from becoming too hard. In order to achieve a brilliant white colour, lemon juice is added to the mixture. It is important to note that Royal Icing should not be mixed in a metal bowl as this results in the icing becoming grey in colour. Royal Icing is used extensively by the confectioner, baker and patissier as a decorating medium: for example, to decorate and ice traditional celebration cakes such as wedding, christening and birthday cakes.

History

It is a French creation and was originally called Sucre Royal during the time of Antoine Carême. The French name later changed to Glace Royal (the French word *glace* meaning ice or glaze), hence the English name Royal Icing.

∽ RUM – RHUM ∽

Rum is an alcohol distilled from fermented sugar cane. It is perhaps the alcohol most widely used by the patissier. It is used as a flavouring in such classic pastries as Rum Baba, Mocha Gâteau and Gâteau Paris-Brest.

History

It took a great deal of experimentation before the alcohol was obtained from sugar cane, since the syrup had a tendency to ferment. The French alcohol Rhum was created in the middle of the seventeenth century by a French missionary called Father Labat, who perfected the distillation process on the island of Haiti, which was a French colony. It was christened Taffia. Labat stated that 'it is a drink of fire which will give strength to men and happiness to women'.

Sugar cane had been introduced to the island from the Canary Islands in 1493 by the explorer, Christopher Columbus. By 1635, it had reached the French colony of Martinique. The English-speaking islands in the Caribbean also distilled alcohol from sugar cane, which was later called Rum. The

Spanish also distilled the alcohol. The famous white rum known as Bacardi is today produced on the island of Puerto Rico.

❧ RUM BUTTER ❧

Is a mixture of unsalted butter, sugar and rum. It is traditionally served as an accompaniment to Christmas Pudding in Britain.

History

There are two versions as to how Rum Butter was created. The first version is that a sailing ship, on a return journey from the Spice Islands, ran into a storm, during which the ship's cargo was damaged. The resourceful sailors mixed the spilt commodities together, and the result was Rum Butter! The second version is that Rum Butter was a regional speciality which was created in Cumberland, a region in the north of England. It was made to celebrate the birth of a new baby. Friends visiting the new arrival were welcomed with tea and baked goods spread with the delicious butter.

S

∾ SACCHARIN ∾

Saccharin is a sweetening agent. It is four hundred times sweeter than sucrose, which is found in fruits, sugar cane and sugar beet. It is rarely used by the patissier. It is recommended by doctors to people who wish to slim and use it as a substitute for sugar.

History

Saccharin was invented by an American called Constantin Fahlberg while he was studying at the University of Baltimore in 1789.

∾ SACHER TORTE – SACHER GÂTEAU ∾

There are several variations in the production of this gâteau. The traditional Sacher Torte is a rich chocolate sponge, consisting of plain flour, ground almonds, eggs, caster sugar, butter and chocolate. The mixture is baked in a well greased and floured Genoese tin, which can be either round or square in shape. The filling consists of whipped cream or Italian meringue flavoured with chocolate, or a butter cream richly flavoured with a ganache. The sponge is usually soaked with syrup which has been flavoured with rum. The gâteau is masked with the same mixture used for the filling and is very often glazed with melted chocolate. Finally, it is decorated with chocolate ganache which is piped into various patterns. The name 'Sacher' is usually piped on the surface of the gâteau.

History

The Sacher Torte is of Austrian origin. It was created in Vienna in 1832, by a young apprentice patissier called Franz Sacher. At that time, he was in the employ of Prince Clemens Wenzel Metternich. The story of how the cake was created is very interesting. The Executive Chef of the Prince quite unexpectedly became extremely ill one evening. A large dinner party had been arranged by the Prince for a number of very important guests, among whom were members of the royal family. Young Sacher was given the responsibility of creating a very special dessert for the dinner. The result was the Sacher Torte, which was made with a chocolate cake batter, glazed with apricot jam and covered with chocolate icing. The dinner guests adored the new dessert, and it became an overnight sensation!

Young Franz quickly realized the potential of his new creation and terminated his employment. He left Pressburg, known today as Bratislava, and found a position as a Chief Patissier in Budapest. His reputation as a patissier of some excellence grew, and during this period he received considerable recognition.

In 1848 he returned to his native Vienna and opened his own salon de thé and patisserie. It soon became the fashionable rendezvous of the Viennese nobility. The recipe for the Sacher Torte had changed by that time and the gâteau now contained a filling.

In 1857, Franz Joseph (1830–1916), who was Emperor of Austria-Hungary from 1848, decided to extend the interior of Vienna. This meant the demolition of the city's walls and also the destruction of a famous Viennese theatre. The people of the city protested in vain against the demolition of the theatre, but in 1869 it was flattened to the ground. A new building was designed and erected to take its place, but it remained empty for years.

Eventually, some years later, Franz Sacher and his son Edward, who was also a patissier, purchased the building. The Sacher Hotel was born! The Sacher Hotel and the Sacher Torte have become synonymous with Vienna.

∾ Saint-Honoré Gâteau ∾

This is a type of flan, which is decorated with choux buns and has a cream filling. The base of the gâteau is made with shortcrust pastry or puff pastry trimmings. Choux pastry is then piped around the pastry base and the remainder is piped into small individual choux buns. The base and the buns are then baked in the oven. The filling consists of a rich pastry cream which is mixed with an Italian meringue. During the summer months, gelatine is added to the cream to ensure that the mixture holds better. The little choux buns are then filled with the cream mixture and glazed with a light caramel. Finally, the bases of the buns are dipped in a caramel solution and they are then placed on the outer edge of the circular pastry base in order to form a flan. The gâteau is then filled with Saint-Honoré cream. The Saint-Honoré Gâteau is often decorated with sugar flowers and leaves, or a veil of spun sugar may be placed on top of the gâteau. Small individual gâteaux may also be made with a whipped cream filling, and are often decorated with glacé cherries and angelica.

History

The Saint-Honoré Gâteau originated in a small pastry shop in the Rue Saint Honoré in Paris in 1840. Saint Honoré is the patron saint of bakers, hence the gâteau's name. The owner was a patissier called Chiboust. At that time, the gâteau was made with brioche paste; the base, the crown and the buns were all made from brioche. The filling was pastry cream flavoured with vanilla, coffee or chocolate.

Shortly afterwards, the piping bag and the pastry nozzle were invented.

This heralded a transformation of the Saint-Honoré Gâteau. Instead of brioche paste, the base was made of shortcrust pastry and choux pastry was piped around the base. Choux pastry buns were used as the decoration around the gâteau. The filling was changed and was made from pastry cream, gelatine and meringue or whisked egg whites. The gâteau became an immediate sensation and was sold by the hundreds. As the popularity of the gâteau grew, it was to become the source of many cases of food poisoning at that time, as knowledge of hygiene in the kitchen was extremely limited. The egg whites were kept in hot temperatures within the kitchen, and often came into contact with dirty bowls.

∾ SALLY LUNN ∾

Is a plain teacake made with a yeast dough which consists of the following ingredients: butter, milk, caster sugar, eggs, fresh yeast, plain flour and a little salt. The dough is placed into greased cake tins, covered with oiled paper and allowed to rise until the dough fills the tins. This process takes approximately one hour. They are then baked and can be served hot, with butter or cold, glazed with water icing.

History

The teacake originated in the city of Bath in England, during the eighteenth century. It was named after the proprietress of a bakery in Lilliput Alley. The buns became extremely fashionable during this period, and their popularity soon spread throughout Britain.

∾ SALT – SEL ∾

Salt, or Sodium Chloride, is a mineral deposit which is used in the seasoning of food. Salt is found in solid form such as rock salt and in solutions of seawater and brine wells. Most of the salt which is produced in Great Britain comes from Cheshire. Salt is essential to life: this is highlighted during high temperatures or in times of great exertion. The body loses salt through perspiration, resulting in cramps and fatigue. However, too much salt in the body can lead to high blood pressure, with an increased risk of heart attacks.

History

Salt has been documented as long ago as Sodom and Gomorrah, when the Hebrews reached the cities, salt became the most important source of wealth. During that period, sacrifices were made, and salt was also offered as a gift to the gods. During the time of Troy, salt was regarded as a precious commodity and was always served with meat dishes. At the time of the Roman Empire, the traditional wedding cake was salted. During the twelfth century, the Norsemen imported salt in order to store and keep fish such as cod and herring. In the Middle Ages, sea salt was gathered along the Atlantic coast in France at ports such as Granville, Dieppe and Boulogne. In France, heavy taxes were imposed on the sale of salt from the fourteenth century until the end of the French Revolution in 1799.

∽ SALTED SPICED ALMONDS ∽

The almonds are placed in a large bowl with egg whites, salt, paprika and cayenne pepper, mixed well, then placed on a baking tray and allowed to dry in an oven at a temperature of 100 °C.

History

In England, the spiced almonds were served as an appetizer together with an aperitif as far back as 1830.

∽ SANDWICHES ∽

The great British snack of today! It literally means any type of food, for example, meat or vegetable, which has been sandwiched between two slices of bread. The variety of different types of sandwiches has become endless, as new types of bread are introduced to the market and new and more exotic fillings are concocted. Millions of sandwiches are sold each day in Britain, and the sandwich has become an accepted part of our everyday menu.

History

The sandwich was invented by John Montagu, Fourth Earl of Sandwich (1718–1792), who was a British politician. It is said that as he was an obsessive gambler and often did not wish to leave his game, he asked his master chef to prepare him food which could be eaten at the gambling table, thus enabling him to continue with his game without interruption. Thus the great British sandwich was born!

∽ SAVARIN ∽

A Savarin is quite simply a rich, fermented dough which is placed in a special savarin mould in the shape of a ring. The dough is allowed to prove before it is baked. It is then soaked in a sweet syrup which is flavoured with rum, then glazed with apricot jam and filled with fruit or whipped cream, or a combination of both. The Savarin can be made in a variety of sizes, small ones can be served as petits fours, which are then called Marignans, or they can be served as individual Savarins, or as a large Savarin consisting of up to twenty or more portions. Individual Savarins are usually filled with fruit or pastry cream and glazed with boiling apricot jam. They can also be filled with Crème Chantilly and decorated with glacé cherries and angelica.

History

In 1834, one of the famous Julien brothers, Monsieur Auguste (1821–1887), who was one of the greatest patissiers of his time, saw some patissiers in Bordeaux soaking Genoese sponges with flavoured syrup to make a gâteau which was called 'The Fribourg'. Inspired by this idea, he decided to open a business with his two brothers in the Place de la Bourse, in Paris. His brothers already had a successful and thriving business in Rue d'Antin in Paris. Monsieur Auguste continued to experiment with new recipes and different types of syrup. One of his brothers' creations was the Savarin, which initially was made with wheat flour, butter, eggs, diced orange peel, salt, sugar, yeast and milk. The mixture was then put into a mould and the bottom of the mould was sprinkled with nibbed almonds. The Savarin was then soaked in the syrup specially created by Monsieur Auguste for the new sweet. The Julien brothers made a fortune with their new creations and were responsible for creating numerous other cakes and pastries. Like Antoine Carême, they promoted the profession of a patissier as an enviable one.

∾ SAVARIN, JEAN ANTHELME BRILLAT ∾

Savarin was French and a renowned gastronome. He was also a magistrate.

History

He was born in 1755 in Bellay, a small town near the city of Lyon in the south-east of France. His political career was short-lived, as he opposed the party which supported capital punishment during the French Revolution. He stated that capital punishment should be banned. This was viewed as an act of heresy, and he was forced to flee to avoid possible arrest. He fled to Germany and then to Switzerland, acting as an ambassador for French cuisine. He then sailed to the New World and became a teacher of the violin and the French language in New York.

He returned to France in 1796, to discover that most of his wealth had been seized by the government. Undeterred, he regained his position and was eventually promoted to General Secretary of the French army in Germany.

He was regarded not only as a gastronome because of his great love of food, but also as an intellectual. He spoke several languages fluently and was interested in archaeology, astronomy and chemistry. He wrote several essays, one on political economy and another on duels.

His main interest, however, was food, and he was a valued customer at Procope and Tortoli, which was an extremely fashionable eating place in Paris. He was a great promoter of the new restaurants which offered a menu at a fixed price, a revolutionary idea at the time. He also entertained a great deal in his hotel suite in Rue de Richelieu. Among his guests was Alexandre Balthazar Laurent Grimod de la Revnière (a well-known French gastronome and writer) who praised his table. However, gastronomes such as Antoine Carême criticized his behaviour at the table, stating, that 'invariably after a meal, Savarin fell asleep'.

In 1825 he published a book which immortalized him. It was called *The Physiology of Taste*. On 20 January 1826, he died of pneumonia. Although Savarin had not created his own recipes, he was regarded as one of the greatest promoters of French cuisine.

～ SAVILLUM ～

It was a type of pudding and was eaten with a spoon. It was made from wheat flour, curd cheese, honey and eggs. The mixture was baked in an oiled earthenware mould which was covered with a lid. When cooked, it was brushed with melted honey and dredged with poppy seeds.

History

The pudding dates back to Roman times.

～ SAVOY CAKE – GÂTEAU DE SAVOIE ～

Savoy Cake is a type of sponge made with the yolks of eggs, flour, sugar and cornflour, to which whisked egg whites are added to make the sponge mixture lighter. The mixture can be made into a cake, or it can also be made into small individual biscuits. The cake or biscuits are usually served for afternoon tea. The sponge can also be used in the production of small fancy cakes, petits fours glacés or large decorated gâteaux.

History

Savoy Cake was created by the Executive Chef of Count Amedée VI of Germany, Count of the Duchy of Savoy (1373–1383). The chef decided to name the cake Savoie, in honour of his master. When it was first created the cake was baked in a thick wooden mould, at a low temperature, and was cooked for a relatively long time.

The cake enjoyed a great reputation in the eighteenth century in France. In 1788, the Marquis de Sade (1740–1814), who was imprisoned in the Bastille in Paris for a series of sexual offences, wrote to his wife complaining about the quality of the Savoy Cake which she had sent to him. Its popularity grew throughout the nineteenth and twentieth centuries, not only in France, but spreading across the Channel to Britain and inland across Europe. In Europe the cake is known as Gâteau de Savoie; in Britain it is known simply as Savoy Cake.

∾ SCONES –
GALETTES ÉCOSSAISES ∾

Scones are made with a mixture of flour, eggs, fat, milk, salt and a raising agent. The raising agent is essential in this recipe. Originally buttermilk was used in the recipe. The ingredients are mixed to a sticky dough, which is turned out onto a well floured board. The dough should be handled as little as possible and should be rolled lightly into a round. Using a small round pastry cutter to cut into individual shapes, the scones are then egg-washed and baked quickly in a very hot oven or on a girdle. Scones can be either sweet or savoury. Sweet scones can be made by adding ingredients such as treacle and raisins to the basic dough. Savoury scones are usually made with the addition of cheese. Scones are usually served with afternoon tea and they can be eaten either hot or cold with butter, jam, honey or cream.

History

Scones are an old traditional Scottish recipe. The word 'scone' comes from the Gaelic word *Sgonn*. Originally scones were baked over hot stones. Large round shapes were made with the dough and were then marked with a blade to make the sign of the cross, which allowed them to be easily broken into four cakes when cooked. During that time they were known as a Bannock, a derivative of the Gaelic word *Bannach*, which translated into English means cake. The Bannock may also at that time have been referred to as Communion Bread.

Scones are cut into small individual shapes with a pastry cutter before baking. Another term which is often used is Drop Scones. These are quite different, and are made from a batter mixture which is dropped onto the girdle, hence the name Drop Scones. They are thin, light and spongy.

Over the centuries, the original hard biscuit has changed into the much lighter, softer cake of today, achieved by the introduction of bicarbonate of soda, buttermilk and a finer flour into the original recipe.

∾ SELKIRK BANNOCK ∾

This is a rich yeast bun which is shaped like a cob loaf. It is made with bread flour, lard, butter, milk, yeast, sugar, sultanas, raisins and mixed peel. The ingredients are mixed into a soft dough which is kneaded and then allowed to go through a process of fermentation. It is then shaped into a ball, proved and baked in the oven until golden brown in colour. When cool, the bannock is glazed with a syrup of sugar and water. It is served in slices with butter.

History

The Selkirk Bannock is a Scottish speciality. The recipe was created by a Scottish baker called Robert Douglas who had a small bakery in the market town of Selkirk in the Scottish borders. This delicious Bannock is not only popular in Scotland, but is known and appreciated worldwide.

∾ SHORTBREAD ∾

Shortbread is an old traditional Scottish recipe for biscuits which were associated with Christmas and Hogmanay, the name for the Scottish New Year. The biscuit is made of sweet paste of a very short texture, consisting of plain flour, salt, sugar and butter. The proportion of butter to flour is high: three-quarters of fat to one-quarter of flour. Butter is always used as the fat in the mixture, therefore it is extremely rich in flavour. Shortbread is baked in a slow oven. The shape of the biscuit varies; ingredients and recipe also vary from region to region in Scotland. In Edinburgh it is decorated with peel and almonds, whilst in Ayrshire the recipe is enhanced by the addition of cream and eggs. Another recipe, which is called Bride's Bun, comes from the Orkneys and Shetland Islands and contains caraway seeds.

History

Shortbread originated in Scotland. It is a descendant of the ancient Yale Bannock, a large round cake which was decorated with notches around the outer edge to symbolize the rays of the sun. Originally it was made with rough, untreated flour; however, as white flour became available, bakers tried out different recipes and shapes, giving us the Shortbread we know today. The most popular shapes are Shortbread Fingers and Petticoat Tails. There are many interesting stories as to how the different shapes and names were derived. For example, several theories exist as to how the shape of Petticoat Tails evolved. One theory is that in Edinburgh, during the Elizabethan era, it was extremely fashionable for the gentrified ladies of the city to wear petticoat hoops underneath their dresses, to enhance the full gored skirt of that era. An enterprising Scottish baker copied the shape of the ladies' dresses with the Shortbread paste, and the biscuits became a popular novelty. Another explanation is that in France a similar type of small biscuit was made purely with butter and were known as Petites Gatelles, but through mispronunciation of the French name by the Scottish, it became known as Petticoat Tails. This theory is quite feasible, as Scotland and France had a very strong link with each other during that period.

Today, Shortbread is available and eaten throughout the year. Originally, however, the biscuit was served only at Christmas and Hogmanay. Bakers would decorate the Shortbread with heather or with festive messages, and many were sent as gifts to the hundreds of Scottish families who had emigrated to the New World. However, the majority of bakers left the Shortbread unadorned except for the traditional notched edge. Traditionally the Shortbread biscuit, or a generous slice of black bun, was given with a dram of whisky to the first person who visited a house after the stroke of twelve midnight on New Year's Eve (a 'first footer'). This custom is still practised in many households in Scotland today. Shortbread was also served as a speciality cake at the wedding feast. The Bride's Bun, which also originated in Scotland, was a large biscuit which contained caraway seeds and was either cooked in the oven or on a girdle. A large sweet was placed in the centre to decorate it, and guests would simply break off a piece of the biscuit to eat.

∾ SHORTCRUST PASTRY – PÂTE BRISÉE ∾

Shortcrust pastry can be used to make either sweet or savoury dishes. It is made with plain flour, butter or cake margarine, a pinch of salt and very cold water. The quantity of fat used to flour is half. The method used to make shortcrust pastry is called the 'rubbing in' method. In order to incorporate the fat into the flour, it is rubbed into the flour between the fingertips until the mixture has reached a crumbly texture, almost like breadcrumbs. Cold water is then added slowly to the mixture, which is worked carefully until the pastry has reached a short texture. The pastry is allowed to rest before use. Shortcrust pastry is used in the production of sweet and savoury baked goods such as pies, flans and tarts. In France and Italy, this pastry is often enriched by adding eggs and sugar and is called Pâte à Foncer.

History

Pliny the Elder, a Roman cookery writer and social historian, recorded that a type of shortcrust pastry was made during Roman times, using rough flour, water and oil.

As early as 1250, a type of shortcrust pastry was made in France. The recipe for the pastry included flour, animal fat, salt and sugar. The famous medieval chef and cookery writer, Taillevent (1314–1395), in his book *Le Viandier*, which was published in 1379, explains that shortcrust pastry was made extensively during that time and was used in the production of sweet and savoury pies, tarts and flans.

In Elizabethan England, tarts were made with a rich shortcrust pastry with a filling of fruit and flowers. The pastry was also used to make Florentines, which had either a sweet or savoury filling.

∾ SHREWSBURY CAKES ∾

The cakes are made with plain flour, butter, caster sugar, eggs and salt and are flavoured with the zest of lemon, caraway seeds or ratafia. The ingredients are mixed into a paste which is rolled out on a board sprinkled with sugar. The paste is then cut into shapes with a plain or serrated pastry cutter. The little cakes are gently baked until light brown in colour.

Shrewsbury Cakes and biscuits have most certainly put the town of Shrewsbury on the map! These delightful little cakes and biscuits originated in the town in the sixteenth century or perhaps before, because by that date they had been well documented in records kept during that period. They continued to be popular throughout the centuries. Today, the cakes and biscuits remain a speciality of the town of Shrewsbury.

∾ SIMNEL CAKE ∾

Is a fruit cake which has a thin layer of marzipan on the top.

History

The English word 'simnel' is a derivative of the French word *simenel*, which comes from the Latin word *siminellus*, meaning fine bread. Originally the Simnel was a type of bread and was popular in medieval England. By the seventeenth century, the word 'simnel' described a rich fruit cake which had a strip of marzipan running through the middle of the cake. It resembled the German speciality cake called Stollen, which was traditionally eaten at Christmas. The rich English Simnel Cake is made especially to celebrate Easter in England. The recipe changed over the years; the marzipan filling disappeared and the fruit cake was given a marzipan topping instead.

∾ SINGIN' HINNY ∾

Is made with plain flour, baking powder, lard, currants, milk, cream, sugar and a little salt. The dry ingredients are mixed in a bowl and the fat is rubbed into the flour. The currants are added and then the milk and cream are stirred into the mixture to make a soft dough. The dough is rolled into a large round and cooked slowly on a girdle until golden brown on both sides. It is served in slices with butter.

History

This is an old northeast of England recipe dating back hundreds of years. It is the English equivalent of a Scottish scone. The name, Singin' Hinny, refers to the sizzling sound the Hinny makes while it is cooking, and Hinny is a term of endearment used by Geordies which simply means honey. The term Hinny is still used widely by the people in this northern region of England.

∾ SOUFFLÉ ∾

Soufflés may be hot or cold and can be either sweet or savoury. The following recipes are the main types of soufflés.

Sweet Hot Soufflé

This is made with a rich, hot pastry cream which is flavoured. The pastry cream can be flavoured with coffee, chocolate, liqueurs or zest of fruits. Whisked egg whites are folded into the mixture, which is then poured into a prepared ramekin dish which has been buttered and sugared. It is then baked in the oven. The sweet hot soufflé is usually served with an accompanying sauce.

Example: Soufflé Grand Marnier.

Hot Soufflé Pudding

Hot soufflé puddings are made from a mixture of flour, cornflour or unsweetened custard powder. These ingredients are creamed together with butter and sweetened boiling milk is then added slowly to the creamed mixture. The mixture is then poured back into the pan and allowed to boil until it thickens. It is removed from the heat and allowed to cool before the egg yolks are added to the mixture. Whisked egg whites are folded into the mixture, which is then poured into ramekin moulds which have been greased with butter and coated with sugar. The soufflés are partly cooked in a bain-marie and finished off in a moderate oven. When cooked, they are turned out of the moulds onto a dessert plate and served with a hot sauce, for example, Crème Anglaise. Hot soufflé puddings are made in a variety of flavours; each flavour determines the name of the soufflé.

Examples: Hot Lemon Soufflé, Hot Chocolate Soufflé.

Sweet Cold Soufflé

This is a mixture of egg yolks and sugar which are whisked together over a bain-marie until light and fluffy. Melted gelatine is added to the mixture. It is then removed from the heat and flavoured with fruit zest, fruit purée, fruit juice or a combination of all of these. The mixture is whisked until it is cool. Whipped cream is then added to the mixture. Either whisked egg whites or an Italian meringue is also added. The mixture is then poured into ramekin dishes which have been lined on the outside with greaseproof paper. The paper should be several centimetres above the level of the dish and secured with an elastic band. The mixture should reach a level of at least two centimetres above the dish. The soufflés are then placed in the refrigerator to set.

Example: Soufflé Milanaise.

Sweet Iced Soufflé

This is a mixture of whipped cream and Italian meringue with the addition of fruit purée. It can also be made with egg yolks, syrup, whisked egg whites and whipped cream, and is always flavoured with a liqueur.

Example: Iced Strawberry Soufflé.

Savoury Hot Soufflé

This soufflé is made with a basic white sauce or a Béchamel sauce, to which a variety of different ingredients may be added to flavour the soufflé. For example, popular flavourings are cheese, shellfish and game purée. Whisked egg whites are then added to the sauce and the mixture is poured into greased ramekin dishes and then baked in the oven. It is essential that hot soufflés, either sweet or savoury, be served immediately when they come out of the oven, as when the soufflé, which has risen considerably, comes into contact with the cold air it begins to fall.

Example: Cheese Soufflé.

History

Soufflé is a French word and comes from the verb *souffler*, which translated into English means to puff or to blow up, referring to the way the mixture increases in volume. The classic soufflé which we know today was the creation of Antoine Carême (1784–1833). However, puddings had been made light and fluffy by the addition of meringue for a considerable number of years before his soufflé creation.

The soufflé was originally made in a croustade, which was a straight-sided pastry case into which the soufflé mixture was poured. The croustade was not eaten, but was only used as a container in which to bake the soufflé. The idea of the croustade resulted in the invention of our present soufflé dishes with straight sides. Antoine Carême's creation was helped by the fact that the new ovens introduced at that time were heated by air draft, replacing the old ovens which had been fuelled by hot coals. The old ovens did not provide a regulated heat, whereas the new ovens provided a regulated heat which was essential for the soufflé mixture to rise to perfection.

∾ SOUFFLÉ ROTHSCHILD ∾

This is a hot soufflé consisting of a rich confectioner's custard, mixed with candied fruit which is macerated in a liqueur, usually Denziger Coldswasser, which contains minute particles of gold metal and whisked egg whites. When cooked, the soufflé is dredged with icing sugar before serving.

History

The soufflé is named after the illustrious Jewish banking family. Originally the family were moneylenders and eventually moved into the world of banking and finance. The name Rothschild became a synonym of wealth. Today, the Rothschild family are associated not only with the world of banking but are also famous for their excellent vineyards, which produce some of the world's finest wines, such as Château Lafitte and Château Mouton-Rothschild.

∾ SOURIS MERINGUE ∾

This is a little cake which is made with French meringue. The meringue is placed into a piping bag and the mixture is piped into small shapes to resemble the body of a mouse. The shapes are then baked in a slow oven. When cooked, the meringues are allowed to cool and are brushed with soft butter cream and rolled in chocolate vermicelli. To complete the illusion, currants are used for the eyes, almonds are used to imitate the ears and a small tail is made with a thin strip of angelica.

History

Souris, translated into English, means mouse. The small cakes are known simply as Meringue Mice in France. They were created in France in the middle of the nineteenth century and remain a popular novelty cake today, especially for children. In Britain in the early twentieth century, small cakes were made in the shape of mice using pink and white sugar fondant and remained extremely popular until the middle of the twentieth century.

∾ SOYER, ALEX BENOIT ∾

Soyer was one of the greatest chefs in the nineteenth century. He was born in Meaux-en-Brie, a small town near Paris. He created the Sauce Espagnol and the Demi-glace sauce, which remain the most important basic sauces in French cookery. He made a fortune by patenting his sauces and writing books. However, he became bankrupt after opening his own restaurant, and died penniless in 1858 at the age of forty-nine.

∾ SPONGE ∾

The term 'Sponge' is used to describe a light-textured cake which is made with a mixture of four main ingredients of flour, sugar, fat and eggs. The quantities of the ingredients used differ in each recipe. Also, a variety of other ingredients may be added to flavour the basic sponge mixture. The two main methods used to make the lightest textured sponge cakes are the whisking method and the creaming method. These are methods of aeration to enable the mixture to rise. Chemical raising agents may also be used in the recipe. These methods produce the classic Victoria Sponge and the Genoese Sponge.

History

The cake was probably called a sponge because of its close resemblance to the texture and colour of the natural sponge, the small marine animal. The first types of sponge batters were created in France. However, it was not until after the beginning of the eighteenth century that the sponge became much lighter, using eggs as a method of aeration. It became common practice to beat the egg yolks and egg whites separately before mixing them together. Sponge cakes and sponge puddings became popular in England in the middle of the eighteenth century.

∾ SPOTTED DICK ∾

This is a sweet suet pudding which is made with self-raising flour, breadcrumbs, shredded suet, sugar, currants and milk, which are mixed together in a bowl. The soft dough is shaped in the form of a roll and wrapped loosely in greased greaseproof paper or silicon paper. It is finally wrapped in silver foil and steamed for up to two hours. Spotted Dick is usually served with a custard sauce.

History

At one time the pudding was called Spotted Dog. The origin of the name Spotted Dick is not clear. It is an English creation, and is firmly established as a classic English pudding of some renown. The heavy, sweet pudding dates back to the early nineteenth century. Served with lashings of thick custard, it is quite a substantial dish!

∾ STEAM AND PRESSURE COOKER – AUTOCLAVE ∾

This is a metal pan with a lid in which food is cooked in a liquid, usually water. The food is cooked under pressure from the steam of the liquid which reaches a higher temperature than 100 °C, which is boiling point. Modern pressure cookers have a safety valve which can be adjusted to control the steam pressure.

History

It was invented by the French scientist, Denis Papin (1647–1712). He was born in Chitenay, not far from the city of Blois. He worked extensively on the steam and pressure machine, resulting in the first cooker of its type.

∾ STOLLEN CAKE ∾

Is a spicy loaf cake made with fruits which have been steeped in rum. An added delight is a strip of marzipan which runs through the centre of the cake. The cake is baked in a loaf tin and, when cooked, is generously dredged with sugar.

History

Stollen Cake originated in Germany. For centuries this cake has been eaten in Germany during the Christmas season. The spicy loaf was originally round in shape. The Stollen, which is thought to date back to the fourteenth century, is often referred to as Christollen or Striezel. It was introduced to the British by Prince Albert, a member of the German royal family who in 1840 married Victoria, Queen of Great Britain and Ireland from 1837. The Prince Consort not only brought the Stollen Cake to the British, but was also responsible for introducing many other Christmas symbols and traditions – notably the Christmas tree, which he popularized in this country.

✑ STOVE ✑

The stove was invented by an Anglo-American physicist called Benjamin Thompson who was born in 1753 in Massachusetts, in the United States of America. He was made Count Rumford in 1791.

✑ STRAWBERRY – FRAISE ✑

Is the fruit of the plant genus *Fragaria*. There are hundreds of different varieties of the strawberry. The fruit is highly flavoured and delicious when eaten raw. Strawberries are a very good source of vitamin C. Commercially cultivated strawberries have only one crop during the summer.

The patissier uses the fruit widely in the production of fruit tarts, mousses, shortcake, ice cream, fools and numerous desserts. Its beautiful rich red colour and unusual shape make it ideal for decoration purposes in gâteaux and a variety of desserts. The fruit is also wonderful for jam making. And a British summer without seasonal strawberries served with cream would not be the same!

History

Strawberries have grown in the wild in temperate climates for thousands of years. During the time of the Roman Empire, several fruit were well documented; however, strawberries were rarely mentioned. For example, in Italy during this period a gastronome and poet called Quintus Horatius praised wild blackberries as a wonderful fruit which could be eaten at the end of a meal or used for medicinal purposes in the form of a syrup. Yet strawberries, which must have grown in abundance at that time, are not mentioned.

However, it was not until the fourteenth century that strawberries were cultivated. It is documented that a wild strawberry plant called *Fragaria Vesca* was planted in the Louvre garden in Paris for Charles V (1337–1380), who was King of France from 1364. By the eighteenth century, strawberries had become extremely popular as a fruit in France and are frequently mentioned in French literature of that period. For example, Madame

Pompadour (1721–1764), one of Louis XV's mistresses (he reputedly had sixty-four mistresses), instructed her gardeners to grow strawberries in hot-houses in the Garden of Trianon at the château of Versailles. Louis XV adored the fruit, and by 1760 ten different types of strawberries were grown at Versailles. The most popular varieties were known as the Strawberry of Versailles (1761), and the Alp Strawberry, which was cultivated in England in 1762.

Another interesting story regarding the fruit which is well documented in history books was at the Battle of Waterloo in 1815. Emperor Napoleon Bonaparte was engaged in battle with the English led by the Duke of Wellington. He desperately awaited reinforcements who were marching towards Waterloo, headed by Marshal Grouchy. In desperation, Napoleon sent a messenger, General Gerard, begging Grouchy to make haste. Gerard reputedly found Marshal Grouchy in the village of Sart-a-Wachain, on the road to Namur, eating his favourite fruit, strawberries, from a basket. Grouchy refused to march to help his Emperor, and consequently the thirty thousand reinforcements arrived too late to save the day and Napoleon lost the battle. The strawberry has a lot to answer for!

In the early seventeenth century, new hybrids from America were imported from the state of Virginia. In the late eighteenth century, the first Scottish strawberry appeared.

∾ STRAWBERRY ROMANOFF – FRAISE ROMANOFF ∾

The sweet consists of fresh orange segments and fresh strawberries which are soaked in fresh orange juice flavoured with the orange liqueur Curaçao. The sweet is served in fluted glasses and decorated with piped Crème Chantilly and roasted flaked almonds.

History

Strawberry Romanoff is named after the Imperial Russian family name of Romanoff of 1613, which remained the royal name until the assassination of Tsar Nicholas II (1868–1918), Tsarina Alexandra and their entire family during the Russian Revolution in 1918.

∾ STRUDEL, APPLE ∾

This is made with a very elastic pastry which consists of flour, water, salt, sugar, eggs and oil. It is very important to give as much elasticity to the pastry as possible. Once made, the pastry is brushed with oil and allowed to rest for about one hour. The pastry is worked by hand, using the finger-tips, which have been dipped in oil. Gradually the pastry is stretched from underneath until it is in the shape of a square and is paper-thin. This process should take place over a large tablecloth which has been dusted with flour. The pastry is then generously brushed with melted butter and spread with a filling of apple slices, cinnamon, flavoured sugar and raisins. Melted butter is then poured over the filling. Breadcrumbs are sometimes added to absorb the extra moisture which is created by the juice extracted from the fresh apples during baking. The pastry is then rolled into a large sausage shape, almost like a Swiss Roll, and very carefully, because it is extremely fragile, and is placed onto a baking tray in the shape of an S. It is then brushed with melted butter and baked in the oven. Apple Strudel is served hot, cut into slices and accompanied by fresh cream. Strudel can also be made with a savoury filling.

History

The word 'Strudel' is a derivative of the old German word *Streden. Streden,* translated into English, means to boil or bubble. This is an apt description of the pastry, as after baking it often appears very wrinkly and bubbly on the surface. The pastry is thought to have originated in Bavaria in the south of Germany or in Austria, and was the creation of a Hungarian patissier. It has also been suggested that the recipe for Strudel is an adaptation of the Turkish sweet, Baklava, which consists of thin layers of filo pastry sandwiched together with a filling of chopped nuts. The pastry is coated in a very sweet syrup.

∽ SUET PASTRY ∽

This is made with self-raising flour, or plain flour may be used with the addition of baking powder, salt, shredded suet and very cold water to mix. The quantity of fat to flour is half. Suet is the fat surrounding the kidneys of animals; beef suet is the most common type of suet used. All the ingredients are mixed together in a bowl and very cold water is added until a dough which has an elastic consistency has been achieved. It is then kneaded until smooth. This pastry can be used for both sweet and savoury dishes. If the pastry is for a sweet dish, sugar is added to the recipe and cold milk replaces the water. For best results, the pastry should be boiled or steamed; however, suet pastry dishes take a long time to cook using this method. Sometimes the pastry is baked, but it tends to become hard using this method of cooking. Classic sweet dishes such as Jam Roly Poly, Baked Apple Dumpling and Spotted Dick are made with suet pastry. Savoury dishes include Steak and Kidney Pie and Leek Pudding.

History

Hundreds of years ago, suet puddings were boiled in metal pots which were placed on a support over a fire. At the beginning of the seventeenth century in England, the pudding cloth was invented. All the ingredients to make the suet pudding were placed in the cloth and then steamed or boiled.

This simple invention was to herald the creation of an endless selection of English puddings, both sweet and savoury. England became the home of the pudding!

In 1714 England had a new King, George I (1660–1727), who was the first Hanoverian King of Great Britain and Ireland. He did not like England and never even attempted to learn the language. George disliked English food and brought with him to England his own German chefs. He adored suet puddings; these heavy steamed puddings were a speciality in his homeland. During his reign, a variety of new steamed suet puddings were introduced to the British. One of his favourite recipes was the Apple Dumpling, and this was to become a classic English steamed pudding.

In the nineteenth century, countless recipes for steamed suet puddings, both sweet and savoury, appeared in a number of English cookery books. By that date, the Plum Pudding was firmly established as the British national dish!

∽ SUGAR – SUCRE ∽

Sugar is a carbohydrate which gives energy. It is obtained from plants. The two main plants from which it is extracted are sugar cane and sugar beet. All sugars which are refined contain 100 per cent sucrose. Crude brown sugar contains traces of proteins and minerals.

History

The word for sugar in French is *sucre*. Sucre is a derivative of the old French word *sukere*, from where the English word 'sugar' comes. Sugar was discovered by a Persian military expedition in the valley of the Indus. The Polynesians used sugar cane as a source of food. In the fourth century, Alexander the Great (356–323 BC) conquered Asia, and the sugar cane was given the name of Sacred Reed and brought back to the West. The process of refining sugar is of Persian origin. Sugar then found its way into Egypt and Arabia, and by the time the Romans had conquered Europe sugar cane had already been introduced.

In the Middle Ages, sugar was sold in France as *poudre de sucre*, which translated into English means powdered sugar. Of course, it was not as pure as the sugar sold today. During this period, sugar was also used as a method of payment. In 1323, the sugar from Cyprus and Alexandria was an article of brokerage in Pisa in Italy. Sugar consignments from Cyprus, Rhodes, Syria and Alexandria arrived at the French port of Marseilles in the south of France. The sugar was still brown and unrefined and was called *cassonade*. Sugar was also at that time shaped into cones of which there were a few different types; however, these cones broke easily during transportation.

In the fifteenth century, it is documented that Charles VII of France (1403–1461), who was King of France from 1422, received a consignment of sugar from Venice in Italy which was estimated at a value of one million pounds. In 1493 Christopher Columbus introduced sugar cane to Santo Domingo in the Canary Islands.

By the seventeenth century, England dominated the sugar market of the world. Britain and France were in constant conflict. Britain had supremacy over the French at sea, and France subsequently lost colonies to the British. Sugar became a very expensive commodity. In 1807, for one year, Napoleon Bonaparte (1769–1821) started the Continental Blockade, forbidding entry of British goods into Europe. Sugar prices soared, and sugar became rare. On 2 January 1812, Benjamin Delessert (1773–1847), encouraged by Napoleon, opened a factory in Passy, not far from Paris, where for the first time sugar was successfully extracted from sugar beet rather than from sugar cane. In 1747, some sixty-five years earlier, a German scientist, Maraggraf, successfully extracted sugar from beetroot as an experiment, but not as a commercial venture. In England, the first factory to process sugar beet was opened in Maldon in 1832. However, many years were to pass before pure sugar was obtained in the form we know today.

Sugar Beet – Sucre de Betteraves

This is extracted from the genus *Beta Vulgaris*, belonging to the *Chenapodiaceae* family. Sugar beet grows in temperate climates in Europe, the USA, and Canada. The seeds are planted in March to early April and the sugar beet is harvested from the end of September to early December. The sugar is extracted from the white flesh of the root which contains approximately 16 per cent of raw sugar. During the process of refining the sugar beet, syrup, molasses and sugar crystals are the main by-products. Almost ten million tons of raw sugar beet are produced by farmers in Britain each year. It provides more than half of the home market's sugar requirement; the other half is imported from tropical countries where the sugar is extracted from sugar cane.

The patissier uses the refined sugar extracted from sugar beet in an extensive list of cakes and pastries. However, many patissiers prefer the refined sugar extracted from sugar cane to make cooked sugar solutions such as pulled sugar, blown sugar and spun sugar. Large manufacturers in bakery, confectionery and ice cream goods use sugar which has been extracted from sugar beet. The sugar beet industry was established in the early twentieth century in Britain.

Sugar Cane – Sucre de Canne

It comes from the genus *Saccharum Officinarum*, belonging to the *Gentianaceae* family. The sugar cane plant requires rich moist soil, plenty of sunlight and a lot of water. The plant is grown in Mauritius, Barbados, Jamaica, Madagascar and other countries which have a climate suitable for its growth. The sugar cane needs to be planted and allowed to grow for twelve to eighteen months before it is harvested and cut. The dry leaves are known as trash and are often burned off before harvesting begins. The canes are cut as close to the ground as possible. Once cut, the cane is delivered to the factory, where it is washed and the extracted juices are processed to produce the raw sugar. The sugar is sent in its raw state to factories throughout the world for further refining.

In the production of sugar from sugar cane, there is no waste. All the by-products of the sugar cane processing industry are used. Left-over cane pulp, called bagasse, is burned as renewable non-fossil fuel in the boilers and furnaces of the factories to power the mill. The other by-product, known as cane molasses, is converted into rum, baker's yeast, or industrial alcohol.

Types of Sugar and their uses in patisserie

Loaf or Cube Sugar

Because of its pure state, this type of sugar is free from unwanted matter such as dust from the atmosphere. It is the ideal choice for the patissier in the production of cooked sugar solutions.

Preserving Sugar

This type of sugar is suitable for jam and jelly making. Preserving sugar which is manufactured today has pectin added to it during the manufacturing process. Pectin helps the jam or jelly to set. It is therefore extremely useful when making jams with fruit which are low in pectin content.

Granulated Sugar

Granulated sugar is used extensively by patissiers in the production of syrups, fruit sorbets and sweet coulis.

Caster Sugar

Because of its fine particles, this sugar is ideal for the production of cakes, sponges, meringues and pastry goods.

Icing Sugar

This sugar, which comes in a fine white powdered form, is mainly used by the patissier in the production of Swiss meringues, pastillage, royal icing and water icing, which are used for decoration purposes.

Light Brown and Brown Sugar

This type of sugar is extracted from sugar cane and sugar beet. Because of their mild flavour they are used extensively by the patissier in the production of cakes, biscuits, fruit cocktails and such classic desserts as Crème Brûlée and Crème Caramel.

Nibbed Sugar

These are tiny sugar particles, about three millimetres in diameter. They are white in colour and are used mainly by the patissier to decorate cakes and pastry goods, for example, Bath Buns and Gâteau d'Artois.

Raw Sugar (Unrefined)

Sugars which come under this heading are Demerara, Dark Muscovado and Golden Granulated. These sugars are excellent for the production of rich fruit cakes and Christmas Pudding.

Maple Sugar

This sugar is used mainly in the production of maple syrup, which is usually served as an accompaniment to waffles and pancakes. The syrup can also be used as a filling in steamed sponges.

Malt Sugar or Extract

Is used in the production of cakes, puddings, and also in bread making.

These are the main forms of sugar. However, the patissier also uses other sugars, such as glucose, fructose, lactose and honey.

By-products obtained during the refining of Sugar

Golden Syrup

This is used by patissiers in the production of sponge puddings, Florentines and steamed puddings.

Treacle

It is used in the production of baked goods such as gingerbread, treacle scones and treacle tarts.

Molasses

This by-product is rarely used by the patissier.

Sugar Syrup – Sirop de Sucre

A sugar syrup is basically a solution of water and sugar, approximately 300 to 400 ml of water to each kilogramme of sugar. The solution is brought to the boil. If agitated the sugar solution would crystallize and produce a mass of coarse crystals. To prevent this occurring chemicals are added, for example glucose syrup, cream of tartar or lemon juice.

Density and its uses

According to the amount of sugar present in a syrup, its uses will be varied. See the table overleaf.

Sugar syrup – Sirop de sucre
Allow syrups to boil for 30 seconds before taking readings

Density		Approximate		Saccharometer Densimetre (French)			
Baume		Sugar	Water	Quantity		Density Reading	Uses
							Some syrups will be used
Hot	Cold	Grs.	Ml.	Hot Ml.	Cold Ml.	Boiling	hot, some will be used cold, depending upon their uses
10							
11							
12	16					1.0907	Ice granité
13	17	200	500	625	575		Ice granité
14	18	250	500	650	600	1.1074	Ice granité
15	19					1.1159	Wine and/or alcohol sorbets
16	20	275	500	670	625	1.1247	Fruit sorbets, babas, savarins
17	21	300	500	680	635	1.1335	Fruit sorbets, babas, savarins
18	22	325	500	700	645	1.1425	Large savarins
19	23	350	500	710	660	1.1515	
20	24	375	500	730	680	1.1609	Large babas
21	25	400	500	740	685	1.1699	
22	26	425	500	750	710	1.1799	
23	28	475	500	780	740	1.1896	
24	29	525	500	820	770	1.1995	
25						1.2095	
26	30	575	500	850	800	1.2197	
27	31½	625	500	890	840	1.2301	
28	32½	675	500	910	850	1.2407	100°C/212°F Iced parfaits
29	33	360	250	480	430	1.2515	
30	34	385	250	490	450	1.2624	101°C/274°F Fruit coulis, butter cream, iced parfaits
31	35	410	250	500	460	1.2736	
31½	35½	435	250	510	480		
32	36	450	250	520	485	1.2850	
32½	36½	475	250	540	495		
33½	37½	525	250	565	510	1.3023	103°C/218°F = 33°B Candied sugar
34	39½	575	250	600	550	1.3082	104°C/220°F Candied sugar
35						1.3199	105°C/222°F Candied sugar
36	40	630	250	630	580	1.3310	
36½	40½	680	250	680	600		
37	41	730	250	690	610		
38	41½	780	250	700	620	1.3574	107°C/225°F Iced mousses Very thick syrup
39	43	830	250	720	630		
39½	43½	880	250	760	640		
40	44	960	250	780	660	1.3834	110°C/230°F

Sugar, Rock – Sucre Rocher

As its name implies, this is sugar which gives an extremely attractive rock effect which is most effective for display purposes, especially if it is decorated with sugar flowers and leaves. Sucre Rocher is a cooked sugar solution which consists of crystallized sugar, water and colouring. It is cooked to a temperature of 145°C and then royal icing is added to the solution. The addition of royal icing forces the mass to crystallize. Once cold, it is fairly easy to shape.

History

Sucre Rocher was created by a Spanish patissier called Bartolomeo in 1838, in the city of Barcelona in Spain. He was experimenting with sugar solutions and decided to add royal icing to a cooked sugar solution. After a great deal of trial and error he managed to obtain a white sugar crystallized mass which he coloured. The sugar was cut into various lengths and sizes and sold as a confectionery. He named his new creation Trocadéro, to commemorate the victorious battle won by the Duke of Angoulême at the fortress of the L'Ile de Leon in 1823. In 1842 the sugar was used by the renowned French patissier Chiboust to produce elaborate display pieces.

Sugar, Blown – Sucre Soufflé

This is a solution of sugar, water and glucose. It is cooked to a temperature of between 148°C and 150°C. The sugar mass is poured onto a clean, oiled marble slab and worked until the sugar becomes satinized. To blow the sugar, a ball is cut off from the mass; the ball should still be warm, firm and malleable. A special nozzle and rubber pump are essential to achieve the required shape. The nozzle is inserted into the ball and the ball is then pumped gently and regularly by hand until it gradually swells into a bubble of the desired shape and size. Sugar displays of fruit, fish or birds are popular subjects obtained by this method. They are then cooled quickly by an electric fan and coloured by hand with fine paint brushes and food colourings.

History

Sucre Soufflé was invented by a French patissier called Webel. In the early days, the sugar was blown by inserting a metal tube into the sugar and placing the other end of the tube into the mouth and blowing gently. For reasons of hygiene, a rubber pump with a nozzle is now used.

Sugar, Pulled – Sucre Tiré

This is made from a sugar solution made up of sugar, water, glucose and lemon juice. The addition of glucose and lemon juice prevents the crystallization of the mass. It is cooked at a temperature of between 148°C and 160°C, depending on its use. When it has reached the correct temperature, the sugar mass is allowed to cool by plunging the pan in a bowl of cold water for a few seconds. It is then allowed to stand for a few minutes before pouring. It is then pulled between the fingers while still malleable into the shape desired, for example, flower petals, leaves and ribbons. Sucre Tiré is mostly used for display pieces and confectionery work.

History

Sucre Tiré was invented by a French patissier called Landry in 1883. The greatest patissier in the art of Sucre Tiré in the twentieth century was a Frenchman called Monsieur Tholonait, who created the most elaborate sugar displays.

Sugar, Spun – Sucre Voilé

This is a sugar solution of water, sugar and glucose which is cooked to a temperature of between 155 °C and 165 °C. The solution is allowed to cool until the desired consistency is obtained, approximately two minutes. A work area should be prepared. Lay several sheets of paper over the floor and place two or three lightly oiled broom handles across a table, projecting over the edge. A balloon-shaped metal hand whisk, which has had the top part of the balloon cut off in order to loosen the metal strips, is the most effective piece of equipment to use in order to obtain the desired effect. Dip the whisk into the sugar and, with a quick flicking movement backwards and forwards above the broom handles, allow the sugar to fall or spin into fine sugar threads over the broom handles. This process is where the name Spun Sugar originated. Collect all the fine sugar threads and place on a greased baking tray or silicon paper. Spun Sugar is used in the presentation of large cakes such as Croquembouche or Gâteau Saint-Honoré, as well as in iced confectionery and Petits Fours.

History

Sucre Voilé was created by a French chef called Sabatier, who was the Executive Chef of Louis XVI (1754–1793), King of France from 1774. However, some patissiers claim that the creation belonged to the famous French gastronome, Jules Gouffé (1807–1877).

Sugar Almonds – Dragées

Are almonds coated with a boiled sugar solution. The sugar solution is made in a variety of different colours.

History

There is a great deal of controversy as to exactly where the dragée origi- nated. However, it is documented that in 177 BC the dragée was created by Julius Dragatus, who was the chef of a prominent and wealthy Roman family called Fabius. At that time, the dragées were given to family and friends when a child was born, or at a wedding. The recipe for the sweets during this period was very similar to the recipe which is used today. However, at that time, the almonds were dipped in honey or coated in cane sugar syrup and then allowed to dry. The dragées would not be coloured in the lovely pastel shades we know today. Centuries would pass before improvements were seen in the process of making and presentation of this delicate confectionery.

In France during the seventeenth century, dragées became popular with the aristocracy. Henry III and Henry IV of France were given decorated boxes of dragées at their coronations. Louis XIV (1638–1715), King of France from 1643, started a custom during his reign: at the beginning of each New Year the sweets were distributed to all schoolchildren. This gesture from the King set a fashion. Dragées immediately became more popular, and were to become a symbol of peace, happiness and joy.

In 1750, a master confectioner named Pecquet opened the first shop to specialize in dragées in the Rue des Lombards in Paris. The popularity of the sugar sweets grew, and they were still regarded as tokens of peace, happiness and joy during that period. For example, Frederick William II (1744–1797), King of Prussia from 1786, who occupied the city of Verdun in France in 1792, was presented with a box of dragées by a group of young ladies as a sign of peace. In 1808, Napoleon Bonaparte was presented with a huge cake in the form of an arch. The cake was elaborately decorated with sugar dragées, to commemorate his victory against the Prussians at the Battle of Jena in 1806.

It was years later in France that a patissier modified the original recipe and coated the almonds in cooked sugar. The success of the new recipe was immediate. The production of dragées increased greatly as factories opened and new machinery was invented. They became a speciality, and each city had its own variety. For example, Metz, Nancy, Toulouse, Verdun and Paris produced their own particular recipes for the sweet.

Gradually new ingredients were introduced in the making of dragées, such as chocolate, croquant, marzipan and fondant. Today, some are flavoured with different alcohols and are made in a variety of pastel shades. The sweets are also decorated with silver balls and mimosa. The silvery coating on the balls is made with pure silver and the mimosa decoration encloses a seed of the mimosa flower. They are still given as tokens at weddings and christenings. The traditional French wedding cake, the Croquembouche, is decorated with dragées. France is the biggest manufacturer of the dragée in the world today and exports tons of the sweet each year. Britain also manufactures the sweet, but on a much smaller scale.

Sugar Paste – Pâte Sucrée
and Pâte Sablée

Sugar paste (Pâte Sucrée) is made with plain flour, cake margarine or butter, sugar, eggs and a little salt. Sometimes a raising agent is added to the paste. The method used to make the sugar paste is called the creaming method.

The fat and sugar are creamed together until very light and fluffy. The eggs are then added slowly, and finally the sifted flour, salt and baking powder are folded into the mixture. Because of its very soft consistency, the paste is mixed with a spatula until thoroughly mixed. The pastry should be allowed to rest in a refrigerator before use; this makes it easier to handle. Sugar paste is used in the production of fruit flans, fruit pies and petits fours.

Pâte Sablée can be obtained by using the same ingredients and method as for Pâte Sucrée; however, less sugar is used and a greater quantity of fat. It is very short in texture and is very difficult to work with, and needs to be handled with care. The pastry should be allowed to rest in the refrigerator. Pâte Sablée is used in the production of petits fours secs, small cakes and to make bases for gâteaux and tortens.

History

The Roman social historian, Pliny the Elder (AD 23–AD 79), recorded that a type of sugar paste was made during Roman times, using rough flour, water, oil and honey.

∾ SURPRISE ∾

The name given to a savoury or sweet dish whose ingredients and contents are unknown, for example, Soufflé Surprise.

∾ SWEETS, BOILED – BONBONS ∾

Boiled sweets are made from a solution of sugar and water which is boiled and to which flavouring is added. The list of boiled sweets is endless.

History

Boiled sweets date back to over three thousand years ago, during the time of the Egyptians. The sweets, however, were not made with sugar, but with honey, as sugar had not yet been discovered. During the time of the Crusades, the Christians discovered the use of sugar when invading the East during the twelfth century in the Holy Wars against the Infidels.

It was not until the Renaissance, in the fifteenth century, that sugar replaced honey as a sweetener. However, it was used as a sweetener during that period only by the wealthy, as it was expensive. It was also used at that time for medicinal purposes. A well known remedy for breathing problems was a sugar solution flavoured with liquorice. Another remedy, for stomach pains, was a sugar solution flavoured with violets.

In the seventeenth and eighteenth centuries, Paris was the capital of confectionery, but sugar was not used in its production until the middle of the nineteenth century, when sugar beet was commercially grown in order to produce sugar.

∽ SWISS ROLL – ROULADE / BISCUIT ROULÉ ∽

It is made with a basic Genoese sponge mixture which can be flavoured with either chocolate, coffee or vanilla. Often glycerine is added to the eggs in the sponge mixture in order to soften the structure of the sponge, thus making it easier to roll. The sponge mixture is spread onto a baking tray lined with greaseproof paper which has been well greased. It is baked very quickly in a hot oven. When cooked, the sponge is removed from the tin and allowed to cool before rolling. The surface of the sponge is then spread with the desired filling. A variety of different fillings may be used, for example, flavoured butter cream, ganache, jam, fruit purée or whipped cream. Often a combination of two or more fillings is used. The sponge is then rolled, decorated and served in individual slices.

History

The English name for this cake is very misleading, as it is not in fact a Swiss creation but a French creation! It originated in the French Alps. The French name for the cake, Roulade, comes from the French verb *rouler*, which in English means to roll. The recipe was brought back from France at the beginning of the twentieth century and was christened Swiss Roll by the English. It was probably created in France towards the end of the nineteenth century.

∽ SYLLABUB ∽

Is an old English sweet which was originally made by pouring fresh cows' milk over cider, fruit juice, wine or sherry which resulted in the milk curdling. The curdled mixture was then sweetened with sugar or honey and flavoured with spices. There were many variations of the sweet. The original syllabub was served in glasses accompanied with ratafia biscuits.

Syllabub is making a comeback today in the form of a semi-thick cream dessert which consists of sherry or sweet white wine which is sweetened with sugar and flavoured with lemon zest. The liquid is then mixed with thick cream and whisked until light and frothy. It is served cold in fluted wine glasses and decorated with lemon rind or zest.

History

The Syllabub was a favourite sweet during the reign of Charles II (1630–1685), King of Great Britain and Ireland from 1660.

T

~ TAILLEVENT, GUILLAUME TIREL ~

He was a French Master Chef and medieval cookery writer.

History

Taillevent was born in 1314 in France. His exact date of birth is unknown, as his birth was not recorded. His real name was Guillaume Tirel. Taillevent was a nickname given to him in adolescence.

He started his career at the age of fourteen in the great kitchens of the French royal household of Queen Jeanne d'Évreux and Charles IV (1294–1328), who was King of France from 1322. In 1346, he was promoted to the position of Head Chef and was employed by Philippe de Valois, a French aristocrat. In 1355, he was made a Squire within the household, and years later he was promoted to First Squire.

In the middle of the fourteenth century, his book, *Le Viandier*, was published: it was to be the first medieval cookery book of its kind. In the book he describes in detail the types of food which were eaten by the French during that time. It is a wealth of information which provides an insight into what life for wealthy people in France was like during that period. The book established him not only as a cook of some repute, but also as a social historian. *Le Viandier* was unique, because it covered all aspects of catering during that period. Taillevent, through his writing, contributed immensely to the promotion of French cuisine.

In 1392, he was made Master Chef to Charles VI (1368–1422), who was King of France from 1380. He was held in such high esteem by the French royal household that he was made a noble. Taillevent died in 1395 and was buried with all the honours which reflected his elevated position within the French aristocracy. His tomb is not far from Saint-Germain-en-Laye, on the outskirts of Paris.

~ TALLEYRAND ~

This is made with a savarin dough to which chopped pineapple is added. The dough is placed into a special savarin mould and baked. It is then soaked in syrup and glazed with boiling apricot jam and decorated with pineapple.

History

The Talleyrand was the creation of a French patissier called Avice. He named the pastry after the famous French gastronome and politician, Talleyrand (1754–1838) (see below). Talleyrand was extremely well respected and had a formidable reputation as a gastronome of great knowledge. He helped to promote the reputation of Brie cheese as one of the finest quality cheeses in France. He stated in 1815, 'le Brie est le roi des fromages', which translated into English means, 'Brie is the king of all cheeses'.

∾ TALLEYRAND, PRINCE DE ∾

He was a famous French gastronome and politician.

History

The Prince de Talleyrand was born in France in 1754 into an aristocratic family. His first love was food, and his life was dedicated to promoting French cuisine. During the French Revolution (1789–1799), he was reputed to have the best table in the whole of France. During this period, French cookery was at its most lavish. In 1808, he was employed by Napoleon Bonaparte and given the responsibility for the organization of the catering for all the grand state occasions. In 1832, he was made French Ambassador to England. At his home in London, his reputation as a true gastronome was well and truly established as he hosted a succession of formal dinner parties and banquets which could not be surpassed. He succeeded in illustrating to the English the true excellence and superiority of French cuisine during that period.

∾ TALMOUSE ∾

A Talmouse is made with puff pastry which is rolled out and then cut into rounds with a pastry cutter. The edges of the pastry rounds are brushed with egg-wash and a filling, consisting of choux pastry, Brie cheese and fresh cream, is placed in the middle. The edges of the pastry round are drawn back up into the centre and pinched to close, in order to obtain a ball shape. The small pastry is allowed to rest. It is then brushed with egg-wash and baked in the oven. Before it is served, it is dredged with icing sugar. The pastry is served hot.

History

The pastry dates back to medieval times in France, where it was created. Gastronomic historians have documented in their writings that the savoury pastry reached the height of its popularity in Paris, in the year 1420. Therefore, the Talmouse must have been created before that date. The Talmouse was the favourite pastry of Louis XI (1423–1483), King of France from 1461. During that period, the pastry was made with Brie cheese, cottage cheese and eggs. Brie cheese was used in pastry recipes in France as far back as the eighth century.

Today, Talmouses are not widely popular in France. However, they are still made in a small number of hotels and restaurants.

∾ TANT POUR TANT ∾

Is a mixture made up of equal amounts of caster sugar and ground almonds. It is used extensively by the patissier in the production of desserts, cakes, creams and gâteaux.

History

The mixture was created in 1845 in Bordeaux, by a French patissier named Gareau.

∾ TARTE ANGLAISE ∾

This is made with shortcrust pastry. A flan ring is lined with the pastry and a filling of sweetened apple purée is added to the tart. Starting at the outer edge of the flan ring and working towards the centre, evenly cut apple slices are arranged, slightly overlapping, in a series of circles until the whole surface of the tart is covered with apple slices. The circles of sliced apples create a wonderful decoration. The decoration is the main characteristic of the Tarte Anglaise and distinguishes it from other tarts. The tart is then baked in an oven. It is allowed to cool and is removed from the flan ring. The surface of the tart is brushed with boiling apricot jam to glaze.

History

In 1847, a Polish patissier called Mariote opened a patisserie in Paris in the Rue Lafitte. He introduced to his Parisian customers the Flan Polonais, which was made with brioche dough and had an apple filling. In 1870, he created the Flan Anglais. The original Flan Anglais was made with brioche dough and differed from the Flan Polonais in shape as it was made in a round flan ring. At a later date, it became known as Tarte Anglaise and was made with shortcrust pastry instead of brioche dough.

∾ TARTE TATIN ∾

The tarte is made in a pan or a dish which has a very thick bottom. The bottom of the dish is heavily greased with butter and dredged generously with caster sugar, and cooked to a caramel over a fierce heat. The peeled and cored apples are cut into halves, arranged in layers in the pan and cooked gently. The apples are then covered with a thin layer of pastry. Puff pastry or shortcrust pastry can be used. The tarte is then baked in the oven. When cooked, the surfaces of the pastry are dredged with sugar and can be caramelized either in the oven or under a salamander. It is then turned out of the dish, upside down, and served piping hot. The apple surface can be caramelized with a hot poker as a final decoration, if desired. The hot apple tarte should be served with double cream. Tarte Tatin is an extremely popular dessert in France today, and is regarded as a classic French dessert.

History

Tarte is a fourteenth-century French word which is a derivative of the thirteenth-century French word *tourte*, meaning a savoury or sweet pie.

Tarte Tatin was created in 1850 by two sisters called Stephanie and Caroline Tatin, who ran a small family hotel in Motte-Beuvron, which is south of the city of Orleans in the Loire et Cher district of France. The recipe for Tarte Tatin resulted from an accident in the small restaurant kitchen. Caroline, when taking the apple tarte out of the oven, accidentally dropped the dish onto the table top. It landed upside down, with the cooked apples on the surface and the pastry underneath. Caroline thought it looked quite attractive, and as there was no time to make another tarte she served the tarte to her customers upside down. It was an instant success!

∾ THERMOMETER – THERMOMÈTRE ∾

This is an instrument which is used to measure temperature in either degrees Centigrade or degrees Fahrenheit.

History

The Greek mathematician, Archimedes (287–212 BC), who was born in Syracuse in Sicily, was the first person to formulate a low liquid displacement, known as the Archimedes Principle.

In the sixteenth century, an Italian mathematician, Galileo Galilei (1564–1642), invented in 1589 a thermometer which was an air device. Around the same period, the clinical thermometer, which measured body heat, was invented by another Italian, Sanctorius (1561–1636).

In the eighteenth century, the Réamur, Fahrenheit and Centigrade thermometers were all invented. The French physician, René Antoine Réamur (1683–1757), invented the Réamur thermometer, which measured from 0 degrees, which is freezing point, to 80 degrees, which is boiling point. In 1714, the German physicist, Gabriel Daniel Fahrenheit (1686–1736), invented the Fahrenheit thermometer. Twenty-eight years later, the Swedish astronomer, Anders Celsius (1701–1744), invented the Celsius or Centigrade thermometer (100 degrees Celsius being boiling point).

At a later date, the French chemist, Antoine Baumé (1728–1804), invented a thermometer which measured the density of liquids, based on the Archimedes Principle. This type of thermometer is called a hydrometer.

The Centigrade and Fahrenheit thermometers are widely used by the patissier in the following preparations: Italian meringue, Nougat de

Montélimar, petits fours déguisés, fondant, fudge, pulled sugar and spun sugar. The saccharometer, which measures the density of liquid, is used extensively by the patissier in the production of ice sorbets, granités, fruit coulis and candied fruit. The saccharometer is a hydrometer which measures the density of sugar in Brix or Baumé degrees.

Terminology of thermometers and their uses

Physical mass terms used	Baumé (°B)	Réamur (R)	Celsius (°C) Centigrade	Fahrenheit (°F)	Water %	Uses
Pearl Grand lissé	30	80	101	214		Butter cream Candied fruit Fruit coulis
Small thread Filet	33.5	85	103	218	40	Candied fruit
Thread	34	86	104	220		Candied fruit Jam
Soft ball Petit boulé	38	90	107	225		Candied fruit Jam Mousses
Small ball Boulé moyen	40	92	110	230		Candied fruit (last stage)
Ball Boulé		96	115	240	12	
Hard ball Gros boulé		96 to 100	115 to 120	240 to 248	8	Fondant, butter cream, Italian meringue, almond paste
Hard crack Grand cassé		113 to 116	141 to 145	286 to 294	4.25	Nougat de Montélimar
Above 40°B – very thick syrup solution		116 to 122	145 to 152	294 to 306	3.45	Blown sugar Glazed petits fours Pulled sugar

∽ TOQUE – CHEF'S HAT ∽

Is the French name given to the white cotton hat which is part of a chef's standard uniform.

History

The word *toque* dates back to 1462 in France (Ref.: *Le Petit Robert 1*, 1972). However, the word was not used to describe a chef's hat until a much later date. The shape of the chef's hat has changed considerably over the centuries, and seems to have been dictated by the fashion of each particular period in history. The hat which was originally worn by chefs resembled a nightcap, and this particular style was worn by chefs for over two hundred years. At a later date, the beret was the height of fashion in France. The French chefs followed suite, and the shape of the chef's hat changed to a beret.

In the early nineteenth century in France, the most fashionable ladies of that time wore a hat which was called a toque, and under the influence of the great French chef, Antoine Câreme (1784–1833), French chefs adopted the style of the ladies' fashionable hat. The name 'toque' was also adopted by the chefs during that period.

In the year 1840, the chef's hat saw another transformation. The flat crown of the toque disappeared and was replaced with a high crown of almost thirty centimetres. Because of the height of the crown it was necessary to stiffen it with starch in order for the hat to stand upright. It is in fact the same style of hat that is worn by chefs today. Although the style of the hat changed, the name 'toque' remained the same in France.

Today, chefs' hats vary in style and size. There is a hierarchy within the kitchen, and the height of the hat worn by the chef denotes the importance of his rank within the kitchen. For example, an Executive Chef wears a hat with a high crown, whereas a Commis Chef will wear a hat with a flat crown.

∾ TORTEN ∾

This is a type of gâteau which consists of a base made with a variety of meringue-based mixtures. There are three different types of meringue mixtures used for the base, known as Succès, Progrès and the most commonly known, Japonaise. Bases for the Torten can also be made with sugar paste or shortbread. The base is baked in the oven and placed on a cake board. A Genoese sponge, the same size as the base, is also made and baked in the oven. When cooked, the Genoese sponge is cut into three equal sponge circles. The sponges are then soaked in a syrup which has been flavoured with either a liqueur or as alcohol. The three sponges are sandwiched together with butter cream or a ganache, or a combination of both. A mixture of jam, cream and fruits can also be used, depending on the type of Torten. The sponge is then placed on top of the base, the surface and sides of the Torten are then masked with whipped cream or butter cream and coated with chocolate vermicelli, nibbed almonds or roasted flaked almonds.

History

The word *Torten* comes from the German word *Torte*, which translated into English means a tart or a pastry flan with a filling. The original Torte was a savoury dish, a type of pie made with pastry and baked in a dish. It was not until the sixteenth century that the Torte became a sweet dish and was made from an almond mixture which was glazed with jam and coated with water icing. By the nineteenth century there were many recipes for the Torten. The bases were made with a variety of mixtures, and new fillings such as butter cream and ganache were introduced into the recipes instead of jam. Classic Tortens which were created during that period include the world-famous Sacher Torte and Gâteau Sarah Bernhardt, which was French.

The terms Torten and Gâteau are often confused. One of the main differences is that the surface of the Torten is marked into individual portions with a Torten marker and each portion of a Torten is decorated individually, whereas the whole surface of a gâteau is decorated and then cut into portions after it has been decorated.

∽ TREACLE ∽

Is the sticky liquid which remains after sugar cane has been processed. Treacle is a carbohydrate. It provides energy and is a good source of calcium and iron. The patissier and baker use treacle as a sweetener in rich fruit cakes, suet puddings, desserts, scones and gingerbreads. Although it has considerable sweetening properties, it is not as sweet as sugar.

History

Treacle dates back to the sixteenth century. In the eighteenth century, it was used by the poor working classes as a sweetener instead of ordinary white sugar candy or refined white sugar which, although superior in quality, were much more expensive. It was used as a sugar substitute up until the nineteenth century, when sugar became much cheaper because of the removal of the tax on it in 1874 by the Prime Minister of the time, Mr Gladstone. In the nineteenth century, treacle was often used for medicinal purposes; for example, sulphur was sweetened with treacle to create a well-known nineteenth century concoction commonly known as brimstone and treacle.

∽ TRIFLE ∽

This is a cold dessert which consists of stale sponge pieces, jelly, fruit and whipped cream. The sponge pieces are often soaked in sherry and are then placed in a large bowl with fresh fruit which has been peeled and cut into small pieces. A fruit jelly is poured into the bowl to cover the sponge and fruit and is allowed to set. Custard is then poured on top of the mixture and it is also allowed to set before the surface is decorated with whipped cream and glacé cherries. There is no set recipe for making this dessert and there are endless variations. It can also be made in individual glasses.

History

Trifle is a British creation! Originally the Trifle was simply a cream which was warmed and then flavoured with sugar and spices. The early Scottish version of the dessert was called a Whim-Wham and consisted of cream, white wine, Naples biscuits, redcurrant jelly and candied fruits.

At the end of the eighteenth century, the recipe for the dessert included such ingredients as ratafia biscuits, macaroons, custard and fruits. Hannah Glasse (1708–1770), the famous English cookery writer, published several recipes for Trifles containing a myriad of exotic new ingredients. The Trifle was a true concoction of delights during that period! It was extremely popular as a dessert during the reign of Victoria (1819–1901), Queen of Great Britain and Ireland from 1837, and remained so up until the early twentieth century.

Today, Trifle is a poor imitation of the luxurious dessert of the eighteenth century, consisting usually of convenience custard, tinned fruit and table jelly. Its popularity with the British public has greatly diminished.

V

∾ VACHERIN ∾

This is a round meringue shell which has a filling of fruit, sponge and jam. It is decorated elaborately with fresh whipped cream. The type of meringue used to make the shell is optional, but a Swiss meringue holds much better than the other types of meringue. To make the meringue shell, the meringue mixture is placed into a piping bag. A round base is piped first of all. Three circles of meringue exactly the same size as the base are then piped. These form the outer walls of the meringue shell. The meringues are allowed to dry out in a very slow oven, approximately 100 °C, or in a hot, dry prover. Another batch of meringue is then made and put into the piping bag. The walls of the shell are achieved by piping a series of meringue whirls between the base and between each of the three meringue circles. The meringue shell is once again allowed to dry out in a slow oven or hot, dry prover as before. When completely dry, the filling is put into the shell and decorated with piped whipped cream.

History

The Vacherin was created in France around 1906. As to why the sweet was called a Vacherin is open to suggestion. One school of thought is that the round, hard, white meringue shell with its soft interior resembled the range of French soft white cheeses called Vacherins, which are circular in shape, with a soft interior and a semi-hard crust. The cheeses are made from cow's milk. The French word for cow is *vache*, resulting in the name Vacherin. The Vacherin cheese originated in Switzerland. However, the name Vacherin spread to France to cover numerous soft cheeses made throughout France, for example, Vacherin d'Abundance.

∾ VALENTINE'S DAY – JOUR DE LA SAINT VALENTIN ∾

Valentine was a priest of Rome who was beheaded in AD 270 and became a martyr. He was then canonized and became a saint. St. Valentine's Day Festival was held on 14 February. However, this does not explain the custom of sending a valentine or a gift as a token of love.

One explanation of this popular celebration is that during Roman times, on 15 February, the day after St. Valentine's Day, the Romans held a fertility festival called Lupercalia. On this day, priests paraded around the streets of

Rome dressed in animal skins. It was believed that infertile women, if struck by the priests, would become fertile and would be given the gift of a baby. It is a highly plausible explanation that these two Roman festivals which were so close together eventually, through time, became one, becoming our present celebration known as St. Valentine's Day.

Today, the custom has become extremely popular, with lovers exchanging gifts, cards, pastries and chocolates. All the pastries, cakes and chocolates are either made in the shape of a heart or decorated with hearts as a symbol of love. St. Valentine's Day is celebrated throughout the world and has become a multi-million-pound industry. It is one of the busiest days in the patissiers' calendar.

∾ VANILLA – VANILLE ∾

The vanilla pod is about twenty centimetres in length. It is gathered when still green and allowed to develop to allow fermentation. During the process of fermentation, the flavour becomes increasingly pronounced. The vanilla pod belongs to the family of the orchid.

The pod produces vanilla essence, which is one of the most popular essences used in baking. The essence, although distinctive, is quite light and is used in all types of baked goods to enhance the main flavour of the goods.

History

The vanilla pod originated in Mexico. There are about a hundred and ten species, most of which grow in the wild. Only three species have been cultivated. The first was *Vanilla Pompona*, which has been cultivated in Guadeloupe and Martinique since the early eighteenth century. The second, *Vanilla Tahiten*, was cultivated in Tahiti in the middle of the nineteenth century, and the third, *Fragrans*, previously known as *Planifolia*. were cultivated in Mexico, Uganda, Mauritius, the Seychelles and Madagascar around 1820 to 1880.

The conquistadors who called the plant Vanilla were the first to bring back the plant to Spain from South America. Vanilla was not the only thing brought back to Spain from the Aztec civilization. The Indians drank a concoction of a cocoa drink flavoured with vanilla which became very popular in Spain in the early sixteenth century. The cocoa-flavoured drink was introduced into France in the seventeenth century.

In 1861, a young black slave called Edmond Albius, who lived in the French-ruled island of Réunion, which is approximately four hundred miles east of Madagascar and a hundred miles south-west of Mauritius, had the idea to pollinate both male and female flowers which were growing on the same plant. This cross-pollination between male and female flowers resulted in a new, highly flavoured vanilla pod that we know today.

⌘ VATEL, JEAN-FRANÇOIS ⌘

Jean-François Vatel was a famous French chef. He was born in Paris on 14 June, 1631. His family were poor and his father worked as a roofer in Paris. Because he was afraid of heights, Vatel was unable to follow in his father's trade.

At the age of fourteen, his father found a position for him as an apprentice patissier in a patisserie in Paris. Within a few years, Vatel had gained a considerable reputation within his chosen profession for the excellence of his work. As a young man he worked as a chef for such illustrious personages as the French politician Fouquet (1615–1680). This was a considerable achievement for such a young man.

Years later, he worked as an Executive Chef for the Prince of Condé and was later promoted to Head Waiter, responsible for the planning and organization of all social occasions within the House of Condé. He was now regarded as one of the aristocracy and accepted by the élite of French society. As recognition of his high rank he was granted permission to officially wear a sword, a great honour to bestow upon a commoner at that time. During this period he created many recipes; perhaps his greatest creation was Crème Chantilly.

On 21 April 1671, Vatel committed suicide by piercing his heart three times with his own sword. The circumstances surrounding his suicide were tragic. He had been given the responsibility for organizing a wedding banquet given by the King which was to be held at the Palace of Chantilly, twenty-five kilometres to the north of Paris. It was a prestigious occasion, and the guests included members of European royalty and the élite of French society. Vatel had ordered fresh fish from a small fishing port on the north coast of France, but disaster struck – the tide was late and it was impossible to transport the fish from the coast to the Palace of Chantilly in time for the chefs to prepare the fish course for the banquet. It was unthinkable at that time to have a royal banquet without the customary fish course. This caused absolute chaos to his well organized plans. He was utterly humiliated, and felt so dishonoured that he took his own life. He was only forty years of age.

⌘ VICTORIA SANDWICH OR SPONGE ⌘

The Victoria Sponge is made with the same quantities of sugar, fat and flour to which whole eggs are added. Baking powder is used as a raising agent. The rich sponge is made by using the creaming method, and is often cut into slices and served with afternoon tea. Another variation of serving the rich cake is to sandwich two sponges together with jam and freshly whipped cream. The surface of the sponge is dredged with icing sugar. It is then called a Victoria Sponge Sandwich.

The Victoria Sandwich or Victoria Sponge, as it is most commonly known, was created during the reign of Queen Victoria (1819–1901), Queen of Great Britain and Ireland from 1837. The recipe for this popular English sponge was first published in a cookery book called *Household Management*, by the famous Victorian cook, Isabella Beeton, in 1860.

⤳ VOL-AU-VENT ⤳

This is a puff pastry case which has a variety of different savoury fillings. Special graduated pastry cutters are available to make Vol-au-Vents and determine the size of the Vol-au-Vents. The meaning of the term 'Vol-au-Vent' differs slightly in Britain and France.

The British have adopted the term to describe a small individual pastry case with a savoury filling which is usually served at finger buffets.

In France, the term Vol-au-Vent is used to describe a larger pastry case with a savoury filling which is served as an entrée. The size of the Vol-au-Vent can vary and can serve between two and ten persons. The French use the term Bouchée to describe the small puff pastry case with a savoury filling which is served at finger buffets.

Vive la difference!

History

The Vol-au-Vent was a creation of one of the world's greatest chefs of all time, Antoine Carême (1784–1833). Carême created most of the world's great classic dishes, and was always experimenting in his kitchen in order to create new dishes.

Whilst working in a patisserie in the Rue de Gaillon in Paris, he had a new idea. He wanted to make a different shaped product with the use of puff pastry. He worked with the puff pastry, making a variety of shapes. Taking two of the small circular shapes which he had made, he decided to lay one circle on top of the other and bind them with egg-wash, hoping to create additional layers by using two layers of pastry.

He left the baking of the shapes to his Fournier, which is the name of a pastry chef who is in charge of the baking process within a patisserie, requesting to be called about the progress of his new creation. The Fournier, also called Antoine, summoned Carême to the kitchen, explaining excitedly that the pastry shapes were 'flying with the wind'. He was attempting to describe how the small pastry shapes had risen to such a height and were shaking slightly with the draught caused by the fuel-stoked ovens. From that day, the small pastry cases were known as Vol-au-Vents, which translated into English means 'flying with the wind'. Carême commissioned special cutters to be made in order to perfect the Vol-au-Vent cases.

ᕲ WAFFLE – GAUFRE ᕲ

This is made with plain flour, sugar, eggs, milk and melted butter, which is mixed into a pouring consistency. The batter is flavoured with vanilla and seasoned with salt. The mixture is poured into square-shaped honeycombed iron moulds which are heated, and the moulds are pressed together in order to cook the Waffles.

History

The French word for waffle is *gaufre*, which is a derivative of the Latin word *gafrun*. The English word for this type of cake comes from the German word *Waffel*, a derivative of the twelfth-century German word *walfre*, which later became *wafel* and eventually *waffle*. *Wafel* translated into English means honey's arrows.

A type of waffle was made during the time of the Ancient Greeks, around 500 BC, and was called *obolios*. The cakes were cooked between two sheets of iron. Between the twelfth and thirteenth centuries, waffles were introduced into Germany, France and Holland by the Crusaders, who brought the recipe back from the Holy Wars in the East.

In the Middle Ages in France, the peasants ate waffles or gaufres which were made from very rough flour to which salt and water were added. It was the French aristocracy who added eggs, sugar and milk to the recipe. The gaufres were cooked in moulds made of steel or wrought iron. They were made in a variety of designs, in the shape of flowers, stars and crescent moons.

The patissiers during that period were called Oubloyeurs, a word which originated from the Greek word *obolios*. They cooked the gaufres in the streets of the city. In the year 1400 in Paris alone, there were twenty-nine Oubloyeurs working in the city. Each of them could make more than a thousand gaufres each day. By the sixteenth century the number of Oubloyeurs had risen dramatically and it was necessary for Charles IX (1550–1574), King of France from 1559, to pass an edict that there had to be a distance of twelve metres between each stall.

Francois I (1494–1547), who was King of France from 1515, had such a passion for the sweet cakes that he commissioned a silversmith to make special moulds in solid silver in order to make gaufres purely for his own consumption. During this period, the French aristocracy commissioned blacksmiths to design special moulds with their family coat of arms or with the initials of their name.

Three hundred years later, the blacksmiths in France designed special iron moulds in a series of ambitious designs such as steam trains, châteaux and horse-drawn carriages. It was not until a later date that a blacksmith designed the familiar square-honeycombed mould with which we are familiar today.

In the twentieth century, the popularity of waffles in Britain has grown. Waffles were introduced to Britain from America. The recipe for waffles was taken over to America by the early European settlers. Today, waffles are made commercially in large quantities in factories in America, France and Germany. However, recently waffle irons have become available on the market in order to make waffles in the home.

In France today, the gaufre remains as popular as it was in the past. Each district has its own speciality of gaufre. For example, in the north of France gaufres are referred to as etrennes. Gaufres in France can be either sweet or savoury.

∾ WALNUT – NOIX ∾

The walnut tree, *Specie Juglans Regia*, belongs to the family *Juglandaceae*. The tree grows to a height of over thirty metres and produces a full crop of nuts twelve years after planting. The shell of the nut differs greatly in colour, ranging from pale golden to dark brown. The lighter the shade of the shell, the higher the quality of the nut. France has the reputation of producing the finest walnuts in the world, especially those grown in the Dordogne region. Walnuts are grown in numerous countries throughout the world. The United States of America is the largest producer of walnuts in the world today.

Walnuts are used extensively by the patissier as a flavouring or for decoration purposes. As a flavouring, the walnuts are usually ground or chopped and used in the production of bakery goods and desserts. Walnut halves are used to decorate gâteaux, pastry goods and petits fours. Countries such as Mexico, Turkey and Italy use the nuts a great deal in cookery; many old traditional recipes from these countries include walnuts. The nuts also produce a very distinctive and aromatic oil which is used in the production of bakery goods. The oil is also wonderful for making salad dressings. However, production of this versatile oil is very small; therefore it is an expensive commodity.

History

The walnut tree originated in Asia and in countries in south-eastern Europe. For thousands of years the walnut has been known to man as a source of food, and this has been well documented throughout history. The early Greeks used the walnut. During Roman times, specifically at the time of Pliny the Elder (AD 23–AD 79), the walnut was not at all appreciated as a food, and therefore walnut trees were not cultivated by the Romans until a later date. However, walnuts were greatly valued for their oil during that period, and the nuts were gathered from the wild walnut trees. The oil was used purely for medicinal purposes. During their invasion of Britain, the Romans introduced the walnut tree to the southern part of England; however, cultivation proved extremely difficult due to the unsuitable climate.

In the fifteenth century, France reintroduced the walnut tree to England and, despite the difficult climatic conditions previously experienced by the Romans, the growers persevered and this time were more successful. During this period, walnuts were eaten whole after a meal, as it was thought to aid digestion. In Elizabethan England, walnut trees were grown as ornamental trees and were regarded as a special feature in the garden. By the eighteenth century, walnuts were widely available and were used in cookery. A delicacy of that period was pickled walnuts.

Walnuts have always been valued by Eastern European countries. For example, in Turkey the walnut is an essential ingredient in such classic dishes as the savoury Tarator and the delicious dessert Baklava.

∾ WHEAT – BLÉ ∾

Wheat is a cereal plant, *Triticum*, which is a member of the grass family. It is the most cultivated cereal in the world today. The plant is grown in countries which have temperate climates suitable to its growth. Wheat is used mainly in the production of flour. Although thousands of varieties of wheat exist, there are three main varieties which are cultivated for the production of flour. *Triticum Vulgare* is grown mainly to produce flour which is used in the making of bakery goods such as bread. This flour is high in gluten content. *Triticum Durum*, commonly known as Durum wheat, is mainly used in the production of pastas. *Triticum Compactum* produces a much softer flour which is low in gluten content and is not suitable for bread making, but is excellent for the production of bakery goods such as cakes and biscuits. It is also used extensively in the production of breakfast cereals. Semolina, which is also prepared from wheat, is obtained from the process of flour manufacturing and is used to make milk puddings. Wheat is also used in the production of cattle feed.

The whole grain contains vitamin B, which is a combination of other vitamins such as B1 and B2. It is also rich in vitamin E. Wheat is high in fibre content; therefore the whole grain is extremely nutritious. Wholemeal flour is made from the whole grain of wheat and is used widely in the production of bread and pastries.

History

The cereal plant is native to the Middle East. As early as the year 10,000 BC, the Neolithic people gathered wild wheat. It is believed that the farming of wild wheat started around 6000 BC.

The early Egyptians, in the year 3100 BC, grew wheat and barley. During that time, more than a dozen different types of bread were made. A type of girdle cake was also made by the Egyptians. The harvesting and milling of wheat was under the direct control of the Pharaoh. The Pharaoh's bakers were not paid in money, but with bread and girdle cakes. Bread was so highly valued during that period that it was placed in the tombs of the Pharaohs. Bread was life!

The ancient Greeks, in the year 1600 BC, made a type of leavened bread using hops as a leaven. Early manuscripts reveal that more than fifty different types of bread were made at that time. The wealthy Greeks ate white bread which contained fruit such as pears or blackberries.

In 750 BC, the Romans grew wheat in large quantities. They were also responsible for modernizing the milling process. The quality of the flour produced by that time had improved a great deal. The classical Roman bread made during that period was made in the shape of a bun. Before the bun was baked, the surface was marked with a knife in the shape of a cross. It resembled the Hot Cross Bun with which we are familiar today. During Roman times, bread was distributed free of charge to the poor and to those who were unable to work. The Roman soldier was allowed 850 grams of wheat as part of his allocated daily ration whilst on campaign. He was expected to make his own girdle cakes or bread when the army camped. The Roman politician and social historian, Marcus Porcius Cato (234 BC–149 BC), wrote that slaves received 900 grams of cereal as a daily ration and, like the Roman soldier, were expected to make their own bread. However, they were also responsible for milling the grain! It is interesting to note that before the Romans, their ancestors, the Etruscans, ate millet.

In Europe, the grain was widely cultivated by the tenth century. In twelfth-century Europe, the peasants grew their own wheat, but had to carry their crop to the nearest castle in order to have the wheat milled. A tax was imposed by the lord of the castle for this service.

In the sixteenth century, wheat was introduced into South America by the Spanish. The Spanish Conquistador, Hernando Cortés (1485–1547), overthrew the Aztec empire and secured Mexico for his country. The ships belonging to the Spanish fleet had cargoes of food, among which was a consignment of rice. A Franciscan father, a missionary to the New World, found in the cargo of rice some grains of wheat. Out of curiosity, he decided to plant the grains of wheat in a pot and was delighted when small plants appeared. He then harvested the grains from the original plants and planted them in a small area of garden adjacent to the church. The process was repeated over a few years until he had sufficient grains to plant a whole field. Wheat had arrived in the New World!

Today, the main wheat-producing countries in the world are the United States of America, India, Canada, Argentina, France and Russia.

∾ WHISK – FOUET ∾

This is a utensil used in cookery. It has a wooden or metal handle to which a series of fine metallic wires are attached to form a balloon shape. The name 'whisk' is from the verb to whisk, which means to beat. The whisk is used in cookery to whisk a variety of mixtures; for example, egg whites are whisked in order to incorporate air into the mixture to increase its volume.

History

Originally the whisk was made from heather. It was later made from cytisus wood, commonly known as broom. During the reign of Louis XIV (1638–1715), who was King of France from 1643, the whisk was made from boxwood. It was not until 1860 that the metallic whisk was invented.

Y

∾ YEAST – LEVURE ∾

Yeast is a microscopic fungus. When a sugar solution is added to it, the small oval fungal cells multiply and change the sugar into alcohol and carbon dioxide. It is used in the fermentation of beers, wines and industrial alcohol. Yeast is also used extensively by the patissier and baker in the production of bread, cakes and pastries. When yeast is added to dough, it comes into contact with the carbohydrates present, causing the mixture to rise.

History

It is believed that the ancient Egyptians were the first to produce a leavened bread by using yeast. The process they used was quite simple; they made a fresh bread dough each day and incorporated into the mixture a piece of left-over dough from the previous day. They then allowed the dough to stand for a period of time, to allow fermentation to take place.

It was not until 1792, in England, that a gentleman called Mason prepared the first compressed yeast. However, the Dutch claim that compressed yeast had been created in Holland eleven years earlier, in 1781.

∾ YULE CAKES AND BREAD ∾

Are small cakes which are made with a rich yeast dough. The dough is made with flour, butter, lard, brown sugar, currants, yeast, eggs, milk, salt and nutmeg. The dough is made in a series of stages, between which fermentation is allowed to take place. It is then divided into pieces and rolled into small round shapes. The cakes are allowed to prove for a further thirty minutes before they are baked in a hot oven.

Yule Bread can also be made by placing the dough in a large bread tin. When cooked, it is served in slices.

History

Yule Cakes and Yule Bread were created in Yorkshire. The cakes were usually made during Christmas and New Year and were a traditional part of the Christmas meal in the past. The bread and cakes were usually served with the cheese course, often replacing bread at the table. Yule is an old Scottish word meaning Christmas. The cakes and bread are often compared with the Scottish Bannock.

Z

∾ ZABAGLIONE – SABAYON ∾

Zabaglione is a very light cream which is made with egg yolks and sweetened with sugar. The mixture is heated over a bain-marie until light and frothy. It is then sweetened with sweet white wine, such as Marsala or Sauterne, which is added very slowly to the mixture. It is served warm in glasses with petit fours. Whipped cream may also be added to the mixture. Zabaglione can also be served iced. This is a very recent idea and has become very popular.

History

The sweet originated in Italy. The word Zambaglione comes from the Italian word *zampar*, which means to froth. It later changed to Zabaglione. In France, the sweet is called Sabayon.

The sweet is not mentioned in cookery books of the eighteenth century, and it is not until the early nineteenth century that the recipe is to be found. However, the recipe of that time differs greatly from the recipe of today. It was not made with wine, egg yolks and sugar, but with a mixture of milk and sugar, to which alcohol such as rum or Kirsch was added.

A similar mixture is made in Scotland and is called Whipkull. The only difference in the recipe from that of Zabaglione is that rum or malt whisky is added to the cream mixture. The recipe is an old one and was created in the Shetland Islands, a group of islands which lie off the north coast of Scotland. Whipkull is traditionally served in Scotland with shortbread biscuits at Christmas. It may be served hot or cold.

It is also interesting to note that a type of Zabaglione is made in Norway and is called Eggedosis. Eggedosis is flavoured with rum.

∾ ZEST ∾

Is the thin peel of the outer skin of citrus fruits such as lemons, oranges and limes. Zest is used mainly as a flavouring in desserts, cakes and puddings. It is also used in the production of liqueurs such as Grand-Marnier and Curaçao.

History

The word 'zest' is a French word which dates back to 1611, and is a derivative of the French word *sec* or *zec* (Ref.: *Le Petit Robert 1*, 1972), which translated into English means dry. However, the use of the word zest to describe the peel of citrus fruits dates back to 1660 in France.

In the English dictionary, the meaning of zest is given as 'something which gives excitement or interest'. The citrus peel was aptly named, as it certainly does add excitement and interest to a variety of recipes throughout the world.

BIBLIOGRAPHY

British Beet Sugar Industry, British Sugar PLC, Peterborough.

Hutchinson Encyclopedia (1986) Helicon, Oxford.

International Coffee Organization (ICO).

The Incorporated National Association of British and Irish Millers Limited.

Le Pâtissier Moderne Magazines, Paris.

Le Petit Robert 1 (1972) Dictionaries Le Robert, Paris.

Residuary Milk Marketing Board, Surrey.

Tate and Lyle, BTA Publications Limited.

INDEX